To the Jims and Lauries of the world;

to the Andrews and Sophies,

the Marks and Joyces;

to the Cliffords,

and the Rickys and Susans, with love;

And to almost four billion other people

who chronically strengthen problem behaviors

without intending to do so.

Without them all,

this book would never have had to be written.

WINNING
THE GAMES
PEOPLE PLAY:

HOW TO MASTER THE ART
OF
CHANGING PEOPLE'S BEHAVIOR

Nathan B. Miron, Ph.D.

MISSION PRESS

Box 740   Sonoma, California 95476

158.2
M678w

First Edition
Copyright © 1977 by Nathan B. Miron, Ph.D.

Library of Congress Catalog Card Number 76-52149

ISBN: 0-918418-01-1 (Hard Cover)
ISBN: 0-918418-02-X (Soft Cover)

MISSION PRESS

Box 740   Sonoma, California 95476

Table of Contents
Part One: The Rules of the Games
(Principles of Human Behavior)

Part Two: Programming For Change

Preface

This book is not intended to be a course in one-upmanship. I am not trying to teach the reader how to play games, nor to compete with others for the dubious pleasure of winning such games. Rather, I hope to help people who have been trapped by games—their own or those of other people. This book was written for the non-psychologist who would like to take advantage of the scientist's knowledge of human behavior to make some favorable changes in his life. It deals with how human behavior can be changed, either by accident, in natural settings, or deliberately, by means of certain things you can learn. This book is for the person who is not content to let his life happen accidentally. If you are interested in how you can guide your life in such a way that more of your life will come out as you planned it, read on. I have written this book for the person who wants to be more in control of his life than he was before—for the person who has been frustrated by his lack of power to determine what his future will shape up to be. The person who wants more power to determine his own future will have to learn some simple rules about how to control other people, as well as himself. And that is what this book is about.

People have always suffered at the hands of other people, and not always by design, either. Most of the problems people have are caused by their own behavior, or by the behavior of their mates, families, employers, acquaintances, or other people important to them. But these behaviors can be changed for the better, if one knows the rules and follows them consistently. Even what people call *mental illness* is often nothing more than a long-standing series of behavior patterns which are self-defeating. The behaviors may be the result of unsuccessful attempts to deal with small annoyances which had not been handled properly, and built up until their cumulative effect was overpowering. Even extremes, such as "crazy" behaviors, represent the best efforts people have developed for dealing with their problems. These behaviors may be partially successful attempts to deal with unresolved annoyances. Like attention-getting behaviors, they can permit someone to survive crises, or fill needs that might not have otherwise been filled. But in the long run they may make the problems still worse. Yet these behaviors can usually be changed, when someone knows what to do and what not to do.

This book consists of two main parts, which should be read and studied in sequence. Most of the important principles of human behavior are found in the first ten chapters, which make up Part One. The language is non-technical, because this is a book for the person without training in clinical psychology. I am not writing for the scholar, although I hope he too will find it enjoyable to read, and will not be turned away by the informal, sometimes conversational style.

Part Two tells you specific rules to follow, like a cookbook. These rules are the recipes for cooking up changes in the way people act. I have tried to make the process as simple as possible. Most of the rules *are* simple, but their application is sometimes not so easy. Not all of it will be fun, either, but with the proper use of the information here, you will get most of the changes you want. That is, you will be in control. Of course, this will mean you have developed more personal power. It is to be hoped that the lives of those people you contact will also benefit. This is the reason I have written the final chapter, which is a philosophical one, dealing with the rights and wrongs of one person's controlling another person. It was written in the hope of preventing you from inadvertently abusing your new power.

You will find many stories throughout the book. All of them are true—at least in part. But I have changed details, sometimes to make them more understandable, readable, or interesting, or for reasons of confidentiality. In some cases, the stories are actually combinations of two or more separate incidents. I was less interested in presenting historically accurate cases than in teaching something by the use of the story, and after all, I could have used totally fictional stories too, had I wanted to do so.

All names are fictitious, with the exception of three of my favorite people: My wife Susan, and my children, Ricky and Emily.

I would like to thank a number of people who helped in the preparation stages of this book. Byron La Goy, Ph.D., and Edith Morledge, M.A., helped with some of the many earlier revisions. They steered me away from some blind alleys I was about to follow, and gave me helpful feedback for many months. I wish to thank a number of co-workers who helped develop and/or carry out some of the programs I discuss in this book: George Daly, P.T.II, for his help with Ralph's program; Linda Olsen, for helping train Louie to walk; John Wise, Ph.D., for help in training Hobart; and Ida (Van Dyke) Givens, for supervising Nancy.

I would like to thank my students and co-workers over the past twelve years or more, for taking a lot of the burden off me, doing much of the hard work, giving me a lot of good ideas, and sharing the glory with me.

Thank you too, Susan, Ricky, and Emily, for your courage in allowing me to share some rather personal experiences with my readers, and incidentally, for tolerating some of my own problem behaviors while I wrote and prepared this book for publication.

It is my hope that this book will help many readers develop more control over their lives, in directions which will result in favorable growth for them and the people around them, and that my work will help them achieve more personal power, without hurting other people. To those I might have hurt in the past, I am sorry. Perhaps I would have been kinder if I had known the contents of this book at those times, and followed its instructions.

Nathan B. Miron, Ph.D.

December 28, 1976

Part One:

The Rules of the Games

(Principles of Human Behavior)

Chapter 1

Winning the Games People Play

Our language is always changing, as people give new meanings to old words. There was a time when the word *game* meant entertainment. Since people sometimes hunted or gambled for entertainment, the word *game* began to mean other things as well. A new branch of mathematics called *game theory* was invented to explain how certain games were structured. But it was Dr. Eric Berne who made a new meaning of *game* popular, in his best-selling book, *Games People Play*[1]. These games are not played for entertainment. They are usually unconscious—that is, we do not realize we play them. What are called *games* are actually certain behavior patterns we develop for our own reasons, and these reasons may be selfish ones, which exploit others. They may also be protective. For the most part, these games are dishonest, because they hide the player's true feelings; but they represent the best we can do. Finally, they are essentially ways we try to control other people—and usually succeed, up to a point.

Because these games are so common, and because every one of us "play" them to control other people, it is just as likely that others are playing their games with us. When a child throws a tantrum to get his wish, it is his way of controlling people. We may think of it as a game he plays. You will read later of the way I eliminated a tantrum-game my son played, by deliberately not responding to it. You may, if you wish, say that I played an ignoring -game, but of course, I did so deliberately. In other words, I chose my game consciously, because I knew the rules, and expected my game to be successful. It was. Playing games is a way of controlling people, and others will play their games to control you. It is likely that you have developed some counter-games of your own, to prevent you from becoming someone else's prey, and being completely under his power. When we talk about power we mean a person's ability to control other people's behavior.

A person has power when he can use his wealth, physical strength, connections, looks, position, or his own behavior to get people to do what he wants. Of these, only behavior can be changed relatively quickly, and as you will see, you *can* teach an old dog new tricks. Furthermore, when you know the rules of the games, it is often a lot easier to change behavior than you might have thought. You don't always have to be the one who is exploited. You can learn to control others, too, and you can learn to control yourself better in the process. Not only that, but you can control people in ways which are of a great deal of benefit to them. In other words, you can use your control to help others as well as yourself. Control need not be exploitive and cruel.

You may be thinking that it is terrible that people control other people, and you might wish for a world in which nobody controls anybody else. You might not like the idea that you too control people, just like everyone else in the world. But wait. Not all control is bad, as I implied in the previous paragraph. Everything we or other people do is controlled by something, even when the behavior seems haphazard and chaotic. For the most part, this control comes from outside our bodies. The way any person acts is largely governed, or *controlled*, by the things which happen to him. Even things we often think were brought about by some mysterious internal process which we might call our "will," "desire," "wish," or "volition" actually involve a lot of external control, for we learn to desire or will things because of what has happened to us in the past. Everything we do is strengthened (or weakened) by forces you will understand better when you have read this book. Most of these forces are social—that is, they result from the actions of people. You might feel that you have very little control over other people, but you are probably wrong. You have a lot of control, just like the driver of a car. There are good drivers and there are bad drivers. The bad ones move the same steering wheels as the good ones, but they move them in different ways. They sometimes force the car to do things which hurt people, including the driver himself. Without knowing it, you could be making others do things which are not in your own best interest, or theirs—things which end up hurting you, or preventing you from having what you want, or becoming what you would like to be. This book will tell you how to become a good driver, in control of your life. But you will choose the road you wish to travel.

You will be able to control better—that is, play the games—when you know the rules thoroughly and apply them consistently. But your games will not have to be phony, or sneaky. You can be very open and honest about them, for you should deliberately spell out the rules to others in many cases. Right now you are already controlling many people. You might not *feel* like it, possibly because you are not as successful as you would like to be in getting the things you really want. But you are still controlling them, in spite of your feelings to the contrary. Feelings are sometimes useful, but are not very good guides to reality. You should always look for evidence more objective than your own feelings.

Most of the time, the reasons for our behavior are not mysterious. They are usually logical, transparent, and easily readable by anyone who knows what to look for. Everyone's behavior follows certain rules which by now are well understood by scientists. These rules are called *scientific laws* of behavior. Most of the laws are simple and easy to understand. You will recognize some from your own experience. This book organizes the most important laws into a practical system that makes it relatively easy to use them. I did not include every rule. To do so would take many years and thousands of pages, filled with technical language, with more being added every day. My goals were simplicity and practicality, not completeness, for this is a book for beginners. You must forgive me if you occasionally run across an exception to some of these rules, for that is the price we pay when we try to simplify. But exceptions shouldn't happen very often, because these laws are surprisingly general, and cover most situations you are likely to encounter.

Naturally, the more consistently you apply the laws, the better they will work for you. Every time you fail to follow instructions, you delay your ultimate success and erode your power just a bit. You will find that even though you will probably not be able to live your entire life as systematically as Chapter 11 and Chapter 12 would recommend, you can always *try* to reach that goal, and you will probably be surprised at how much you can accomplish without absolute consistency. Even without formal programs such as those outlined in Part Two, you can accomplish a lot, if you have made the rules of Part One an important part of your life.

You will rarely be called upon to use punishment. Chapter 8 is about punishment, and should convince you that my reasons for de-emphasizing punishment are practical as well as humanitarian. Punishment usually promises more than it delivers. A successful person is one who can control easily without the use of punishment, or threat. The more a person must use punishment or threats, the less control (or power) he really has. Count the number of times you have to punish, or say "No," or "Stop that!" If it is more than you can count on your fingers each day, you need to learn how to get in control of the situation and get some power over your life. You need to learn to win the games people play.

Power means control, and control means how well you are able to solve the problems which involve your actions or the actions of other people. For that reason, I have tried to keep a problem-solving approach throughout this book and the problems I discuss center around the behavior of some person: You, me, or someone else. By *behavior*, I mean the way people act, good or bad—the things people do—the games people play. This book is about changing behavior, because *power* means your ability to control behavior, and in order to control behavior successfully, you must know how to change it.

There is a lot of scientific evidence to back up the laws and rules in this book. It is found in many technical journals and books written for behavioral psychologists. My purpose will be to tell you the rules in working English, and show you how to use them to invent strategies we will call *programs*. Such programs might be written to teach you new behaviors you would like to have or improve (such as better concentration, saying more positive things to your friends or employees, better work habits, or standing up for your rights). Or you might wish to eliminate some things you don't want (such as the number of times you blow up, the number of things your children leave lying around, the number of times your husband keeps you waiting, the number of times your friends take advantage of you, or [for the children] the number of times your parents promise you things they don't give you).

I could have included a long bibliography to help you look up the technical proofs, but I am going to ask you to accept the rules on faith. If you have any doubts, you will have plenty of chance to verify each rule yourself, for the proof will be whether it works for you, and you will learn later how to test your theories to see if they are correct. I am not trying to give you a book on theory, although that would have been easy enough to do. There are already good college textbooks on behavior modification theory. You should not have to depend on the theories of other people—not even the greatest scientists on earth, although if you're wise, you will let them help you as much as you can. But only you can tell if a program is working to your satisfaction. If it is, you'll know it very soon. If it's not, you'll know that too, and should then revise it so that it will work. You will have the final say, not some scientist in his laboratory. He will give you the tools from that laboratory, but you must do the building yourself. And when you get the results, the house will belong to you, not to the hardware store that sold you the hammer and nails. If your results do not stand up to your expectations, you will learn how to change your program (or your expectations) until they begin to match.

Does that sound fair enough? Then continue to read. It will not always be easy, even though it is beginner's stuff. But it will be easy most of the time, and anyway, I am not promising to turn really difficult problems into pushovers—although that often happens too. You should be able to get early results in most cases, but remember that some problems have been building up for many years. These will probably take more than just a few days to work out. And some problems will remain so difficult that you might need the help of a skilled and highly trained professional behavior therapist. But even with problems as tough as these, the rules you will learn in this book will help make his job easier. The information in this book is compatible with the best clinical advice he will be giving you.

Well, let's get started learning something you will need to know about human behavior, sometimes called "human nature." But first, you must learn to speak a language that will help you solve your problems.

Chapter 2

Learning a Language That Can Help You
Solve Your Problems

Our behavior is influenced not only by what goes on inside of us, but also things outside of our bodies. These outside forces are part of our environment, and the most important parts of our environment are the other people we encounter, and what they do to us. In spite of this fact, many people still believe that most of our behavior is generated deep within us, by mysterious qualities or forces they call our "psyches," "minds," or "souls." Even our everyday language reflects this misconception. For example, we often use terms such as "self-discipline" and "will power" to explain why some people stick to a job, especially one they do not like to do, and "force themselves" to continue when others in their position might have stopped. They are not very good explanations, because they really do not explain anything. All we have done is take a fact (that some people are persistent) and give that fact a name (self-discipline). We then use that name to explain the fact ("He is very persistent because he has a lot of self-discipline"). People who are not persistent, we may say, must lack self-discipline. Therefore, lack of self-discipline must be the reason they are not persistent. All this really means is that a person who is not very persistent is not very persistent. We have learned nothing new from such exercise. This is called *circular reasoning*, and it fools people into thinking they understand something they have not yet explained adequately. The new names have added nothing to their ability to solve the problem. Sometimes these phrases may communicate something about the way people feel, but they do not usually help people change those things, despite their descriptiveness or the poetic beauty of the description. Because people think they know something they don't know, they stop trying to find the real answers.

For those of you who are serious and wish to make some changes in your life, it is important that you first understand what is happening to you, or to other people whose behavior affects you. And in order to do that, the first step you must take is to learn how to use your native language to help you, rather than hide facts from you.

One reason why scientists such as chemists, astronomers, physicists, and engineers have made such outstanding progress is because they have usually managed to avoid using circular reasoning. But when we deal with personal areas, we tend to use our language in a loose and sloppy way, which is often circular, and places emphasis upon inner, psychic processes. No physicist would ever say that a brick falls to the earth when dropped because it had an urge to do so. An airplane doesn't crash because it hasn't managed to pull itself together, and a watch doesn't indicate the time because it feels it in its gut. Yet, in trying to explain human behavior, we find laymen, and even professional psychologists, who use language just as nonsensical. The way to avoid pitfalls such as those above is to describe problems in language which translates into direct observation, in a form which can be measured, which means you can count it or time it to see how long it lasts.

Using the example above, suppose you decided that you wanted to increase your self-discipline. Let's translate. What you really mean is that you wish you could stick to an unpleasant job until you get it finished. But you cannot measure self-discipline, except by having someone judge how "disciplined" you are. That is not a good way to measure anything, because you are only reflecting someone's opinion. Opinions may change, and two people might not agree very closely. But you can measure how long you stick to your task, and all you need is a clock, a pencil, and some paper to record your results. Once you know how long you usually stick to your task, you may design your program to improve it. You can then know whether you have done better today than yesterday, or tomorrow, because you have an objective record which can be understood by anyone. You do not talk about self-discipline any more, but the length of time you stick to a task. Maybe it is the same thing, but it is now in language which can help you. Incidentally, it might help you learn to describe things better if you realize that you never talk about self-discipline except when you are thinking about something you don't like to do. You never think it takes self-discipline to spend a lot of time working on your model railroad, or reading a good novel, or playing football, or knitting on that afghan, or doing anything else you really enjoy. That is called fun, and sticking to it doesn't take any will power or self-discipline. Therefore, if you are trying to increase self-discipline, you would only measure the amount of time you spent doing things you do not enjoy, but which you feel you must do anyway.

Don't think that professionals don't also use sloppy language! They do, and this has been one of the most important reasons why psychiatry and clinical psychology have been so backward and ineffective in the past. Thousands of psychologists have spent the major part of their professional lives on testing designed only to give them labels they called *diagnoses*. At the least, this practice has resulted in a severe drainage of manpower from a field that was already too short. But at worst, it prevented adequate programs from being developed to treat the disorders. How much more convenient it is to give a behavior a name. Then the problem is solved,

Here are some examples of such terms, used both by professional people and laymen alike:

1. He is schizophrenic. Translation: *His behavior is bizarre.* Even more clear: *He makes weird, inappropriate motions with his hands.* Or: *He stares off into space and talks to himself.* Or: *He giggles at inappropriate times.* Or: Any number of different things people do which cause professionals to give them the name *schizophrenic.* If you ask one of the professionals why he gave the patient such a diagnosis he is likely to tell you something which boils down to: He acts like other schizophrenics, or: That behavior is characteristic of schizophrenics.

2. I am unhappy. This is a descriptive statement which tells how a person feels, but does not tell what is really the problem[2]. We may even use this description to explain why we have failed in other areas, which might have made us happier. For example, if we are doing poorly on our job, this makes us unhappy. Nobody likes to be a failure. We may explain our failure by saying, "I haven't done my best because I have been so unhappy lately." Again, we have not used language which gives us any clue as to how we can become happier, or how we can do better on our job.

3. I lack fulfillment.

4. You must work toward self-actualization.

5. Nothing seems to matter very much.

6. Your trouble is that you don't have your head together.

7. He has a very low self-esteem.

8. You're not in touch with yourself.

9. I can't really start working on my problem until I can work through my feelings.

10. She had a nervous breakdown.

11. You can tell by watching her that she feels inadequate.

12. Try to explain that again, but do it at a gut level.

Notice that every one of these statements tells us that something

needs to be changed. Now, stop reading. Go back and read the list
again. See if you can put your finger on something specific that needs to
be changed in each statement in order to make the person feel his
problem is improved. Ask yourself what somebody is doing that he
shouldn't be doing, or what he should be doing that he isn't. See if you
can think of a way to count or time whatever it is that needs changing.
When you have finished, turn the page and continue reading.

Did you have any luck? Probably not. Those statements were not in language which could translate easily into an action program. Now, let me give you a different list. Each statement is written so there is no mystery about what should be changed. In each case, we would work on someone's *behavior,* so let me interrupt myself by first telling you what I mean when I talk about a behavior:

A behavior is something that somebody does, says, or thinks.

Now back to the list. In each example, I will be talking about something somebody does, says, or thinks. As a clue, the verb in the sentence will usually help identify the behavior. In some cases, it is possible to talk about a missing behavior—that is, something a person does not do, but which you feel he should do. In each statement, look for something that can be observed and measured. Not every statement is about a problem, although the problems I do mention are typical. At times, you might notice more than one possible solution. See how many you can find. By the way, this list was not intended to match the first list, so don't exhaust yourself trying to translate the two as pairs:

1. **Most women I date refuse to go with me a second time.** Anybody who can count can tell how many dates you have with each woman, or how many refuse to go with you again. Measurement here is only a matter of a simple count.

2. **My husband ignores any suggestion I make.** You can learn to count and write down the number of suggestions you make to your husband and how many he ignored, or to be more positive about it, the number he acted upon. This number might be zero, but when we count we are often surprised to realize how much different the problem is than we thought. I have said before that feelings are not a good guide to reality. It often happens, for example, that people count such things as the number of suggestions the husband follows, and they are quite surprised to find he was following more than they had thought. It often happens that your reaction to the time he does not do as you wish may color your interpretation, and make it impossible to be objective enough to realize this. Not getting 100% of our wishes, we sometimes think we are getting nothing at all. Counting and recording makes it clear that we are getting more than we thought—or perhaps, counting and recording may make it clear that we were understating the problem.

3. **She is the only person I know who compliments me so often.** You can count the number of statements you consider compliments.

4. **He is often hostile to me.** You can count the number of acts you consider hostile. You may, if you wish, include hostile statements as well.

5. **She uses too much obscene language.** You can count the number of statements you consider obscene. You are the sole judge of whether you consider her statements to be obscene, or for that matter, hostile or complimentary. Nobody else may agree with you, but for the present that is beside the point. All I'm doing right now is talking about how you can get behaviors into language you can count.

6. **When she doesn't get her way, she screams and cries and throws her toys.** The number of times she throws her toys may be counted, or the number of episodes she has, or the number of minutes each tantrum lasted. You might use any one of those counts at some time or another.

In every case I have stated the problem so that you can decide what somebody does or does not do, put it into words that tell what to look for, and then count it or time it whenever it comes up. This allows you to keep good records, and prevents your falling into the trap of circular reasoning. The language tells us what the behavior is. The measurement tells us how strong it is.

You may have noticed at this point that I have said nothing at all about how to solve any of the problems I mentioned. I did not tell you what you must do to get your husband to treat you with more respect, or listen to more of your suggestions. I said nothing about what you must do to get women to go out with you a second time, or third time. I said nothing about how to stop your child's tantrums and toy throwing. All of this will come later. But first, we must be able to speak a language that will not hide the solutions from us. We must describe the problems in a way that will tell us what to look for and what to measure.

The way you describe your problem has a lot to do with how you will go about solving it. If you are not precise in the way you talk about your problem, it probably means that you do not understand it well enough, and may have been trying to do the wrong things to solve it. It may be one reason you have not been able to deal successfully with it so far. Precise language is not the answer to everything, but it does force you to come to grips with a problem and think it through. Fuzzy thinking shows up quickly when you ask yourself, "What behavior should I look for? And how will I measure it?" You must remember that if your present way of dealing with your problem has not worked, it is going to be necessary for you to do something different the next time around.

After all, if the old way had worked well enough you would not be trying to get my help right now. You would not be reading this book. So be prepared to change your approach. And remember, as long as you still have the problem, your "solution" has not been totally successful. Don't be ashamed of it. Just be ready to change your tactics to something more successful.

Natural catastrophes, physical disability, or "acts of God" are often very distressing, but somehow most people manage to deal with them in ways they often did not suspect were within their power. On the other hand, what people call *emotional problems* are really nothing more than minor, everyday problems which accumulate until they become incapacitating. They are mostly repeated unresolved annoyances—nothing big by themselves—just annoyances—the big and little annoyances caused by friction with other people, by their rejection, by the ways one person exploits another person, by the ways people knowingly or unconsciously hurt other people, by the way people avoid dealing with other people, by the way people avoid dealing with problems resulting from disagreements with other people, by the way people react to things which have been said, or by the way people react because they are afraid of something someone else *might* say, and on and on and on.

These problems are almost always the result of something somebody does or something somebody does not do, which you feel he should do. In the first case, someone is doing something you don't like—something you wish he would not do. You would rather he didn't smoke around you, didn't use obscene language around you, didn't talk quite so loud, didn't let his dog make a mess on your lawn, didn't snap at you when you didn't mean to insult him, didn't push you around quite so freely, or didn't do any of ten million other possible things which can annoy you or make you angry.

In some cases, you have the problem because somebody is not doing something you feel should be done. He *should* listen to my suggestions; he *should* learn to notice the nice things I do for him; he *should* give me a raise; she *should* love me; he *should* compliment me when he sees I have done something well; I *should* speak more confidently; he *should* laugh when I tell a joke; he *should* let me use the car more often; he *should* budget his money better; I *should* study more; he *should* keep his room clean; he *should* take me out more often; she *should* like the things I like; she *should* try to understand me; etc.

I have already told you that a behavior is anything a person does, says, or thinks. Once you have identified a behavior you must be able to measure it. The most common ways are: 1) counting it; and 2) timing it to see how long it lasts. Here are some examples of behaviors which would be relatively easy to measure:

1. **Gives compliments.**
2. **Picks up toys.**
3. **Buys his mother flowers.**
4. **Comes to appointments on time.**
5. **Makes hostile remarks.**
6. **Begins conversations with strangers.**
7. **Disguises a hostile statement as a compliment.**
8. **Hits a classmate.**
9. **Looks into your eyes.**
10. **Writes.**
11. **Bakes his favorite dish for him.**

At this point we are just trying to talk about behavior as descriptively and objectively as possible, and that, as all scientists know, means in a way which can be measured. You cannot measure a problem like, "My husband is not affectionate," but you can count the number of times he buys you flowers, or the number of compliments he gives you. It is easy to count the number of times he spontaneously kisses you. While some people might argue that counting takes all the fun out of it, I am quite positive that this does not have to be the case at all! Moreover, most people can remember if they are kissed once or twice, and record this fact later. Anyone who is kissed too often to keep count probably has no problem in that area anyway!

I will refer to the problem of defining behavior many times, and will spend an entire chapter on the problem of keeping good records. For the time being, just try to put your problem into language that talks about specific behaviors—in other words, you must be able to say what is being done which you don't like, or what is not being done which you would like to take place.

I will use the term *problem behavior* many times. This will mean *anything someone does which someone does not like.* You will notice that this is a very vague definition. What is *anything*? Just what I said. Anything. Who is *someone*? Just what I said. Any person, including you, me, and everyone else. You will also notice that this definition is subjective. That is, it is someone's opinion, and two people might not see it the same way. I did that on purpose, because any time we call a behavior a problem behavior we are being subjective. One person will not be annoyed by the same things which bother someone else. For this reason, there is really no scientific definition of problem behavior. It is in no way different from any other behavior in principle except that someone does not like it. Sometimes, in fact, the only thing wrong with a problem behavior is that it happens too often. It might be alright if it just happened now and then. It becomes a problem at the point where it begins to annoy someone.

Our dislike of a behavior may make us react to it in ways we would not act toward behaviors we like. That is, the consequences of a problem behavior may end up being different from the consequences of a behavior we like. But problem behavior is still behavior. It is still something somebody does or says or thinks. You might think something I do is a problem behavior if you don't like it, even though it is something I like very much. I will mention this point again and again, because I know many people get confused when we call a behavior a problem behavior one time and not at another. To the worried person who tosses and turns for hours during the middle of the night, falling asleep would be a most welcome gift, although most people would call falling asleep a problem behavior if it came during a job interview, or while driving down the Hollywood Freeway. Here is another example:

For many years I looked forward to the day I could afford to dine in a certain expensive restaurant. Finally the day arrived. It was time to celebrate, and I paid more than $50 for the pleasure. The meal was wonderful, the setting was beautiful, the view out the window was breathtaking, and the service was superb. It was well worth every cent I had saved to come to that place. Unfortunately, at the next table, another diner finished his meal and lit a cigar. The moment I smelled its offensive odor, my feelings of pleasure changed to acute discomfort.

To me, his smoking was a problem behavior. (Did you notice that I even used a very emotional word, *offensive*, to describe the smoke? Here is a good example of a message hidden—not too well— in our everyday speech. You should be on the lookout for such messages). On the other hand, he did not consider his smoke offensive at all. In fact, if he had been asked, he might have called it *fragrant!* Smoking his cigar to him was desirable behavior. If I had tried to stop him, he might have been polite to me, and put away his cigar nicely, but he would have considered my intervention an interference, and possibly an insult as well. At any rate, he certainly would have considered it a problem behavior, because he would have preferred that I refrain from interfering.

It is important to understand that there are many behaviors of this type. A child imitating police sirens may be offensive to his neighbors, but to him and his friends, it is just fun. To the neighbors, his making noise is a problem behavior because it annoys them. To him, their interruption and nagging to stop the noise are the problem behaviors. Regardless of what we consider it to be, imitating police sirens will follow the scientific laws that govern other behaviors, and so will nagging and interfering, and smoking cigars, and complaining about people who smoke cigars, and everything else that people do. Behaviors are completely democratic. Good or bad, they follow the same rules. Kings and slaves, the wealthy and the pauper, black, white, yellow, red, child, adult, female, male, brilliant, retarded, young, and old—all follow the same laws. Of course, it would be foolish to deny that the king and some others have more power—that is, more effective means available for making the changes they want. Orwell said, "All animals are equal, but some animals are more equal than others[3]." Nevertheless, all people still behave in ways that are determined by the things which happen to them—in other words, their behavior is controlled by its environment.

The reason I have spent so much time describing problem behaviors is that people often get so upset by them that they begin to feel there is something unique about them. They believe that problem behaviors are mysterious, or magic, and follow special rules, or perhaps no rules at all. Let me assure anyone who feels this way that it simply is not so. Science does not make a distinction between ordinary behaviors and problem behaviors. Just like all other known behaviors, problem behaviors obey scientific laws, and these are the same laws which are followed by desirable behaviors. The only difference is the fact that someone does not like the problem behaviors, and as a result may at times act differently because of them. In other words, the consequences of the problem behaviors are different. They have controlled the behavior of someone else. These consequences will have some bearing on how strong that behavior will be in the future, just as they have on desirable behaviors.

I don't want to drive this point into the ground, but it is very important that you understand that problem behavior is no more magical than any other behavior. You can reward problem behavior and it will become stronger, the same as behavior you might like (see Chapter 3). You can take away the rewards and problem behavior will become weaker. The same would have been true of behaviors you like (see Chapter 6). You can do either one of these deliberately or you can do them without the slightest intention or awareness. Likewise, other people are changing your behaviors, including both the things you like and dislike, and the things they like and dislike, just as you are changing these things. All of this can happen without either of you knowing it is happening, and in fact that is exactly the way it usually does happen. The only difference between problem behavior and desirable behavior is that a person reacts differently to behaviors he finds pleasing than to behaviors he hates. But the effects of the things you will be learning about in the rest of this book—things like rewards and punishment— apply equally well to desirable behavior and to problem behavior. Others might strengthen or weaken your behaviors in different ways because of how they feel about those behaviors. But rest assured. Behaviors are still democratic, as I said before. They follow the same laws. In fact, you might be surprised to learn that one of the main reasons we have so many problem behaviors is that people often make them stronger by the way they respond to them. Likewise, they may weaken the behaviors they like the most, and they are almost never aware that they are doing it. But all this is a story for a later chapter.

I will use the terms *behavior* and *problem behavior* many times in this book. The reason is obvious. Behavior is what we wish to change—to eliminate or to acquire—to reduce, to increase, or to maintain at the same level. And the problem behaviors are the ones we will wish to reduce. In fact, one way we know if a behavior is a problem behavior is that we will want to have less of it. Therefore, we should be sure that we can state our problems in terms of some specific behavior.

I will also use the term *target behavior,* which means *a behavior you wish to increase or strengthen* [4]. That is, *target behavior* will mean only *desirable behavior.* If a wife wishes that her husband would sometimes follow her suggestions, the target behavior would be *following her suggestions.* She wants to increase such behavior. If little Clifford interrupts adults very often during their serious conversations, they would probably call the interruption a problem behavior, because they would like to see it happen less. On the other hand, it would be wise to replace his problem behavior with something better, such as: 1) waiting patiently a few moments for a break in the conversation; and then 2) saying, "I beg your pardon." These two behaviors might both be targets, because we would be aiming at them, trying to increase them. We would call them targets because we feel they are desirable behaviors, and we want more of them. We want them to be stronger.

I repeat: I will call a behavior we don't like a *problem behavior,* and assume we want to weaken it, or get rid of it. I will call a behavior we do like a *target behavior,* and assume we want to strengthen it. We'd like to see it happen more often. Target behaviors will also include behaviors a person has not yet learned, but which you would like him to have.

Athletic coaches, piano teachers, flying instructors, and in fact teachers of all kinds are in the business to obtain certain targets which were not present before, or were not quite as strong, or as good, as we might wish.

One more set of definitions seems in order. I'll use the term *program* to mean *the formal strategy we develop for the purpose of changing a behavior.* It is our blueprint, or battle plan, or script. A program can be designed to weaken, reduce, or eliminate a problem behavior, to strengthen a target behavior, to obtain a new target you did not have before, or a combination of these. We change a person's behavior by teaching him new or different ways of doing things, and he changes because he learns these new behaviors. Therefore, I'll use the term *learner* to mean *the person for whom a program is developed.* That is, the learner is the person whose behavior is to be changed by the program. A teacher arranges a learner's experiences and environment so that the odds are higher that he will learn what the teacher wants him to know. Since changing the learner's behavior means teaching—with or without the knowledge of either party—and teaching means arranging the learner's environment, I will use the term *arranger* to mean a person carrying out a program. The arranger is the person who is actually doing the changing of someone's behavior. You'll learn about *self-control* programs later (Chapter 14). In these programs, the learner is the same person as the arranger.

It is a good idea to concentrate on the target behaviors, rather than the problem behaviors. There are many very good reasons for this, and you'll hear me say it again and again. In Chapter 7 you will find that one good way to reduce a problem behavior is to replace it with one or more target behaviors, just as I pointed out in the case of little Clifford and his interrupting. You'll learn a lot of reasons for this rule later, but for the time being, remember that an old song gave good, sound advice: *Accentuate the Positive*[5]!

Please do not skip the following drills. They are important. Learning is most effective when you actively participate and *do* something, rather than passively hope you'll soak up something you hear or read. As you will soon see, you cannot strengthen a behavior that hasn't happened. A behavior is something someone does, so if you wish a behavior to happen it means someone must do something. Do these exercises, and let the success you experience strengthen the right kinds of behaviors you do.

Read the statements in Column 1. They are fairly vague. Read them one at a time, and after each one, stop and think. Then translate each one into a term which is worded as one or more target behaviors or problem behaviors. Write the new behavioral definition in Column 2. If your translation was correct, you should be able to measure the behaviors, either by counting them or by timing them to see how long they last. You may also be able to describe the behavior at different levels, because some behaviors are really a lot of other, smaller behaviors strung together in what we call a *behavioral chain*. For example, a simple behavior such as *driving to work* might be counted as one problem behavior in a program which tries to get you to walk to work more often. On the other hand, *driving to work* could also be interpreted as a string of separate behaviors, such as: Leaves house, kisses wife (or husband, or other), gets into car, closes door, fastens seat belt, puts key into ignition switch, starts engine, backs out of driveway, looks into rear view mirror, drives west on MacArthur Street, turns right on Fifth Street, etc. In fact, even these can be broken into finer divisions, if necessary. *Turns right* is also a chain of other, smaller behaviors, such as: Lifts the directional signal arm for a right turn, places right foot on the brake to slow the auto, pushes clutch to floor with left foot, shifts down to second gear, releases clutch, pulls steering wheel clockwise with right hand, lifts left hand off wheel and replaces it at the left side of the steering wheel rim, etc. How fine you should break it down depends on the nature of the program you will be devising, and its goals—that is, what you want the program to teach the learner.

Don't worry if your translation comes out different from someone else's. We might be looking at different levels of the same behavior. That is all right. You may need more than one definition later. Define behaviors in the drills in as many ways as you can. Use extra sheets if necessary. And don't worry if the definitions sound silly. I have good reasons for asking you to do these exercises, and you will understand them before very long. Right now, the only important thing is to learn how to translate your native language into a more practical, behavioral language. Your only goal at this time should be to develop the important skill of learning to say exactly what you mean, in a way you can measure. I'll do the first one for you as a sample. You try it too, then do the rest. The key words are italicized. They refer directly to behaviors which can be counted or timed. My solutions are not the only ones possible, and are offered only as a guide.

Statement	Translation into behavioral terms.
He comes on too strong.	He makes too many *hostile remarks.* He *interrupts* too often. He does not make enough *friendly statements.* He *frowns* too much. He *tells others* they are wrong. He does not *smile* enough.
He is too shy. **He is nuts.** **She is weird.** **He is spoiled.** **She is withdrawn.** **He is rude.** **He is scatterbrained.** **I am unhappy.**	

If you do not feel comfortable with your ability to translate into behavioral terms, please stop here and do not go on. Read Chapter 2 once more, and try the drills again. You will find that it will help if you always ask yourself, "What behaviors am I really talking about? What is someone doing, or what should they be doing? How can I count or time the behaviors?" You will probably have little trouble after that. We will go into more detail in Chapters 11 and 12.

Chapter 3

Payoffs, and How They Change What We Do

In this chapter I am going to talk about payoffs. For technical reasons, these payoffs are sometimes called *reinforcers,* because they strengthen, or reinforce the behavior they follow. But I will call them *payoffs,* or *rewards,* to keep things more simple. Every behavior, good or bad, is kept alive by its payoffs. A person receiving a reward after a behavior occurs becomes more likely to repeat that behavior. The opposite is also true. Take away all rewards and the behavior will gradually fade out. Exceptions to this rule of payoffs are so rare you will probably never run across them, unless you are a professional psychologist, working in an experimental laboratory, hospital, or clinic. For all practical purposes, just remember that if the learner gets a payoff, it strengthens whatever behavior happened just before the payoff came. It becomes more likely that the same behavior will then appear again under similar conditions. If you give the payoff to the learner, you will have become an arranger, because you will be changing his behavior.

The payoff rule is probably the most important law in all of human behavior. It is the basis of most, if not all, learning. It is so important that I will repeat it:

If a person gets a payoff right after a behavior appears, that behavior is strengthened. It becomes more likely to occur again under similar conditions.

Another way to say the same thing is:

Any behavior will become stronger when it is followed by a payoff, or reward.

Sometimes the learner knows he is getting a reward and deliberately works for it. That is what a salary is all about. But many times, neither the learner nor the arranger are even aware that behavior is being rewarded, much less being changed. Please notice that we are not only talking about target behaviors—those things you want to do better, or

more of—but also problem behaviors. As you know, the only difference between them is that someone does not like the problem behaviors
and someone does like the target behaviors. But both kinds of behaviors are kept going by their rewards.

I have written a few little stories to show you what I mean about
payoffs. These stories contain payoffs for problem behaviors as well as
target behaviors. Every story is about one or more behaviors, and for
each behavior there is at least one payoff. These rewards are not always
obvious, for they are not always obvious in real life, except to those who
are trained to look for them. This is especially true in the case of
problem behaviors. But keep in mind that if it were not for their
payoffs, all of these behaviors would become weakened and eventually
disappear. While there are many things psychologists do not agree on,
this is one of the least disputed statements a psychologist can make, and
it is backed up by a half century or more of painstaking experimenta-
tion. It is very safe to say that a person learns to expect a payoff for
certain behaviors which have been rewarded in the past.

All of the stories in this book are true, although I have made a lot of
changes, either to simplify them, to make a point more clear, or maybe
just to make them more interesting and entertaining. I have tried to
choose a variety of problems, not only to show how general these laws
are, but also to make at least some of the examples relate more directly
to your own life.

As you read these little stories, try to look for the payoffs which
strengthen the behaviors. In other words, look for the rewards people
got right after certain behaviors took place. You may be able to notice
some rewards I did not include. If so, that is good. I want you to get the
satisfaction of doing each of these things successfully, because success is
one of the most powerful rewards known.

In all of these examples, people have been paid. In most of the
stories, they were not paid with money, which is only one kind of
payoff. There are countless other ways to reward as well, and most of
them don't cost a cent.

Now, please read the stories which follow:

1

A number of years ago I was engaged to marry the lovely young lady
who later became my wife. In marrying Susan, I was also marrying her
four-year old son, for Ricky would be just as much a part of my family
as she was to be. Ricky was and still is one of my favorite people, but just

like everyone else in the world, he had some problem behaviors. Let me describe his first four years of life.

Ricky was a beautiful boy, and his personality was an instant turn-on to nearly everyone who met him. He was therefore given almost everything he wanted, and did not have to earn any of it. If his mother was hesitant deciding whether to give him his way, he could decide for her with a screaming tantrum—not unusual behavior for a child of four.

When a tantrum seemed about to take place, Susan quickly gave in to his desires. That was his payoff. "It's a lot better than fighting all the time about it," she said.

And so things went rather nicely most of the time. She didn't mind keeping busy taking care of his whims, because Ricky often did thoughtful things for her, and he filled a lot of her needs. She had always dreamed of being a mother, and now she had a beautiful boy. She couldn't do enough for him. She had just left an unsuccessful marriage, and her son kept her from being lonely. He made her feel needed, important, and worthwhile—payoffs for her. In return, she fed him and took care of him—his payoffs. Through her he could also get things he didn't actually need, but just wanted, such as toys, or a trip to the park. She also gave him things that everybody needs, like love and attention. These are big payoffs. Never underestimate how important attention, love, and the so-called *social rewards* can be. To a normal child, such as Ricky, adult attention (or its removal) is one of the most important motivating forces known. In other words, attention is a very strong payoff.

Their arrangement was a good one. It usually worked, because each person contributed to the needs of the other. But it taught Ricky a few behaviors which would not be good for him in the long run. It taught him to be demanding at times, and to scream if he did not get his way. He learned that when he screamed people gave in, eager to avoid an unpleasant showdown. Who can blame them? And who can blame him, either? Why shouldn't he scream? He was getting paid for it, wasn't he? He was party to a contract. No lawyer wrote this contract. It was in fact unwritten and unspoken. But it still existed, and it was still binding. If Susan said, "No, Ricky. You can not have any cookies before dinner," he might begin to cry and scream, and she would usually give in. When she gave in, she was using cookies to pay him for crying, although of course she didn't realize that. The result was that he would cry more often under those conditions. When a behavior happens more often we say it has been *strengthened*.

But it worked both ways. Ricky lived up to his part of the bargain. He

paid her for the cookies by becoming quiet. Both parties were reasonably satisfied with the results. This is true of any good contract, entered
freely, and without coercion. But even though he became quiet, situations where he found it necessary to scream occurred more often.
Susan did not realize she had paid Ricky to push her around and
control her. (This story will be continued in Chapter 6).

2

I once taught evening classes in a small college in California. I often
asked the class questions and encouraged them to answer. One night a
girl answered my question especially well, and I told her so. "I enjoyed
your answer, Kathy. It was well thought out, and showed a lot of
creative thinking. You deserve to feel proud of it."

My payoff to Kathy was obvious, and it strengthened her behavior.
She answered questions more often after that. She later enrolled in
another of my classes, and even told me, "You are the best teacher I
ever had."

Kathy admitted she was aware of her payoff, the reason she got it,
and what she should do to repeat the experience. She later told me that
my praise had been one of the main reasons she tried to take every class
I taught at the college.

The second story contrasts with the first, in which nobody was really
aware of the terms of the contract, what the payoffs were, or how they
were earned. In the first story, some problem behaviors were being
strengthened, and this was not the case in the second one. From Ricky's
point of view, however, he was strengthening target behaviors, for he
would have wanted Susan to continue giving out goodies on his command. Kathy wanted more goodies too; she knew exactly how to get the
payoff she wanted, and deliberately enrolled in my class, hoping to get
more praise, although I certainly hope there were other reasons too.

Let's try to analyze what happened: First, Kathy answered my question, which took a bit of courage. She also answered it correctly, which
took a bit of preparation. For making the effort and taking the risk, she
was paid handsomely enough to make her eager to repeat the experience. Answering questions was strengthened, and so was preparation
before class. She did both more often—whenever she got the chance.

3

Bill was a nervous wreck when he arrived home in the evenings. Every day his job put him under extreme pressure, and he was kept in a chronic state of tension. He did not know how to relax and unwind. He worked under those conditions more than three years. On Christmas Eve he went to a party. His host offered him a cocktail, which he drank. The alcohol relaxed him and reduced his tension. The relaxation felt so good that he drank alcohol more often. Alcohol became such an important payoff to him that drinking eventually turned into his most serious problem behavior. Today he drinks so heavily that his job, his marriage, his health, and his respect are all in danger. He knows that he could lose everything he values. Yet, he continues to drink whenever he feels tense, or just before he goes into a situation where he expects to be tense.

4

The children were bored and so were the parents. They had rushed to the airport, eager to greet Grandmother's plane, but the flight was an hour and a half late. Within a short time, the children were running wild. The parents tried to talk, but often had to stop their conversation abruptly in order to run after the children and warn them to get quiet at once. The children quickly forgot the warnings, however, and began to run wild again. The parents did not realize that their attention, coming as it did when the children were wild, made this behavior stronger. It made little difference that the parents were angry with the children. Even angry shouts were more than the children had gotten when they were being "good."

At this time I walked by, having just flown in from back East. I said hello to my friends and we chatted awhile. Soon, the children began to repeat their problem behaviors, and the parents began to repeat their ineffectual shouts and warnings. It was obvious to everyone, including strangers passing by, that the parents had little control of the situation. The mother finally turned to me in frustration and said, "You're a psychologist! What do you think is wrong?"

I explained that the children only got attention when they were running wild. When they were being "good" (that is, doing what the

parents wanted them to do) their parents ignored them. Conversation
was more important. The youngsters got no payoff when they were
good, and they did get attention, plus the fun of running wild, when
they misbehaved.

(This story will be continued in Chapter 7).

5

They had only been married eight months, but something happened
one morning, and the newlyweds began to scream at each other.
Eventually they made up, but the wife shed quite a few tears in the
process. Here is a small sample of what went on, taken from somewhere
in the middle of the argument:

JIM: I work hard all day, but you never give me credit for doing a
            damned thing!
LAURIE: I suppose you think keeping house is all a bed of roses?
JIM: But you're *supposed* to do that.
LAURIE: You smug male chauvinist! You're *supposed* to go to work
            and earn a living, too, so crawl back into your apple.
JIM: Listen here. I make you a good living. If you spent more
            time trying to understand me you'd see that I bring home a
            lot more than Barbara's husband, and you'd stop trying to
            compare me with him all the time.
LAURIE: Maybe you'd stop trying to compare me with Barbara if you
            took your eyes off her low-cut gown. I watched you at the
            New Year's Eve party, and your eyes were stuck there like
            glue.
JIM: I didn't pay her any attention.
LAURIE: Yes you did. You can't fool me. I wouldn't be surprised if the
            two of you paired off in the bedroom. I didn't see much of
            either of you that night.
JIM: Well, I didn't pair off with her, but if you keep pushing me I
            might get tempted. At least, according to what Bob says,
            she's certainly not frigid!
LAURIE: That was a low blow! Maybe I wouldn't be frigid if you were
            more considerate. You never show me the kind of affection
            Bob shows Barbara!
JIM: Damn you, Laurie! I should have known you'd try to twist
            every word I say to make it look like it was all my fault.

LAURIE: This whole thing *was* your fault. I was doing fine, until you came home and started yelling at me right away.

JIM: Who wouldn't yell? I work hard all day and listen to my boss rave, and I take flak from everyone who comes in with a complaint, and then I come home and have a shrew yell at me.

LAURIE: Shrew? That did it!

Does that sound familiar? We'll come back to this incident in Chapter 8, when we talk about punishment, because each person was punishing the other; and we'll talk about it again in Chapter 11, when we talk about developing programs to change behaviors. But for the time being, let's look only for the payoffs.

We are listening again, a few minutes later. In the meantime, Laurie has packed her bags. "I'm going home to mother," she said.

She cried a lot, and this made Jim uncomfortable, so he finally made up with her. The conversation went something like this:

LAURIE: I know you don't love me any more, or you wouldn't talk that way to me.

JIM: *(Putting his arm around her waist and kissing her).* Aw, honey. You know I didn't mean all those things I said. I was just under a lot of pressure from my job. I was taking it out on you because you were a convenient target. You know I still love you.

LAURIE: Mmmm. I wish you'd put your arms around me and kiss me more often. Do you really love me? I don't always feel you do. You hardly ever say it to me any more.

JIM: Sure, sweet. Of course I love you.

LAURIE: And you wouldn't pair off with Barbara if you had the chance?

JIM: Of course not. I just said it to make you jealous. I wouldn't pair off with any other woman in the world. You know that.

LAURIE: Honey, let's not fight any more. I want you to know I still love you. If I didn't, I wouldn't get so upset over everything that happened.
            (They embrace and kiss. They walk into the bedroom together, arms around each others' waists).

LAURIE: You just wait. You'll never call me frigid again after this!
            (The door closes).

A few hours later Laurie received a beautiful bouquet of red roses, with a card from Jim. The card read:

"Orchids mean a romance
That lives but for a day.
But even a few faded roses
Mean love that won't fade away[6]."

Now let's analyze what has happened in terms of payoffs. Laurie got quite a few, and so did Jim. The important point is that when things were going well, neither got as many payoffs. The big rewards came after an argument. We should expect arguments to come more often, under the circumstances, and they did.

Of course, we don't know who started the fight, but it really doesn't matter. Both kept it going, and they both managed to get in a few good solid hits. But in the end, Jim gave in and told Laurie he didn't mean what he had said. In other words, she won the argument, primarily with tears. This is why tears are sometimes called, "women's weapons." The term is unfair, because men can use the same device. In the present case, however, Laurie did use them as a weapon. The term was appropriate, not because she was a woman, but because she used the tears to manipulate Jim. Laurie also won by threatening to leave Jim. After he backed down, the yelling and screaming stopped. Another payoff Laurie received was the fact that Jim became more affectionate. That is, he put his arm around her and kissed her. To judge by her comment, this was a rare act. Then, of course, came the roses and the card, which were payoffs she would not have gotten if they had not first argued. With all those riches at once, is it any wonder that Laurie began to argue more often? Who can blame her for crying and using threats? They worked, didn't they? She did not know her problem behaviors had been strengthened, and probably would have been shocked and horrified if she had been told. She would have denied it. She probably didn't realize she was playing a controlling game. But it still makes no difference, for Jim rewarded her, right after the behaviors, and he didn't stop to ask her whether she knew what she was doing.

But before we start putting too much blame on Laurie, let's take a look at some of Jim's payoffs. He did get quite a few. It is true that they were more subtle, but that doesn't stop them from being just as real and just as powerful. Here were some of his rewards:

1. He stopped the flow of tears. Right away he felt better.
2. Laurie became affectionate to him.
3. She reaffirmed her love for him. This was followed by
4. A most rewarding episode in the bedroom. Possibly most important of all,
5. Jim felt less guilty about the way he had been treating Laurie.

But did you notice? His payoffs also came after the argument. On an ordinary day, when he was being reasonably good to her, he would not have gotten these payoffs. It is little wonder that Jim not only began to argue more often with Laurie, but once the arguments had started, he gave in more often as well.

You should understand that neither one of them deliberately started arguments so they could get rewards. These little payoffs slipped in without either person knowing what they were doing, or why. Many times we learn little lessons without the slightest awareness that we have learned the little lessons.

If we are aware, it might or might not change things. It could work either way, depending on circumstances. But my point is that people do not *have* to be aware of what they are learning in order to learn it. Many psychological experiments have shown that people can learn without knowing they are learning. Aware or not, we go right on learning what we get paid for. We are more likely to repeat behaviors which in the past have been followed by payoffs, regardless of whether we know we are getting paid, or why we are getting paid. Awareness can, of course, make the learning faster, but lack of awareness doesn't stop the learning from taking place.

6

We put one foot in front of the other foot. Left foot ahead of the right. Then the right foot ahead of the left. Each time we repeated this process fifty times, we ended up a bit higher on the mountain. Another fifty times and we were higher still. Hour after hour we put one foot in front of the other. The sun beat down unmercifully, and our packs dragged us down without shame. The loose rocks sometimes rolled underneath our feet, causing us to fall heavily against the sharp stones, and only our stout ropes prevented us from sliding another half mile to the New Mexico plains far below. After many hours of this effort, we emerged on the ridge, and suddenly there was no more rock to climb. We were on top. We had climbed Shiprock!

Why did we drive hundreds of miles to this desolate corner of New Mexico, just to climb to the top of a rock? Why had we voluntarily spent two days in physical torture? Why had we spent the night in sleeping bags tied to steel pitons driven into the rock, so that we would not roll down eight hundred feet while we slept? In other words, what were our payoffs?

First of all, the view took our breath away! From where I stood I could see a small cloud beneath my feet, and to the north I could see into Colorado and Utah. To the west I could see into Arizona, and down below me I could see more than one thousand feet of lava called *Shiprock*. But other things happened which also paid us for our efforts.

At many places along the way, we were able to challenge our skill and strength as we climbed first this cliff, then that chimney, and pushed our way up through a crack that brought us another sixty feet nearer the sky. We did not have to wait to get on top before we got any payoffs, but once there we signed our names in a cairn on the summit. By doing so we joined an exclusive group of men and women who, whether sensible or not, would be able to look back with pleasure. It was a privilege to be able to say, "Yes, I climbed Shiprock!" The wonder and the glory and the admiration which always follow are very strong social rewards (in the everyday language I talked about avoiding, it was an ego trip!).

We were bruised, tired, sunburned, thirsty, and skinned. But would we do it again?

You bet we would! If someone asked me why, I would not say, "Because it is there." I would answer in my own words, "Because it was worth it." In other words, I did it because, in spite of the danger and the discomfort and the extreme effort, it was still fun.

I felt tired, but I felt relaxed, and it felt good. It also felt good to know that Nature had challenged me and I had met the challenge, survived, and mastered it. And I did it all on my own strength, skill, brains, and the superb teamwork, of which I was proud to be a part.

Payoffs? There were plenty, and they were big ones, too!

7

We may talk about how we love our work, but if the paycheck stops, so do most employees. For most people, the paycheck is the most tangible reward they have for their work.

Here I am now, three days after payday, sitting at my desk with a stack of bills nearby. I am writing one check after another. In a few minutes my paycheck will be gone. I worked a month for it, and now I watch while various payments take nibbles out of it: A payment on the house, the car, my wife's new dresses, my child's orthodontist, some oil companies, a new set of tires, utilities, insurance, and records of the Brahms Symphonies, the Beatles, and a nostalgic collection of Glen Miller.

You may wonder what payoffs keep me writing those checks. I got my payoffs when I bought the merchandise, not when I am paying for it weeks later. Some of the payoffs will not even take place until the future (the insurance, or my child's straight teeth). My tires are nearly worn out, the car is depreciated, and my wife's dresses are already out of style, yet here I am still giving away my paycheck. Why? As you will learn in the next chapter, if payoffs are to be most effective, they should come immediately after the behavior they are strengthening. Yet, there must be some payoffs for paying the bills, or paying bills would die out. What could these payoffs be?

Paying bills is a nasty job, and most people hate doing it. They are punished for it by seeing their hard-earned paycheck dwindle rapidly. But they sweat out the job, perhaps for an hour or more, and then they are finished. They breathe a sigh of relief. "Thank heavens that's out of the way for another month," they say, and then relax. That feeling of relief is a big payoff. You'll hear me talk about relief from stress or relief from pain or annoyance many times in this book. It is an important kind of payoff.

What might be some alternatives to paying bills? You could, of course, forget all about paying, as a small minority of people actually do. But what would happen then? Or what if you intend to pay, but you are so busy that you have no time to sit down and write checks? There are many other, more pleasant ways to spend that time. Before you know it, a month has gone by and the creditors begin to stamp *Previous Balance Not Paid* on their statements. Meanwhile, the payments have doubled, because you must now pay for two months instead of one.

What if this turns out to be a very busy month? You work so hard that when you come home you are too tired to do anything but eat dinner, relax a few minutes, watch the evening news, and go to bed. Another month soon passes, and this time you get *Friendly Reminder* letters which are not really very friendly. The tension begins to build. "I really should get to this right away," you say, and one evening you finally do. By this time, the debts have stacked up so high that there isn't enough money to go around. You now have another problem: How to pluck the goose that squawks the least. "Who shall I pay, and how much? Who means business, and who can I put off a bit longer?" You get more and more anxious and tense. Soon the friendly reminders become stern and threatening.

Does that sound familiar? Now, you begin to think, "I could have avoided all this hassle just by paying those bills on time," and you add guilt to your other discomforts.

Finally, you write some checks. You may still owe much, but at least you have done something. It is the best you can do under the circumstances, but you are as relieved as Atlas, taking the world off his shoulders and handing it to Hercules.

That feeling of relief is a payoff for paying bills. So is the knowledge that you have avoided a lot of punishment. Payoffs like these can be strong enough to keep you writing checks every month for the rest of your life.

What about your creditors? We need to explain their behavior too. It took them some effort, but they got paid. Of course, they added interest and finance charges, so they ended with even more money than they might have had if you had paid on time. Their threats are now forgotten. The stores are still your good friends, and still cherish your business. They continue to extend credit. They know that by doing so they can depend on you to buy more, at higher prices, and pay them for the privilege. From their point of view, they can afford to take the risk. Almost all debtors eventually pay up, and the added charges from those who do will more than offset the losses from the small percentage who do not pay at all.

8

"My gosh," I thought! "What on earth can that be?"

But I felt under some pressure to taste it anyway. My boss's wife had worked many hours to prepare this meal for us, and she is a very sensitive person, easily offended. To my surprise, I not only liked the dish, but I eagerly took second helpings.

That was how I learned to love squid. My payoff? I can't say that it looked very good at first, but it was so delicious that today I order squid whenever I see it on the menu.

There were other payoffs too. I managed to avoid embarrassing the boss's wife, and creating an unpleasant scene, with possiblities of future repercussions.

9

I pressed my foot harder on the accelerator. Normally, it takes me twenty four minutes to get to work. I'm just now leaving the house, only eleven minutes before eight o'clock. What can I tell my boss? Being on time is very important to him, and he hates excuses. I'm sure he'll see me, because I must pass right by his desk to get to my office. I've got to face the music.

As it happened, some workmen had blocked off the hallway leading to my office, and I had to come in through the rear entrance. I sat at my desk and began working. A few minutes later, my boss happened to wander back and he saw me. He was impressed.

"Goodness!" he exclaimed. "I didn't see you come in this morning. I was twenty minutes early myself, and you must have been here when I arrived. I'm glad to see you're so conscientious. You know, I've been reconsidering, and I think this proves I should have given you the raise you asked me for last week."

Let's look at my payoffs. First, I avoided being reprimanded, and even got the fringe benefit of a raise. What do you think I could have learned from this?

I could have learned one way to sneak into the office in case I'm late again! I also could have learned to keep my mouth shut when someone compliments me by mistake. In short, I could have learned some dishonest ways of behaving.

But neither of these lessons are particularly worthwhile, even for self-serving reasons. There is always the possibility I'll get caught at it in the future. But even if I let my conscience be my guide, and tell the boss he made a mistake, the *temptation* to escape will still be there. After receiving payoffs for doing something wrong, it would become harder to do the right thing. It would become harder to tell him, "I appreciate your generosity, but I have to confess that the reason you didn't see me come in is because I used the back door. I was really thirteen minutes late. I can't undo that mistake, but I can promise you I'll do my best to keep it from happening in the future. And I can promise you I will try to make the time I spend here count, so that I can be of more benefit to you. After all, that is even more important than coming in on time."

Of course, there would be the risk that the boss might have withdrawn the raise and reprimanded me for being late. But the odds are more heavily in favor of his being positive. He would be more likely to say, "Well, I think that I should forgive you this time. I don't like people being late, but I do need to be able to trust my employees. I am glad to see that you did not take advantage of me when you could have gotten away with it. I like punctuality, but I like loyalty even more. I think you deserve your raise anyway, and your honesty convinces me I'm doing the right thing."

His payoff would be my loyalty, and the trust he could place in me. He would not have to spend most of his time watching me suspiciously to make sure I wasn't taking advantage of him. The payoffs I had gotten would make it more likely that I would try to be honest in the future when someone confronts me with a situation I know I can exploit.

But what if my employer had withdrawn the raise in a nasty tone of voice and docked my pay for thirteen minutes? I would have been punished instead of rewarded. Something like that would make loyalty and truthful behavior much more difficult. "That's the last time I'll try to level with him," would run through my mind. We may know these thoughts are morally wrong, and try to resist them, perhaps successfully. But the thoughts would still be there. Wouldn't you feel betrayed? Wouldn't something like that occur to you under those conditions?

Let's think about that for awhile. Don't we often treat our own children, friends, spouse, or employees that way? Don't we sometimes tell a child, "All right, now. I want you to tell me the truth. Did you throw mud on Mr. Webster's garage?" When the child finally confesses, do we home in on the fact that he was honest, and told the truth? Do we say, "It wasn't easy to tell the truth just then, and I'm very proud that you were able to do it. I am really glad to know I can trust you. That means everything to me. I'm so pleased with your honesty that I'll tell you what. Since there is no way we can get out of your cleaning off the mess you made, I'll at least help you do it, and if you do a really good job, maybe after we've finished we can go to the Confectory and get an ice cream cone. What do you say?"

A lot of parents would not reward the honesty. Would you? They would be too hung up on punishing the child for throwing mud. When the child told the truth, they might say, "Ah ha! I thought so! You can't fool me! I always know when you've been bad, and I can spot a lie a mile away. Well, just for that, you have to clean off his garage, and you don't get to watch TV for two weeks."

If you were the child, would that make you want to tell the truth? I doubt it. The parent must decide whether he wants his child to tell the truth because he *wants* to tell the truth or whether he wants him to tell the truth only because he is afraid of getting caught lying, and being punished for it. Being punished for honesty gives rise to the Watergate philosophy that nothing is wrong unless you are caught at it. Next time you punish your child for telling the truth, stop and ask yourself if you are not building toward another Watergate in the year 2000, just in case your child should become president. A parent must decide whether revenge for throwing mud (or some other problem behavior) is so important that it is worth teaching his child a lifetime of lying. The parent can punish the child because he is mad, and punishing him gets rid of some of his own hostile feelings. But is it worth it?

Of course, there will be many times when punishment will come anyway, but if telling the truth has been rewarded enough, it will become very strong. You will be building a strong foundation for a lifetime of honesty. How much better off everyone would be today if the mothers and fathers of recent presidents had taken more pains to reward honesty in their children!

It would be easy to describe hundreds, or millions, of examples of payoffs, because they happen to everyone, every day. In every case, some behavior, either good or bad, is followed by a reward, and the behavior is strengthened. Notice that I did not say that the behavior is inevitably repeated. Life is seldom that simple. Reward is only one of many things which affect the strength of a behavior, although it is probably by far the most important one. With each reward, the odds will go up that the behavior will be repeated when conditions are similar. The odds probably never reach 100%, but with repeated payoff, a behavior can become predictable enough to count on.

This is what is meant when we say that a person has a habit. Habits are behaviors which have had enough payoff to make them strong. If a problem behavior becomes too strong, we call it a *bad habit*. But bad habits can be weakened, just like any other behavior, and you will learn how in Chapter 5. Likewise, good habits may be cultivated by making sure they are rewarded often enough.

Don't overlook the possibility that unpleasant things can also be rewards. Sometimes, yelling at a person strengthens his problem behavior. This is more likely to happen if the person doesn't have many other ways of getting attention. For example, children may escalate their attention-getting behavior until the parent blows up and shows that he notices them. Sometimes, people would rather be punished than ignored. A person who has been punished a lot may be willing to be punished again, if it means that he can annoy his punisher. The annoyance is his reward. He enjoys seeing his punisher suffer. When Red Skelton, in the role of the mischievous boy, used to say, "If I do, I get a whipping. . . . I dood it!", he was saying that the pleasure of getting someone's goat was such a strong payoff that he didn't mind the spanking, especially if the mischief itself was fun. I have worked with many parents who, unknowingly, had strengthened bad behavior in their children by being brutal to them, and punishing them needlessly. People who have been punished will want to retaliate in some way. I'll talk about punishment in Chapter 8, but for the time being, it is enough to know that retaliation can itself be a payoff.

In the examples I gave you I deliberately chose both good and bad behaviors, because all people have them both, and all people reward them both. In my last story, there was a good chance that sneaking and lying could have been strengthened, even though it is the last thing the boss would have wanted to do. The parents punishing their child for telling the truth about throwing mud would surely not *want* to teach their child to lie. Jim strengthened Laurie's habit of controlling him with tears and threats, and calling him bad names. He certainly didn't want her to treat him that way! Laurie strengthened Jim's arguing more often, and giving in more of the time. While she might have preferred that he give in more, she surely did not want him to argue more. Bill strengthened his own drinking, and he certainly did not want to turn himself into a chronic alcoholic. Susan strengthened Ricky's tantrums when he was younger. The fact that she was able to change her own behavior to make it possible for Ricky's behavior to improve is enough evidence that tantrums were not what she wanted, either.

The moral to the story is this: Behavior which is rewarded is strengthened, regardless of the intentions of the arranger. There is really nothing new about this. If you are observant you can see it every day. But the role of the reward is probably the most important fact about human behavior, even though it is so often overlooked some people can manage to ignore its importance nearly their entire lives. Payoffs strengthen bad behavior and good behavior alike, and taking away payoffs weakens both good and bad behaviors. There is nothing wrong with wanting and working for rewards, and there is nothing immoral about it. It is as natural and moral as breathing and eating. It only becomes wrong when a person pays for behaviors he knows will hurt someone. I will go into more detail about weakening behaviors in Chapter 6, and about the rights and wrongs, in Chapter 15. Please don't jump the gun and try to start in on a program to eliminate problem behaviors until you have learned everything in the first ten chapters, and at least read through Chapter 15. There are some important hazards you should know about before you start.

In the meantime, it will help you a lot if you read through all the examples in this chapter a number of times, until you know all the details by heart. Look for behaviors which are not obvious, and learn which behaviors are considered problem behaviors, who considers them problem behaviors, and why. Then, learn which payoffs come with which behaviors, so you can understand why the behavior developed and persisted. Do not go on until you understand how a behavior which can be self-defeating, such as excessive drinking, sarcasm, lying, etc., can still get such strong payoffs at one moment in the present that it becomes very strong in the future. Do not try to read the remainder of this book until you have learned this chapter so well that you can explain it to other people, answer their questions about it, and in fact, answer any objections they (or you) might have. Take every example I have given and try to point out the rewards to someone else.

When you are comfortable with this, go one more step, and try to think of similar, or related examples from your own life. You don't have to be a mountain climber to find examples of things *you* do for fun that take a lot of hard work and result in discomfort, but are fun anyway. Look for the payoffs. Try to figure out the payoffs other people might give you for them, or you give them, or that you give yourself, or they give themselves, and for what behaviors all these payoffs are given. And remember, the payoffs do not have to be something enjoyable, although most of the times they are. Payoffs just have to be something that happens, and something that happens at such a time that it strengthens the behavior it follows.

Then, try to analyze the behaviors of your friends, yourself, your family, or total strangers that you might see in the supermarket, on the street, in the airport, or in restaurants or parks. Try it even with the behaviors of characters in TV skits or movies, plays, or books. Try to see what the payoffs might be which strengthen and maintain some of their behaviors. You will find that good literature pays some attention to these details, which is one reason why the characters in the classics are so much more convincing and believable than those penned by less skillful writers.

And while you are doing all this, write the examples down, using the precise language you learned in Chapter 2.

When you are really good at these new skills, and feel you understand them quite well, proceed to Chapter 4.

Chapter 4

More About Payoffs.

In Chapter 3 you learned that all behaviors are kept alive by their payoffs, but the only thing I told you about payoffs is that they tend to strengthen behaviors they follow. There are other things you should know about them.

First, you can also measure the strength of a payoff by finding out how hard someone will work for it. Work does not have to be constructive, either. A child (or adult) often "works" hard to get attention. People may even tell him, "You're working too hard at it. Go easy." If he works at it, we know that he has been given attention for those behaviors in the past. The attention strengthened those behaviors, so he now uses them to get attention again. If a person works for a salary, it is because he has been rewarded in the past by money.

Second, just rewarding a target behavior is not always enough. You should catch it as quickly as possible. The longer you wait, the weaker it becomes. Careful experiments have shown that rewards tend to lose strength very soon—in some cases even seconds later. So your rule should always be:

Try to reward as soon as possible.

A weak reward right now might have more influence on behavior than a really big one far in the future. That is why a student might go to a movie tonight instead of studying to pass a test which will help him pass a course which will help him earn a degree which will help him get a better job which will result in a better life five or ten years from now. The movie is now. The test is tomorrow. The degree is four years away. The better life is even further into the future. Is it any wonder that people find so many ways to put off important things? We say that the immediate payoffs *compete* with the distant ones. Those that happen now, regardless of what they are, will have an edge over their competition, and all other things being equal, will win out. If you wait too long, a reward loses much of its power to control behavior. Not only that, rewards tend to have more effect on the the more recent behaviors. If you wait too long to reward, other behaviors will arrive before the payoff, and the most recent behaviors will be strengthened more than the one you aimed for. You may miss the target behavior and hit one you didn't really want, thus strengthening the wrong behavior. For example, a schoolteacher often wants the children to sit quietly in their seats. He commands the children to be seated. He may get the target behavior he wants, sometimes simply because of their fear of him. But having gotten his wish, the teacher may then ignore the children until they get noisy again. Too many teachers fail to reward the children while they are quiet. They do not realize that becoming quiet and remaining quiet are actually two separate processes. It would have taken the teacher very little effort to look up from his tasks every few minutes and compliment the children on how nicely they were doing, or perhaps to read one or two paragraphs from their favorite story, saying, "I'll read you more if you remain quiet another few minutes." The children would then be able to get some immediate benefit from sitting quietly, and incidentally for obedience to the teacher, which seems to be the thing most teachers and parents want more than anything else. The teacher who waits too long to reward sitting down is often faced with a number of the children who get up, roam, or create disturbances. If the reward comes at this time, it will strengthen the problem behaviors. Those children will be more likely to get up, roam, or create a disturbance next time.

When you understand the importance of proper timing you will begin to see two things very clearly: 1) **If you want to change a behavior deliberately, you must arrange things so that a payoff comes as soon after the behavior as possible;** and 2) **You have explained a lot of behavior that people sometimes call "crazy."** Although much crazy behavior is simply attention-getting, not all of it is. By crazy behaviors, I mean those that make no immediate sense. That is, their payoffs are not obvious. And the craziest behaviors are those which cause a person to hurt himself—to defeat himself—to lose out on really important things he wants very much. Most people have a hard time understanding behavior which does not seem logical. Laymen "explain" some crazy behaviors by sayings such as, "People are guided by emotion, not intelligence," or, "When your brain and your gut battle, your gut usually wins," or "Women are emotional creatures, not rational ones." (Of course, nonsense like this does not explain why men also have crazy behaviors.)

If you learn to analyze the situation and discover what rewards are present, when they come, and which behaviors they follow, you will have come a long way toward being able to change the things you don't like into things you do like. For example, have you ever wondered why teen-agers sometimes get into serious trouble when they get together with a gang of their friends? Could be that the immediate approval given by their friends comes right now. That makes it stronger than more important, but also more delayed, payoffs. Many "good children" have been enticed into malicious mischief by the immediate payoffs given by their friends. These payoffs were so powerful that they became more important than the strong punishment the children knew would follow.

Have you ever wondered why a man with everything to lose proceeds to lose it all by drinking, gambling, fooling around, destroying his health with tobacco, insulting his friends, borrowing things he never returns, or other ultimately self-defeating habits? It could be that the immediate benefits had more influence than the more important long-range goals. Tense businessmen, bored housewives, or even frustrated children have found the relaxation and temporary relief from problems which they can get from alcohol or other drugs are stronger payoffs than the losses they will suffer, or the goodies which have been offered to them if they stop. The payoffs from the drugs are now, but the goodies are in the future. So are the punishers which come if the problem behavior continues at a high level. These punishers may be severe. They could include loss of job, loss of friends, alienation of families, breakup of marriage, loss of respect, loss of driver's license, loss of physical health, brain damage, a few days in the drunk tank with derelicts he does not like or respect, loss of self-esteem, a life on skid row, a charge of manslaughter for killing someone while under the influence of alcohol, and many other consequences too numerous to mention. And this does not even include the earliest punisher of all, the hangover, nor one of the worst—and certainly the last—namely, the loss of his own life. These terrible things are in the future, so they often matter less than the immediate relief offered by the drug. This explains why nagging an alcoholic by telling him all the frightening things he already knows seldom has any effect, except perhaps to make him reach for the bottle. Payoffs which happen right now can strengthen problem behaviors and wipe out any possibility a person might have of achieving really big and important rewards which lie in the future. In other words, immediate payoffs can strengthen crazy behaviors.

A lot of crazy behavior exists because people *accidentally* strengthened the wrong behavior. You will remember the rule in Chapter 3 stated, *Any behavior will become stronger when followed by a payoff.* The law did not state that any *desirable* behavior will become stronger, nor any behavior we *deliberately* reward. *Any* behavior will become stronger when it is rewarded, accidentally or intentionally. You will find that most crazy behaviors, and in fact almost all problem behaviors have been rewarded by accident only. People do not try to make a problem behavior stronger. And yet, all of us often strengthen problem behaviors entirely without intending to do so.

Behaviors which have been accidentally strengthened are sometimes called *superstitious* behaviors, because they resemble the way superstitious people behave. A man bowling in an important tournament is ready to make a crucial throw. He reaches into his pocket and rubs a rabbit's foot. He then throws five consecutive strikes. The five strikes are his payoff. It becomes more likely that he will rub the rabbit's foot again next time. Of course, he would have made the strikes without the rabbit's foot (unless it gave him a confidence and relaxation he did not have without it. If so, it was not the fault of the rabbit's foot, but rather the things he told himself about the rabbit's foot. He could have told himself the same things, and gotten the same relaxation and confidence, if he believed in a diamond ring, a piece of lava, a toy car, or a piece of cheese).

Sports fans will have no trouble finding many other examples of superstitious behavior. For example, once the bowler has released the ball, he can no longer influence its path in any way. But still, he sometimes "pulls" it to one side by "body english," by talking to it, or by other pointless behaviors. Gamblers "talk" to dice. Race car drivers carry lucky coins, etc.

Superstitious behavior is very common, not only in sports but in any activity where people move their muscles in complicated ways. This is true because we are calling any behavior superstitious if it has been accidentally rewarded. Even people who do not believe in so-called superstitions still have a lot of superstititous behavior. For example, I once drove an old car that was ailing in many ways. There came a time when it no longer shifted out of low gear very easily. I had developed many different and varied means of coping with the problem, such as shifting quickly, pounding the gearshift lever with the palm of my hand, shoving my foot hard on the accelerator and suddenly letting up, etc. Anyone who has had much experience with old cars will recognize some of these behaviors which, it turned out, were entirely pointless, because the problem with the shifting was solved very neatly and permanently by adding some more fluid to the transmission. In other words, all of my complicated rituals were completely irrelevant, but they continued because the transmission just happened to shift about the time I went through the ritual. The ritual was followed by a reward, and it then became stronger as a result, even though it had nothing to do with my receiving the payoff. That is the essence of superstitious behavior. It is strengthened by payoff which comes immediately after, and has nothing to do with cause and effect.

There are two main reasons why I have gone into detail to make you understand that behavior can be strengthened accidentally. The first, as I have already said, is because problem behaviors get payoff by accident. I've already pointed out that nobody deliberately tries to strengthen problem behaviors. But the payoffs still keep happening. The second reason is that you must be careful you don't accidentally teach an undesirable behavior when you teach a target behavior. For example, suppose your goal is to teach a child how to read better. You decide to reward him with raisins, nuts, candy, or bits of cookie each time he reads the word list correctly. So far, that is fine. But it might happen that you give him the goodie just at the moment he grabs. You want to strengthen good reading habits, but you don't want to teach bad manners, or other behaviors which will hurt him in the long run. So be on the lookout, because problem behaviors often appear together with target behaviors, and the same payoff rewards and strengthens both of them simultaneously.

Even though behaviors become weaker when they are not rewarded, most behaviors will not disappear immediately if you fail to reward them. People still learn, even when they miss out on some rewards. When a behavior is still weak, you only need to miss a very few payoffs before the behavior fails to reappear. But a strong behavior can survive a long time without reward. This is a good thing, because getting a payoff every time you do something is rare, outside of psychological laboratories that set up such conditions ideal to study behavior. Most people hardly ever find situations where such frequent payoff is guaranteed, or comes regularly. Yet all of us learn, or maintain our present behavior in spite of this. I love to tell jokes, but sometimes they fall flat. Even though my audience doesn't laugh every time, they do once in awhile, and that has been enough to keep me telling jokes most of my life.

When a behavior is rewarded sometimes and not others, we have a situation I will call *occasional payoff,* or *occasional reward.* Most of the things we do get occasional payoff, or occasional reward. That is, they are rewarded some of the times, but not others. About the closest we commonly come to a payoff every time is when we drop coins into machines especially rigged up to give us food, drink , or telephone calls. With the exception of these special machines, and some psychological laboratories, we almost never get a payoff every time we do something. These machines seldom fail. On the other hand, if we never get a payoff at all, we will eventually stop trying. Almost all situations fall somewhere between *never* and *always,* and those situations are what I have chosen to call *occasional payoff,* or *occasional reward.* I have already mentioned one example: My telling jokes. People laugh sometimes, but not every time. Here are some other examples. In each one, the behavior is rewarded sometimes, but not every time: Ricky asking nicely when he wants something, people asking other people for dates, salesmen knocking on doors to sell encyclopedias, a hunter shooting at a bird, a batter swinging at a ball, a gambler dropping coins into a slot machine, dialing the telephone number of a very busy friend who is seldom home, trying to please someone who is a chronic complainer, playing chess with a partner who is a bit better than you, nagging to change someone's mind, and writing a letter to a friend who sometimes answers but often does not. There are millions of other examples I did not include, but these should be enough to demonstrate my point. The most important thing about occasional payoff is that it results in more persistent behavior.

One type of occasional payoff we should mention is what I will call an *average ratio.* Technically, it is called a *variable-ratio schedule,* and I'll use its abbreviation, VR, when necessary. An average ratio is when there are not exactly the same number of behaviors occurring each time a payoff comes. Rather, there is an average number. For example, a VR 10 schedule (that is, an average ratio of 10) would mean that the payoff comes *about* every tenth time. But it might be after only seven or eight behaviors, and the next time it might be after twelve or thirteen. This sounds more complicated than it really is, but what it should mean to you is that out of every one hundred behaviors, about ten of them get a payoff. The number (VR 10) is simply a shorthand way of writing *occasional payoff, given roughly every tenth time the behavior occurs.* The larger the number, the "thinner" the schedule is considered, and the more persistent you can expect its behavior to become. That is, a VR 10 schcdulc will result in more persistent behavior than a VR 5, and a VR 75 will be so persistent that you will have a tough time eliminating it. But seventy five, or even ten times without a payoff would probably never happen, unless you went through several stages of smaller ratios first. You will learn later that you should try to get as "thin" a ratio as you can. That is, you should try to get as many behaviors between payoffs as possible, because targets which warrant the trouble of a program will probably be important enough that you would not want them to disappear too quickly. When the payoff comes on an average ratio, the learner already knows that the payoff will come, but is never sure just which time it will be. This is the principle that keeps slot machines in business. The average door-to-door salesman is on a ratio of about VR 16. He knocks on an *average* of sixteen doors to make one sale. He might make three sales in a row, or he might knock on fifty doors without a sale. But if he kept good records for a year or more, he would probably find that he made about sixteen times more calls than sales. The habitual slot machine player will probably get about a 50% to 90% return on his money, which means that he can expect from 50¢ to 90¢ in winnings for every $1.00 he spends. Again, I am talking about long-range average. During a short period he might make $25.00 on a $1.00 investment. But he might also spend $50.00 without winning a cent. If he plays long enough, the 10% to 50% loss is inevitable, and the longer he plays, the closer his average will approach those figures. (The reason for the range from 10% to 50% is because different machines are set to different odds). At times, skilled blackjack players can expect to win about 4% to 5% per hour. That is, for every $100.00 they bet, they should finish with an average of $104.00 or $105.00 at the end of the hour, provided they play strictly according to mathematical probabilities, and there is no cheating involved. Even so, on any series of hands, sometimes over periods as long as six or eight hours, their winnings might run far ahead or far behind this figure. If a series of losses comes before the compensating wins, they may deplete their stake without having had a chance to win at all, although this condition is quite rare. The "runs" of "luck" are what make gambling games so exciting to many people. But they don't wipe out the fact that consistent players, or consistent salesmen, or people who are consistent with any behavior, tend to be rewarded on a ratio that comes close to an average figure. As long as their behavior remains about the same, and their program remains about the same, their payoff will stay about the same. The only way to change the level of payoff is to change something in the program. As you will learn in Chapter 11 and in Chapter 12, this means that either the behaviors, the consequences, or the ratios must be changed.

For some behaviors, the payoff comes more often, or it is bigger, or more important when it does come. In such cases, the behaviors are more likely to persist. Other times, a behavior is rewarded so rarely that it no longer occurs. When I was a young boy, I was uncoordinated and nearsighted. When my friends threw the ball, I swung the bat, but I did not connect very often. When the boys chose teams, I was the last one chosen. They knew that my presence on their team was like the kiss of death to their chances of winning games. I have not played baseball since about 1942, and have so little interest in the game that is has completely dropped out of my life. I switch channels away from the World Series, and I never even know the names of the teams playing. In fact, I only learned a few days ago that the Dodgers had left Brooklyn! Baseball had so few rewards for me that I doubt if it would be possible to give me enough payoff to make me start liking it[7].

Years ago, I tried to make a living by door-to-door sales, but the sales did not come often enough, hence the commissions did not come often enough. I did not get enough payoff to keep me in that profession. Other people do, and some make a handsome living from it. But sales are occasional payoffs. Whether or not the salesperson is successful depends on a number of things, such as the person's history. If he got most of what he wanted very easily—especially when he was young—he is not likely to be very persistent when payoffs do not come often. If door-to-door salespersons must make an average of sixteen calls for each sale, they have to learn to take an *average* of fifteen or more failures in a row. In order to average one sale out of sixteen calls, there will be times when you may hit two or three sales in a row, but other time you may make as many as thirty or forty calls without a sale. It is a reality of mathematics all successful salespersons must learn to accept. But when a behavior has been given occasional reward, it tends to become *stronger* than it would be if the rewards had come every time.

This sounds contradictory, because I told you before that a behavior is strengthened by its payoffs. Both statements are true, because strength can be measured in more than one way. You have learned that a behavior is stronger when it occurs more often. But a behavior is also considered strong if it persists for a long time after all rewards are taken away. All behaviors will eventually disappear under those conditions, but a weak behavior drops out more quickly. When a person has learned to knock on an average of sixteen doors to make his sale he is not likely to quit when he hits ten failures in a row. On the other hand, the person who seldom has had more than three or four failures in a row may be done in by a series of ten failures. We will go into more detail in Chapter 6.

Keep in mind that most target behaviors will not be rewarded very often. Our society does not train people to reward positives. I have even met people who argue that it is not important, or not "moral" to reward good behavior. These people are certainly not going to take the extra time and effort to be sure they give immediate payoff to the target behaviors they like. A person who rejects the suggestion to reward desirable behaviors often justifies his rejection by talking about "bribery." He often says something moralistic, such as, "I refuse to pay him for something he should do anyway."

Of course he should do it anyway! But he doesn't. And if you want him to, consistently, your best way will be to see that it is worth his while to do so. If you do not, you must question your own morality, for you have it within your power to help him do the right things. If you do not do it, you are just as responsible for his not doing the right thing as he is. I am not advocating bribery, but payment, which is a different thing. Bribery implies a person is being paid to do something illegal, wrong, bad, or at least of questionable ethics. If it is wrong to pay for the kinds of behaviors we want then every employer who pays a salary, and every employee who receives one is immoral for doing so. The person who objects to paying someone to do something worthwhile and good simply does not understand the laws of behavior. And not understanding them, he will probably not be aware that he is frequently guilty—as is everyone else in the world—of paying off problem behaviors. He may continue to reward problem behaviors without even thinking about bribery, and thus never feel the bite of his conscience. But if it is wrong to pay for good behaviors, how much worse it should be to pay for bad ones!

Often, too, this person might not feel any ethical qualms about using punishment. How often I have heard people beg me for help, saying, "I've tried everything and nothing works. What should I do now?"

If I pin them down and make them describe exactly what they meant by *everything,* it never fails. They describe a wide variety of punishers they have used, or goodies they have taken away. On those rare occasions when they were aware of rewards and tried to use them, they usually used them wrong, in ways such as asking for too much behavior for too little reward, over too long a period of time (see Chapter 11 and Chapter 13). Few people will want to mow a five-acre lawn for only 50¢. But even the incorrect use of reward is so uncommon that whenever I hear. "I've tried everything," I am not afraid to guess that they have really tried nothing at all, except punishment and taking away rewards and privileges.

Most of the rewards people get come more or less by accident, but the whole point of this book is that it doesn't have to be so haphazard, and it won't be, if a person really wants to have something to say about the way behaviors affect his life. Under the present circumstances, the rewards earned by desired target behaviors happen in such a random, unsystematic way that it often surprises me that we learn anything worthwhile at all.

Problem behaviors are usually given occasional reward. The behavior may be learned more slowly than it would be if it had been rewarded every time, but it will also be harder to eliminate, once it has been learned. It will drop out more slowly (see Chapter 6). I have seen many new, weak behaviors disappear after they happened only two or three times without a payoff. I have also seen some problem behaviors which had been rewarded occasionally. Some of these persisted hundreds or even *thousands* of times without being given a single payoff I could recognize. While it is true that this behavior occurred in a state hospital patient with one of the most severe problem behaviors in the country, it is also true that the so-called mentally ill and mentally retarded are human beings, and like all other human beings their behavior follows exactly the same scientific laws. Normal or abnormal, the problem behavior disappeared eventually because we deliberately ignored it and would not give him the payoff he wanted for the behavior.

The bachelor who "scores" quickly is not as likely to be persistent as the one who scores less often, and has to work harder at this pastime. He is more likely to quit sooner when he encounters an unwilling partner. In all likelihood, he has more alternatives as well, so he does not have to put all his eggs in one basket.

The most important things to remember about occasional reward are:

1. *Since the payoff does not come every time the target behavior appears, there are not as many opportunities for the behavior to become strengthened. Learning is therefore somewhat slower;* but

2. *Once learning has taken place, behavior rewarded occasionally tends to become more persistent, and will last a lot longer in situations where little or no payoff is present.*

3. *The thinner the schedule of reward, the more persistent the behavior is likely to become. That is, the more times the behavior occurs between rewards, the less likely it will be to drop out.*

4. Even strong behavior, rewarded on a thin schedule, will ultimately disappear when it happens enough times in the complete absence of rewards.

You should understand that payoffs are very individual things, too. George Bernard Shaw was said to quote his own Golden Rule: *Do not unto others as you would have others do unto you. Their tastes may be different.* There is truth in the saying, *One man's meal is another man's poison.* In other words, I like things you don't like, and vice versa. Different strokes for different folks. All these clichés mean the same thing, and their message should be obvious to everyone. Still, it is surprising how often we try to reward all people as though they have exactly similar tastes and interests. While it is true that some rewards such as money, attention, etc. are in demand by most people much of the time, there are times when people may refuse to do something for these rewards too. For that person, at that time, there are other rewards stronger than money. The reason money is a more or less universal reward is that money can be traded for a wide variety of other things which are actually the true rewards. If you are hungry, money can buy food. If you are thirsty, money can buy you a drink. If you are cold, money can buy you a warm coat. Sad, but true, if you are lonely, money can buy some friendships, and if you are insecure, money can buy status and political power. Yet, there is still no such thing as a *truly* universal reward. What's more, the strength of any reward is constantly changing, as the individual's states of deprivation change.

Food is a strong payoff only to a hungry person, and bits of candy work well with young children, or with some of the residents of mental institutions. But it would be a mistake to think that just because they happen to like it, that it will automatically work as well with you, or with me. It is sometimes a good place to start, when looking for payoffs that work, but there are many times one particular reward will not work at all. Few people—even chronically hungry ones—will work very hard for food just after they have eaten a big meal. Bushmen tribes may go days without food, but when they kill a gemsbok or impala or other big animal, they eat their fill and then rest awhile.

To me, one of the strongest rewards is classical music. There are many people who don't like it at all. How I feel about them doesn't matter in the slightest. While I might happen to think they are unfortunate, or uneducated, or insensitive, or whatever, the fact remains that my own tastes are unimportant, if I am the arranger trying to use classical music as a payoff to teach some behavior to a learner who doesn't like music. If I want to strengthen some of *his* behavior, I must not fool myself into thinking I can do so by playing records of the Metropolitan Opera as a reward. In time, of course, I believe I could teach almost anyone to love it, and it would be no harder than just having him hear the same selections repeatedly, until he became familiar with them. Once the learner likes the music enough, *then* it can be used to reward other behaviors, but not until then.

I haven't really talked about what kinds of payoffs there are. Some of the more obvious ones are attention, money, physical contact, praise, gold stars, or (mostly with children) such goodies as bits of cookie, candy, food, and toys. Needless to say, none of these stay the same strength at all times, although probably money will tend to be one of the most stable over a long period of time. You will have a better idea why after you read Chapter 14, for money is the best example I know of what is called a *token*. I won't try to explain tokens to you now, but I should point out that one of their main values is that they permit an arranger to give the learner more freedom to choose what his reward is going to be.

Physical contact is another strong reward, although it too may sometimes be weak. Children are especially fond of such physical rewards as hugging, back scratching, kissing, running your hand through their hair, squeezing their shoulder gently and reassuringly, and many others. We call things like physical contact, attention, love, kind words, smiles, and encouragement *social rewards*, because all these things involve interactions with other people, and cannot exist without other people. Maybe it is too obvious to mention at all, but there are some types of physical contact which are sexual in nature, and should certainly be confined to consenting adults. Even in these cases they should be used with good judgement, and it should be positively mandatory that such rewards are done for the benefit of the learner, and not just as a means for the arranger to exploit him (or her, as the case may be). The ethics can get very involved and complex. For example, is it permissible for one partner to reward the other by means of sexual acts? My answer is probably too simple to cover many situations, but there are two considerations which come to mind: 1) Many times people already use sexual rewards, to say nothing of the other rewards they give, after problem behaviors by their partners. Remember the story of Laurie and Jim? In cases such as these, both people should be made aware of what they might be doing to their relationship, and take care that there are plenty of opportunities for the same reward after desirable behavior. Sex is often used as a means of exploitation, whether it is the husband threatening to step out if his wife does not give him his way (remember Jim's threat?) or whether it is the petulant wife who suddenly has a headache when she is displeased with her husband (remember Laurie's confession that she was frigid because Jim did not treat her with consideration?), or whether it is Don Giovanni, using Laporello's list of conquests as a means of convincing himself of his masculinity. Essentially, these are all examples of how sex is used as a reward following behaviors which are not always in the best interest of all parties involved; 2) Why not turn things around, and use the same rewards to encourage desirable behaviors? Couples can deliberately set up a specific program, arrived at by mutual agreement, which would require that the partners delay their sexual gratification until certain target behaviors had taken place. Such arrangements should never be done on the spur of the moment, by one partner keeping the terms of the arrangement a secret from the other. All details of such arrangements should be discussed thoroughly and agreed upon in advance, and it should be understood that no agreement, no go. Such programs can be quite effective in improving sexual relations between two people. You will learn more about mutual contracts in Chapter 14.

Each of us has many, many payoffs, and we are always learning new ones. That is just another way of saying that we like many things enough to work for them. But some rewards are what psychologists call *idiosyncratic*, which means that one person will work hard for them, but very few other people get turned on to them. I have seen many severely retarded patients in state hospitals wandering around with strips of cloth, pieces of plastic, or bits of string they twirl for hours at a time. To most of us, these objects would mean very little. But many of the patients would do whatever they could to get one of these goodies. For them, a bit of string or a piece of cloth might be far more valuable than a $100 bill, which would just be something to tear into strips and eat.

I have used idiosyncratic rewards such as flashing a slide or home movie on the wall, letting a child look at his image in a mirror, tossing a child into the air, stretching the neck of a balloon so that the escaping air squawked, petting a puppy, listening to a tape recording of the child's parents, riding a tricycle, or simply letting a child run in a large circle. With adults, I have used payoffs such as arranging time off a job, trading stamps, university credit for work on a research ward, "points" earned toward a trip to Hawaii, a letter of recommendation to the admissions offices of various universities, "bonus packs" to Reno or Lake Tahoe, and other such imaginative rewards. What works best for one person might not work at all for another. We can't use the Met-

ropolitan Opera for everyone. Most children like candy; but I have
seen other children spit it out. I once worked with a young girl who
would not perform the target behaviors when she was rewarded with
ice cream, but we taught her to walk by crinkling a sheet of paper near
her face when she took her first, shaky steps, at the age of twelve. She
seemed to enjoy the noise of the crumpled paper more than she
enjoyed other, more conventional payoffs.

Therefore, we should never take it for granted that just because we
happen to like something, or because most people like something, it
will automatically be a reward for someone else. Remember that for
me, two tickets to the World Series would not be any incentive to work
at anything. But a ticket to hear a Horowitz or Rubinstein piano concert
would be. The very opposite might be true of you.

We must always tailor the program to the needs and desires of the
individual learner. When I was a young boy, my older brother was
dating a girl who occasionally brought me gifts, apparently in hopes
this would earn her a few points with him. Unfortunately for her, she
gave me baseball equipment just at the time I hated baseball most. I
would have enjoyed a telescope, or a book about astronomy much
more. I would have worked very hard to earn a telescope, but not for
baseball equipment, which meant nothing to me. Millions of boys my
age, and girls, too, would have worked just as hard for the baseball
equipment. They might have had just as little interest in a book about
the stars as I had in baseball. Every person likes or wants or needs
certain things, and these will be his rewards, regardless of whether the
arrangers like them or not. In the past twelve years, I have seen many
hospitalized mental patients whose strongest payoffs are cigarettes and
cigars, which I would place near the top of the list of things I hate most.
So you see that rewards are very individualized things, or as I said
before, "Different strokes for different folks."

So far, I have talked about rewards as if they are something a person
likes. Usually they are. That is, a person usually works for the things he
likes. If they are given to him after he has done a certain behavior, they
will strengthen that behavior. Most of the time, the things a person likes
can be used as payoffs, and the other way around, too. He usually likes,
or grows to like those things which strengthen the behaviors they
follow. But this is not always so. For example, there are times when
people have what we call *attention-getting behavior*. Attention is a strong
social reward. Both children and adults have various attention-getting
behaviors. They may talk too much, compete for the limelight, brag,

pick a fight, wear flamboyant clothes, or maybe wear too few of them. All of these behaviors are designed to get someone's attention. But not all attention-getting behavior is bad. Most people will also work for recognition, fame, respect, and status, or for one of the goals philosophers have long considered to be among the most noble—self-improvement, essentially for the same reason: To attract attention.

Some attention-getting behavior may simply be silly, like a boy making faces and noises; or annoying, like whining or nagging; or dangerous, like walking on the ledge of a tall building. It may be all of these. And all of these usually get attention, too, even if the whining and nagging continues until someone screams or slaps the whiner. But remember what I said before. Most people would rather be punished than ignored, so you can't always go by how pleasant something may seem. You must go by the rule: *If a behavior is followed by a payoff, it is more likely to be repeated under the same conditions in the future.* If slapping a child to stop attention-getting behavior actually makes the child do it more often, slapping strengthens the behavior, even though he may stop quickly each time he is slapped. Slapping has the same effect as reward, no matter how much the slap hurt. Many times parents punish children, intending to stop a problem behavior, but their punishment actually strengthens it instead. The pain is no evidence that slapping was not a reward. Rather, it is evidence that the relationship between the parent and the child has become so fouled up that even a slap is more welcome than anything the child got when he was not being annoying.

Each time they punish the child, the behavior stops at once, even though the halt may be temporary. Stopping the episode and preventing the next one from happening might very well be two separate processes, as you will learn in Chapter 9. The relief from the problem convinces the parents they are stopping the problem. And they are, for that moment. Thus, their own behavior is strengthened, so they tend to punish the child more often in the future. But it may also make the problem behavior happen more often, so that the parent must escalate, and use a stronger punisher. If the emphasis is placed upon the desirable, target behaviors, and if the proper records have been kept, you should not fall into that trap very often. Nor would governments escalate wars when it was apparent that the little wars were not successful programs.

So remember: Payoffs are usually things someone enjoys receiving, but not always. Use your eyes. See if the behavior is occurring more often as a result of what has been done. If so, that is the proof that the consequence was really a reward.

Now I want to give you an example of one type of situation in which reward does not work very well. It is sometimes called *backward conditioning*[8], because the payoff is given before the target behavior appears. We often find parents dealing with their children in the following way:

CHILD: May I please go swimming with Buster and Charley and Norma and Margie?

PARENT: I told you before that you can't leave the house for any reason until you have cleaned your room.

CHILD: But they're going to leave without me. Can't I clean my room after I get back?

PARENT: Well, O.K., if you will promise me you'll do it right away when you get back.

CHILD: I promise.

Needless to say, the parent often loses out on this deal. Very few employers pay their workers in advance. Be sure you have not accidentally done some backward conditioning. In other words, be sure you give the payoff *after* the target behavior, and not before. The target behavior is your payoff, and you should be sure you do not miss out on any of it.

But never forget that from the child's eyes, or the employee's, or any other learner's point of view, they are being asked to give you backward conditioning. That is, they are giving you the payoff before you give them theirs. Someone always has to be first. They do the work before they get paid. They are put into the position of trusting you. Do not ever let them down. You must be sure you don't forget to give them their rewards. In other words, don't do it this way:

CHILD: May I please go swimming with Buster and Charley and Norma and Margie?

PARENT: I told you before that you can't leave the house for any reason until you have cleaned your room.

CHILD: But they're going to leave without me. Can't I clean my room after I get back?

PARENT: No. You know the rule. I'm sorry, but I can't make an exception.

          (*The child goes back to his room and cleans it thoroughly*).

CHILD: I cleaned my room. Now I'm going to ride my bike down to the lake and see if I can find Buster and Charley and Norma and Margie. They said they'd be there the rest of the afternoon.

PARENT: No, it is too close to dinner time. You can't go now.

With this kind of payoff, is it any wonder that:
1. The child will not be terribly eager to clean his room next time?
2. The child will feel angry and betrayed? And
3. The child will be less able to trust his parent in the future?

Backward conditioning did not work for him. He gave the parents their rewards but did not receive his own in return. He will probably not break his neck living up to his part of later agreements.

Before we leave the subject of rewards, I would like to discuss a point which might have bothered you, because almost every time I give a lecture, someone in the audience says something to the effect of, "I see how behaviors are strengthened by their payoffs, but I just don't know if I like the idea that everyone is so materialistic, and so mechanical. It rubs me the wrong way."

I can understand the person's concern, and sympathize with it, but the fact that someone does not like a scientific law is irrelevant, and a trifle grandiose and silly. Whether or not you or I or anyone else like it is beside the point. That just happens to be the way it is, and we must either accept it or simply pretend it is not so. Nature is uncompromising, and does not make exceptions for those who feel her laws are unjust, or unflattering. If we wish to pretend, that is our right, but we should understand that this is what we are doing. Still, our behaviors and the behaviors of others around us—and everywhere else, too—will go on following the same laws, despite our protests. It makes no difference if I decide I hate gravity, and think it is immoral or too mechanistic. If I drop my wife's fine china bowl it will still fall. The tides will still flow in and out, and Jupiter will remain in its orbit just as firmly as it would if I did approve. All the king's horses and all the king's men can do nothing at all to change it. To deny what exists means you must live in unreality, and there is certainly no virtue in ignorance. Let the children have their fairy tales for entertainment, but let us not try to deny facts of life just because we do not approve! If we deny what exists, it will only make it harder to give ourselves and others a life more free of problems.

Chapter 5

Weakening Behaviors

So far we have talked about payoffs, what they are, some things about them, and what they do. Strictly speaking, they do one thing. They strengthen, or increase those behaviors they follow. We want to strengthen target behaviors because they are the behaviors we want. We try to *aim* our efforts at them, and *home in* on them. That is why we call them *target behaviors*. But that is only half of the story. Remember that we dislike some behaviors, too. We'd like to decrease, or eliminate them. These are the problem behaviors. They are often present because they have been rewarded, or they wouldn't exist. But you don't want to reward them any more, because they are already too strong.

This chapter is to help you understand that side of the picture: How problem behaviors, or any other behaviors, for that matter, become weakened or eliminated. To make a long story short, there are three ways in which a behavior can be decreased, and the next three chapters will deal with each of them, in more detail. Let me list them first, and tell you something about them. Then we'll quickly move on to Chapter 6.

The most important way to decrease a behavior is simply not to reward it, and not let other people reward it, either. This makes sense. After all, if the problem behavior is strengthened by its rewards, you should be able to weaken it if you make sure that the learner does not get a payoff after the behavior you don't want. If a behavior occurs repeatedly, and each time there is nothing to strengthen it, that behavior will eventually stop reappearing regularly. It may happen quickly, if the behavior is weak, or it may take a long time, if it is strong. But even it it takes thousands of times, the behavior will eventually disappear if it is never rewarded. And by the way, it hardly ever takes thousands of times. So remember that if you want a behavior to become weaker, you must withhold payoffs. The process of weakening a behavior by failure to reward it is technically known as *extinction*, although I will call it *behavioral starvation*, or *starving*, for reasons I will discuss in Chapter 6, when I go into more detail about the process.

The next way in which a behavior is weakened is by strengthening some other behaviors which take its place. These other behaviors are called *competing behaviors*. The name is a good one, because just as in other forms of competition, one person or behavior gets goodies at the expense of another. In economic competition, or political competition, one person gets money, a job, or some other good, at the expense of someone else, because there is not usually enough to go around. Similarly, when one behavior gets rewarded at the expense of another, that is behavioral competition. Sometimes, competing behaviors are called by their technical name, which is *incompatible responses.* This is also a good name, because it tells us what the behaviors are and why they compete. *Incompatible* means that the two behaviors don't go together very well. The way I will use the term, it will mean *two or more behaviors which cannot happen at the same time.* Some examples are: Sitting down and standing up, screaming and whispering, smiling and frowning, holding both hands below your waist and holding them above your head; and lots of others. You should learn to look at any behavior and be able to find some other behavior incompatible with it.

If this seems silly, try to remember that you can often eliminate a problem behavior by increasing competing behaviors. I'll tell you how in Chapter 7, and you'll read about one example in Chapter 6, as well.

Finally, one of the most common ways people try to eliminate behavior is by punishment. I have left it last for a number of reasons. First of all, scientists do not know as much about punishment as they do about reward. It is easy to get people to take part in experiments that dish out rewards, but if you had your choice, would you volunteer as a subject in an experiment that promised you punishment? And whether we like it or not, a large part of scientific knowledge comes from carefully designed experiments.

Aside from the fact that we really don't know as much about punishment, what we do know makes it unmistakably clear that using punishment is a lot trickier than using rewards, the results are less certain, and there are many more side effects, both predictable and unpredictable. There are other reasons that punishment should not be used when you have other choices, and we'll go over them together in detail in Chapter 8. For the time being, I should only state that punishment is probably one of the most common ways people try to deal with their problems, and it is also probably one of the least successful. This is especially true when it is used the way most people use it.

So there you have it. The three ways to decrease a behavior are: 1) *behavioral starvation;* 2) *strengthening of competing behaviors;* and 3) *punishment.* Needless to say, a little thought will convince you that regardless of your main approach in any program you develop, you should always starve the problem behaviors. Even though you might plan to rely primarily on punishing a child for his problem behaviors, it would make no sense to reward that same behavior. You will want to eliminate the payoffs for it just the same, in any case. This is also true of rewarding competing behaviors. Why bother trying to replace a problem behavior with a better target when you're going to continue strengthening the problem behavior you hope to eliminate?

Actually, the best strategy usually involves a combination of the first two methods. Where punishment is necessary, it should never be used except as an addition to the other two, and then only in very clear-cut situations that are well defined beforehand. That is, never use punishment unless it is a part of a well-organized program whose main features include the starving of the problem behaviors and frequent payoff of one or more competing target behaviors. Most of the time, when these two consequences are used, punishment is no longer necessary. You should develop the habit of asking yourself why you are using punishment at all. Usually it means you are failing to reward competing behaviors as well as you should, and you might even be rewarding the problem behaviors, instead of starving them. This situation is so common I am tempted to make it a general statement, but since there are some exceptions, I will not.

One last thought about decreasing behaviors. Remember that we are only talking about problem behaviors, and how to decrease them. They are the ones you want to decrease. Unfortunately, in everyday life, our target behaviors are also exposed to one or more of these three processes, and may also become weakened as a result. It certainly does not make any sense to *try* to teach target behaviors by the use of punishment, which is a method of decreasing behaviors. (For an exception, see Chapter 9). Unfortunately, many teachers and parents have used punishment for so many years that they rarely realize there are other, and much better options available. As I said before, people often tell me, "I've tried *everything*." But they hardly ever mention trying to increase target behaviors. They even seem surprised, and sometimes shocked, or even resentful, if I point this out to them. "Why, I never thought of that before," they might say.

Remember: Even if you are going to use behavioral starvation or punishment as your main tools in a program to decrease a problem behavior, don't forget that your job will be much easier, more effective, and vastly more pleasant if you never forget to replace the problem behavior by frequently rewarding alternative, target behaviors.

Chapter 6

Starving a Behavior: Tune It Out and Let It Die

This is an important chapter, so study it well. Half of your job in changing behaviors will be to increase desirable (target) behaviors, but the other half will be to decrease the undesirable (problem) behaviors. As you will soon learn, increasing target behaviors should be a much bigger half, and it really should take up the majority of your efforts—if I had my way it would be 95% or more. You'll see why in Chapter 7. Meanwhile, as you try to teach a new behavior, it makes no sense to keep the problem behaviors alive by continuing to reward them. You must learn to ignore the problem, or "tune it out." You must not allow the learner to get a social payoff right after his problem behaviors. This can be done without taking extra time, and is the reason I only allowed 5% for that part of the program. But it is still half of the problem.

You can weaken a behavior if you let it happen without reward. You simply let it die out. The technical name of the process is *extinction*, but as I said before, I will call it *behavioral starvation*, or simply, *starving*. You extinguish, or *starve*, a candle flame by removing the oxygen that keeps it alive. You starve a behavior by removing the payoffs that nourish it and keep it alive.

But even when you no longer reward them, only the very weakest behaviors drop out quickly. Most of the problem behaviors that bother you are already strong, or you would not be so concerned with eliminating them. Therefore, you must be patient enough to ignore the behavior repeatedly before it finally drops out completely. Informed parents and teachers have long understood that the best way to eliminate tantrum behavior or attention-getting behavior is to ignore those behaviors as long as necessary. Eventually they must stop. It is a bad mistake to give a person the thing he is throwing the tantrum for. This would give him a payoff, and strengthen his throwing tantrums. Even worse, such payoff probably would not come at the beginning of the tantrum, but usually in the middle. This would make it an occasional payoff which would, as you know, strengthen the problem behavior even more. In Chapter 4, I explained how salespersons work for occasional payoffs. That might be a good reason why the traditional image of the salesperson is one of excessive persistence. Occasional payoff produces persistent behavior. If Susan had rewarded Ricky's screaming after he had continued for thirty minutes, he would have learned that he could get his wish by screaming, but he might have to do it more than a half hour. In other words, she would then have rewarded him for thirty minutes of screaming. It is easy to see why occasional payoff can keep a behavior so strong.

Let me warn you, then. If you decide to eliminate a behavior by starving, you can do it, but you might have to stick with it a long, long, time. Part of that time will be very frustrating, too, because in addition to the necessity for you to subject yourself to a big dose of the problem behavior, you will also feel that you are not getting anywhere. This will happen at the start, especially, but it happens in the final stages as well.

Starving a behavior is sometimes a tricky process. First of all, when a person has been getting a payoff pretty regularly for a certain problem behavior and he suddenly gets none at all, there is often a temporary increase, or *surge* in the strength of the problem behavior. Sometimes, there is also an increase in new, random behaviors. For example: Suppose a parent decides that next time little Doris begins a tantrum, he will deliberately refuse to give in to her demands. The parent may then try to ignore Doris's screaming as much as possible, which is hardly ever an easy thing to do. Doris may, for a time, escalate her tantrum. Getting no results, she may jack up the decibels. She may do more than scream louder. She may kick her feet, hit with her fists, bang her head, or hold her breath. All of these attention-getting behaviors will eventually decrease, if the parent is only patient enough. You should know ahead of time how you expect to protect people or property, to prevent them from becoming casualties of her temporary aggressiveness. If possible, the program should be carried out where no self-inflicted injury, or injury to other people or property can take place. You should be warned ahead of time that behavior sometimes dies out very slowly, and that it may increase for a short time at the very beginning. This sudden surge sometimes fools people into thinking that their basic program is not good, and that ignoring a behavior only makes it worse. I am making a point of telling you this to prepare you for the surge, which might or might not come. Your program will take time, and it will take patience, patience, and still more patience. You may take it from me that there will be many times when it is not easy, and you may feel a lot of guilt over it. I know I often do, and have to catch myself. The child's cries of rage and frustration are designed to pluck at your heart strings and deliberately make you feel bad. I have often heard clinicians call this, "psychic pain," and perhaps it really is pain. But the reason I feel they are crying out is because they are angry that they didn't get what they wanted. They have also learned that at least some of these cries of pain are part of a very effective strategy of control, or coercion, of other people. There are few things that can cause someone's opposition to fold as quickly as guilt!

Still, as long as you know what to expect, and above all, if you know that what you are doing is right, and will eventually result not only in your own comfort but also in benefit for the child, you will find it much easier to keep from giving up the ship before it has had a chance to prove itself seaworthy.

Figure 1 describes a typical case of starving, although not every case will follow it exactly. Notice that near the end the curve flattens out (near D). This means that for some time, the behavior will continue, but at a low rate. The weakening of the behavior past D will be gradual. Sometimes, people are fooled into thinking nothing is happening, so they lose interest and quit. But the prolonged low rate is one of the facts of life, as much as the overall weakening, the surge, or for that matter, the increase which originally resulted from payoffs and brought the

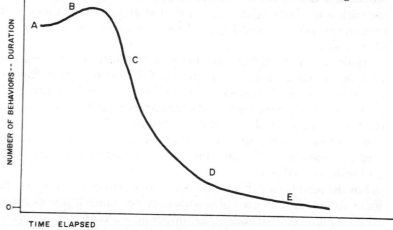

TIME ELAPSED

Figure 1. Typical curve, showing behavioral starvation. Reward is stopped at A. Note the surge, or increase at B. Decrease is fastest around C. With continued starvation, the curve begins to flatten (D). Beyond E, the behavior still weakens slowly, but continues to occur at a low rate for some time to come.

behavior up to its present strength. They are all a part of the way normal people behave under normal conditions of behavioral starvation. If you are also rewarding competing behaviors, however, you can expect the results to be more rapid. You might not even get the beginning surge (B) and maybe you would not get the long period of low-rate behavior, either.

In the first story of Chapter 3, I told you about the payoffs exchanged between Susan and Ricky, and how they helped develop a problem behavior—Ricky's tantrums—that was annoying, but in time would result in problems still worse, and harmful to him as well. Here is the follow-up I promised:

When Susan first asked me for my help in dealing with this problem behavior, I analyzed the situation for her and explained about their mutual payoffs. I told her, "I promise you it won't be easy, but I will help you eliminate the tantrum behavior if you will first agree to two conditions: 1) We must tune out the tantrums." (We must starve them and let them die out. Ricky must never get a payoff when he throws a tantrum); and 2)"We must give him a good alternative way to get his payoffs." In other words, we must lavishly reward the good alternative. We agreed that a suitable target behavior would be his saying, "Please," in a nice, pleasant way. We chose this behavior because it was one which would benefit him for the rest of his life, and because it was incompatible with a tantrum. Think about that statement a moment. Can you scream and ask for something in a nice, pleasant way at the same time? Of course not.

Again, I reminded her that this program would not be easy at first, and that we would have to devote our full time to it. Starving a strong problem behavior is not something which can be done very well on a part-time basis. I have said before that problem behaviors do not always die fast. So we started at a time we both had a holiday and a weekend, and we knew we could devote three consecutive days to the problem. As it turned out, that was really more than enough for the first, hardest, and most crucial part.

For the next two or three days, we went out of our way to do whatever Ricky asked, and to give him whatever he wanted, just as long as he asked for it nicely, without screaming, and with some consideration for the feelings of others. We were using the second method described in Chapter 5: Building and strengthening a desirable, competing alternative behavior. But if Ricky began to scream, we just let him continue, without consequence on our part. We first told him what he could expect as the result of a screaming tantrum, but after we had explained once, we said no more. We did not even look at him or talk to him until he stopped. It was pretty rough, because the good behavior didn't start right away. Here is how it all happened:

We had driven into San Francisco for a pleasant day's outing together. As we walked through Chinatown, Ricky accidentally dropped some of the bubble gum he was chewing. He wanted to pick it up off the sidewalk.

"No, Ricky. That's dirty. We'll have to throw it into the litter can, and get you some more later."

Then the fireworks started! He screamed, "I want my bubble gum!" And he did not stop screaming.

I looked at Susan and nodded. She spoke in a calm voice, and told him, "When you are nice to us we'll be nice to you again. But when you're screaming and crying, we will not even answer you."

He began to scream louder (we were into the surge). Neither of us answered him. I took him by the hand and we walked in silence—that is, as much silence as there could be while he was screaming! We continued walking, pulling him gently by the hand so he would come along with us. He then began to drag his feet, so I lifted him off the ground, holding him aloft by one arm, and we continued to walk. He then wrapped his legs around his mother, almost tripping her. We still did not answer him. He escalated some more. With his free hand he swung and kept hitting. Still, we did not look at him and we did not answer him. Instead, Susan and I did our best to talk together normally, carefully leaving Ricky out of the conversation. Had he stopped screaming, we would of course have included him. But he did not. He began to cry, "Mother, I hate you. You're a killer!"

Strangers passing by would encourage us, "Spank him! Spank him!" Susan looked at me in perplexed agony, while I whispered to her, "Be patient. Just tune it out and let it die. It won't last forever!"

It continued for the next fifty two minutes. But I knew that I could be more stubborn than he, because I knew something about starving a behavior. Sooner or later he would have to stop, and *that* was what I was waiting for. It was inevitable, and I knew it, but he did not. This knowledge gave me an advantage.

As I promised Susan, it was not easy. We walked to the top of Nob Hill (almost four hundred feet of elevation) and back down the other side to our car, and then we drove around, never once talking to him while he screamed. At times he would become quiet for a few seconds. At one such time I told Susan, "I'll be glad when Ricky stops screaming, so that we can talk to him again."

At the mention of the words, *"Stop screaming,"* he began again. He would not give up the battle easily. We continued to ignore his screams, even when he begged, "Mommy, talk to me! Why won't you talk to me?"

Susan's eyes pleaded with me, for neither of us were immune to his distress, nor to the guilt it produced in us both. But we knew before we began that we were right, and this gave us the strength to continue. It would have been easy to give in. But giving in would only have taught him that he could outwait us, and that tantrums really do work after all, if they can only be continued long enough and loud enough. So we continued in silence.

Finally, he seemed to stop for a rest. I then nodded to Susan, and she said, "Ricky, what do you want?"

"I want my bubble gum!" And the tantrum began again.

It is not easy to tell how long a tantrum lasts, because it slows down gradually, like the curve shows any starved behavior to do. After Ricky was silent about two minutes, however, we happened to pass a donut shop. I worded my question carefully, as I did not want to get him started again on the bubble gum. I said, "Ricky, would you like some donuts?"

"Yes."

"Then you may have some if you say, 'Please, may I have some donuts'?"

He asked me nicely, "Please, may I have some donuts?"

"You certainly may! We are glad to give you what you want when you ask for it nicely." We both smiled as we said it, and expressed joy that he was again with us. We hugged him when he said something nice, and we all enjoyed our donuts.

And so ended fifty two minutes of tantrum, and fifty two minutes of chaos, to the relief of everyone involved! You see, tantrums had become Ricky's way of asking for things he could not easily get otherwise. He was not a bad boy. He just didn't know enough alternative ways of arranging his own payoffs. Tantrums had become a habit. But habits can be changed. It took us a full day of ignoring his tantrums to break their back, but our strategy worked, as I knew it would have to.

We carefully recorded the length of each tantrum, and at the end of the day we totalled them. That day he spent one hour and fifty-one minutes (one hundred eleven minutes) in tantrums of various lengths. The longest was the fifty-two minute episode I just described.

"Don't lose faith," I told Susan. "Today we hit the bottom. You watch and see. From now on, it will be much better."

It was. The next day there were only two or three tantrums, and they totalled only twenty six minutes. By the fourth day the worst tantrum we had was a three-minute display, and on the fifth day, none at all. There were a few isolated, brief episodes the next few days, but Ricky learned his lesson and he learned it well. There were no payoffs for his tantrums, so he stopped using them as a tool to get what he wanted.

On the other hand, there were many payoffs for saying, "Please." He got what he wanted, he got social payoffs, and in addition, we put gold stars into a savings stamp book. He was told that when he completed five pages we would take him to the variety store and buy him a toy car. Saying "Please" became a very strong behavior, and occurred nearly every time he wanted something. He said "Please" more than one hundred twenty five times on some days, and of course, he got one hundred twenty five payoffs. We were not concerned with "spoiling" him, because "spoiling" really has very little to do with how many rewards a person receives. A person becomes spoiled only when he gets the rewards for obnoxious behavior. We were glad to give him one hundred twenty five rewards, because it gave us one hundred twenty five chances to teach him good behaviors.

It is obvious, however, that we could not continue to do this forever, nor should we. Nobody ever gets everything he wants, and we would not be doing Ricky a favor if we taught him that he could. Even when he asks nicely—and he soon did that almost every time he wanted something—there will still be times when he cannot get a payoff. Some day the world will awaken him rudely, and he will not know how to deal with his disappointments. He will have no "frustration tolerance" under those conditions.

Our next phase of the program would be to teach Ricky to accept "No" when necessary. We knew we were taking a chance. This might trigger off another tantrum, but we were not too concerned, however, because we knew how to deal with it if it should come, and we frankly didn't expect anything compared to the ones we already had been through. When Ricky finally asked for something he could not have, Susan was ready. She told him, "No, I'm afraid I can't let you have it."

Ricky looked puzzled, and asked, "But why not? I asked nicely."

"You did, and we both appreciate that. But there will always be times when you will not be able to get what you want, no matter how nicely you ask."

That was good enough for him. He went about his play as though nothing had happened, and we got no tantrums. And Susan, with admirable wisdom, didn't forget to reward him for accepting his disappointment. "Ricky, I'm so proud of you! I was afraid you might get angry and start screaming, but you acted like a real man. Here are five stars for you."

He had already learned that tantrums were no longer the answer. He also learned that even though we were unable to give him his wish, we could still treat him with respect, and that was something many parents unfortunately forget.

Today, there are many times we have to turn down his requests. We still try to starve his asking in an unacceptable way, although this is rarely a problem. There have been very few tantrums since that day in Chinatown, more than five years ago. In fact, what we would now call a tantrum is nothing more than an angry response that might even be appropriate under the circumstances. It lasts only a few seconds, and might involve nothing more than a scowl, stamping his feet, muttering something under his breath, and possibly slamming a door. After all, he has the right to get angry, just like anyone else, and he has the right to be angry at us, too. We would not want to take that right away from him. On the other hand, there are a lot of different ways to express that anger, and we wanted to be sure that the way he learned would not use an unacceptable behavior. It is necessary for us to be just as cool about it as we would like him to be. We too must resist the temptation to respond to his anger by instant retaliation. It is alright to let him know we are angry (how else can he learn when he has gone over the limit?), but we must be careful to do so in a way that does not pile up social reward, and strengthen a problem behavior. Usually, if we simply tune out his anger, but remain firm that he behave the best way he knows how that is usually the end of the matter. He quickly cools off and within a short time he is happy again, and so are we.

Could we have taken the advice of the well-meaning strangers, who urged us, "Spank him?"

Well, of course we could have. And it might have even worked. But you'll learn some of the reasons why we did not do so in Chapter 8. For the time being, let me say that we didn't want to pile up retaliations any more than we wanted to pile up social rewards. Retaliation generates counter-retaliation, and the result is inevitable escalation. Moreover, I wanted to demonstrate that punishment wasn't really necessary at all. We got the behaviors we wanted, and eliminated those we did not want. If we had relied on punishment, we would have lost some of the advantages we now had. First of all, we got more permanence than would have been likely with the use of punishment. Also, we got no lasting side effects of anger, and we did not find ourselves in a pitched battle with someone we love. And we did not have to rely on size. We got our results without using our superior strength, other than simply to keep him moving when he tried to drag his feet. We did not want to build a relationship around the fact that we were bigger than he, so that we could bully him by using more force against him than he could use against us. Even if that were not disagreeable to us, what would happen in a few years, when we would no longer be bigger than he? Could we still rely on violence then? Ask the parent of many teen-age boys who have grown into fourteen-year old six-foot giants!

No, it was not necessary to use force, other than what we needed for our own protection. Besides, parents who punish excessively become models for their children to imitate. I did not want to teach Ricky that it is alright for him to bully someone smaller and weaker than he is.

We helped starve his tantrum sooner by rewarding competing behavior, which is more properly a subject for the next chapter. Behavioral starvation alone, even without rewarding "Please," would eventually have gotten rid of the tantrums. But demonstrating the power of starving a behavior was not our goal. That had already been done countless times before, in scores of experimental laboratories for more than fifty years, and there is no longer any question that it works. We wanted to deal with a problem as effectively as we could, and that is just what we did. An aeronautical engineer does not have to test the law of gravitation, or the shear strength of aluminum, or Bernouilli's Principle every time he designs an airplane. He already knows that they are dependable rules, so he simply plugs them into his design. That is what we did. We used whatever laws of human behavior we needed, in order to get our airplane to fly, without tantrums!

If we plot our own data on a daily chart, you will notice how closely

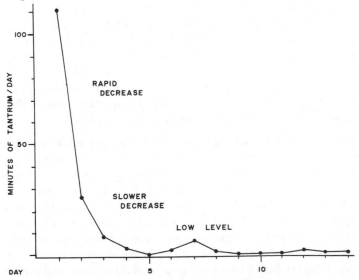

Figure 2. Starving Ricky's tantrums. On Day 1, tantrums continued for a total of 111 minutes, decreasing to only 26 on Day 2. Note that after Day 3, the behavior still occurred, but at a lower level.

the curve resembles Figure 1. We did get a temporary surge, as I described, but it does not show in Figure 2 because it had come and gone before the end of the first day. As you can see, the problem behavior did taper off gradually at first, then much more rapidly. See what happened on days 1 through 3? Then it slowed down again. There was a smaller change between days 3 and 8 than there was from between days 1 and 3.

There are lots of other examples of behavioral starvation which come to mind. I already mentioned how failure to pay off my crude attempts at playing baseball resulted in a lifelong indifference to the game. Many people who begin music lessons do not continue them. Why? Because their playing is not satisfying enough to give them enough payoff to sustain their effort. They do not get adequate reward. It may be fun, but they know it sounds like hell, and eventually the lack of payoff starves their practicing. Without the payoff, their long periods of practice, and eventually their music lessons, begin to drop out. The same applies to a lot of people in high schools. Most people who have dropped out, either from music lessons, public school, or what has been called "the scene" do not take them up again later, unless some intervening experiences direct some payoffs toward those things they had previously abandoned.

It is important that the teacher of the adult beginner be sure to arrange plenty of payoffs for those early efforts, because the adult beginner is likely to be more critical than the child, and not so easily pleased with the behaviors he knows are crude. That is why good teachers try to encourage every little success. We'll go into more detail on this in Chapter 13. Teachers do not *want* the new behaviors to starve and die out. They want the reward to come quickly, before the curve goes into the steep, drop-off stage (Figure 1, at C).

Because we will be working with both target behaviors and problem behaviors, we need to know both how to facilitate behavioral starvation and how to prevent, or impede it. To make a behavior harder to starve, it is necessary to give occasional payoff. But learning is slower when the behavior is not rewarded every time, so you should start by giving payoffs as often as possible. Then, when the behavior is fairly strong, and occurs with reliable regularity, you should skip a payoff occasionally, but only one at a time. When the behavior recovers its strength you may skip a couple of times in a row, and then more and more often, until you are only rewarding infrequently. You will soon get a behavior which is quite strong, and will not immediately starve if someone forgets to give a reward soon enough. That is, the behavior will survive, if you have not thinned out the payoffs too quickly. By then, it is hoped, the behavior itself will have become rewarding enough that it will continue. An example of how a behavior can become rewarding: I once taught a retarded girl to use a playground swing by giving her bits of candy, first for merely sitting on the swing, and then for remaining seated while I pushed the swing gently. She soon learned that it was fun to be a swinger, and from that time on, we were able to teach her other things, such as dressing herself, by letting her swing as a payoff for getting dressed by herself.

Another example: A few months ago, my little daughter, Emily, was just learning to stand by herself. She took one step. It was shaky, but it was a step, and Susan, Ricky, and I all cheered her. She knew she had done something wise and cute and good, and she enjoyed our attention and praise and hugs. Eventually, she walked more and more. Today, she walks and runs as well as you and I. The same thing happened to you, didn't it? And yet, how long has it been since someone told you, "Good boy! That was really good walking!" Probably quite a long time. You may wonder, "Well, if that's the case, why doesn't walking starve?" That is a very good question, and the answer is that walking was given occasional payoff, until it became a strong behavior. By then, walking itself had become enjoyable, and besides, walking never starves because walking leads to all kinds of payoffs. People do a lot of crazy things, like climbing to the top of Shiprock, but I have never heard of anyone crawling up there!

On the other hand, we once taught Louie, a retarded teen-ager, to walk very well, but a few months later when I checked back to follow up on his case, I found him lying in his crib. In this case, the staff would not permit Louie to walk because, "He was getting into things." The staff did not want to permit him to get into the goodies he suddenly found accessible. Cases such as Louie's are exceptional, because walking is usually rewarded, and it stays with us because of the occasional payoffs it gets during the major part of our lives.

Arthur is standing in front of a coke machine. He drops in a quarter, pulls a handle, and out comes a cold bottle of soft drink, which cools him off on this 106° August day. He often comes to this machine for the same reason, and it has never failed him—at least, not until this time. He dropped in his coin, pulled the handle, and reached. This was the same chain of behaviors which had always been rewarded in the past. But for some reason, nothing happened this time. Arthur hit the machine with his palm, shook it, said some words to it, kicked it, tilted it, and came up with a few other new, random behaviors (the surge). But nothing he did changed the consequences. Arthur finally dropped in another coin. He lost it as well. In disgust, he left the machine. Dropping coins starved from lack of payoff, and the behavior died out.

Some time later, Arthur was in Las Vegas, Nevada, standing in front of a machine which looked a bit like the soft drink machine. He performed roughly the same behavior chain. He dropped in a coin, pulled a handle, and reached for his reward. Wheels spun, but no payoffs came out of the opening. He dropped in another, and another, and another. He continued dozens of times. Sometimes, he got a few coins in return, but by the time the sun had slipped behind the desert mountains, Arthur wondered, "Why didn't I stop hours ago?"

We know the answer. The slot machine had given him occasional payoff, and not too often, at that. It made behavioral starvation last a long time. A witty friend commented, "But it hastened Arthur's own starvation!"

Arthur continued to drop coins into the machine. Occasional payoffs made behavioral starvation take a long time. Sometimes they were small and sometimes they were big, but they only came often enough to keep him going, at a handsome profit to the house. By contrast, the coke machine rewarded every time, but when it stopped, so did Arthur.

The moral to the story is that occasional payoff produces persistent behavior. That is, the behavior resists starvation when the rewards fail to come soon enough. It takes a lot longer for a behavior to die out if its payoffs come infrequently. If one of my jokes falls flat, I tell another, and another. Sooner or later someone laughs, not realizing he is giving me occasional payoff. He does not realize he is making it harder to shut me up. On the other hand, my friend William is a true artist, with a lot of first-class training and experience in dramatics, plus an unusual talent for timing, sensitivity, and all the other behaviors that go to make up a fine comedian. When he tells a joke, people laugh almost every time. But occasionally, he may slip up, or his joke may go over his audience's head. They laugh, but only politely. William is sensitive enough to realize he has bombed, and that is the last joke he tells that night. William's payoff comes almost every time. When his expected reward is not forthcoming, he stops, just like Arthur at the machine which failed to deliver a soft drink. It does not matter what he tells himself, nor what I tell myself by way of explanation. The fact remains that our behaviors are governed, or controlled, not only by their payoffs but also by how, when, and under what conditions the behaviors were given their payoff.

Last, but not least, I should mention something which I will talk about again in Chapter 10, and that is the power of the *signal,* or *cue.* A *signal* is anything we see, feel, hear, smell, or in some other way respond to with our senses. When a behavior only happens while certain signals are present, and does not happen at other times, it is being controlled by the signal. I will call a signal that controls a behavior a *cue,* and the behavior under its control will be said to be *on cue.*

For example, most people remove their clothes when they take a shower, but not when they take a bus. We can say that stripping is done on cue. Most football fans will yell and scream in a stadium, but would probably not do so in a library, or funeral parlor. When the light turns red, you step on the brake pedal. When the light turns green, you step on the accelerator. To an infant, the colored lights are only signals, because he can respond to them with his visual apparatus. In other words, he can see them. To a driver, they are also signals, for the same reason, but they have also become cues which control some of his behaviors.

Cues can be reward-signals or starve-signals, as well as more technical ones I will not bother to describe. The reward-signal is present when payoffs come, and it tends to elicit (that is, "trigger off") behaviors that were rewarded in its presence. If the signal does set off the behavior, it has become a cue.

If starving always takes place in certain locations, or around certain people, they will become starve-signals, and the learner's behavior will tend to diminish or stop around those signals. It is at least theoretically possible to reward problem behaviors heavily while presenting unique signals (such as a purple flashing strobe light with sirens), and put the problem behavior under control of those cues. If the signals never appear again (and how often do you see a purple flashing strobe light and hear sirens at the same time?), the behavior should disappear—in theory, at least. Although I have been intrigued by this possibility for more than ten years, it has not been possible for me to do the experimental work necessary to verify this theory, and I have not run across work by any other psychologist who has. It is still anybody's guess whether it would work. Frankly, I have some doubts, because it is possible that still other cues would also control the behavior. Besides, in order to get the behavior on cue, it must be rewarded heavily around one signal and never rewarded around others. If it were possible to insure that it would never be rewarded around other signals, it would also be possible to starve the problem without bothering to get it on cue. That would be a much simpler solution. However, this is just one of those areas where much careful work remains to be done.

Sometimes, after a behavior seems to be completely starved, you can rest for a few hours or days, and sometimes even minutes. Then, when you are again put into the same situation, the behavior will start up, usually weaker than it was at the start of the previous session. This is called *spontaneous recovery*, and should be expected. Thus, even though Ricky finally stopped his tantrums that first day, I expected more the next day, and planned for them. Even though tantrums had disappeared on Day 1, there was spontaneous recovery on Day 2. After another day's starvation, there was spontaneous recovery on Day 3, etc. But each day's starvation weakens the behavior enough that it usually starts out at a lower level than it did on the previous day. Finally, when the behavior no longer recovers spontaneously, we may conclude that starvation is more or less complete.

Let's summarize what we have learned about behavioral starvation:

1. Starving takes place when a behavior occurs but is never rewarded.

2. Strangely enough, it takes longer if the behavior has been rewarded occasionally, and takes place more quickly if the behavior has gotten payoff nearly every time it happened.

3. The thinner the payoff schedule, the more persistent the behavior tends to become, provided also that it was not initially so thin that it starved before it had the chance to become strong.

4. As you would expect, a weak behavior starves much more quickly than a strong behavior.

5. Starving may be put on cue. That is, it may happen under some conditions and not others. The learner then comes to behave in ways that are characteristic of the types of signals he received during starvation.

6. At the start of behavioral starvation, there is often an initial surge of behavior, sometimes of a random nature, and sometimes simply an increase in the rate or intensity of the behaviors already present. Thus, Ricky screamed louder when we didn't give in. Arthur kicked and swore at the balky coke machine.

7. A strong behavior starts dying out slowly, sometimes with a beginning surge. The starvation then speeds up, reaches a maximum rate, and finally begins to taper off, leaving a period of time in which a few behaviors continue to occur at a low rate before the behavior dies out altogether, and starvation is complete.

8. Behavioral starvation may be helped along if you will also strengthen behaviors which are competing with the weakened behavior you are starving.

9. When the strength of a behavior has been reduced, the "starved" behavior may recover spontaneously after a period of rest. If this happens, it usually starts in at a lower rate than it did before, and its decrease is almost always more rapid with each recovery.

10. Strong behaviors die very slowly, so be prepared with a lot of patience, and sometimes protection, if the behavior is at all hazardous.

Now read this chapter again and again. It contains most of what you will need to know in order to reduce your problem behaviors, or those of someone whose behaviors are causing a great deal of unhappiness to you and other people. When you know the material very well, try to think of examples in your own life, of things you do not care for very much, because you did not get enough payoff for them in the past. Not getting enough payoff is the same thing as behavioral starvation. See if this helps explain why you do not practice the piano, play baseball, ask for dates easily, sell a million dollars worth of insurance each year, or score with the opposite sex (or same, if you would like) as often as you would prefer.

And while you are doing it, see if you can uncover any of your own behaviors which you would like to eliminate, that other people keep rewarding. Some examples might be: Telling all your private secrets, or those of other people; making "poor little me" statements; manipulating other people by using guilt; leaving clothes or dishes lying around the house; or any number of other behaviors which you, or other people, might consider to be problem behaviors. In order to eliminate these behaviors, it will somehow be necessary for the behaviors to occur in the complete absence of payoffs, and that is sometimes not very easy to do. But perhaps Chapters 7, 11, and 14 will give you some good hints on how to go about it.

Chapter 7

Crowding Out:

How to Get Less of a Problem
By Getting More of Something Else

The second means of reducing problem behaviors is by rewarding incompatible behaviors, or *competing* behaviors, as I have called them. I sometimes refer to this method as *crowding out*, because it strengthens a good behavior, which then crowds out a problem behavior. This method of reducing problem behavior is by far the method of choice, for a number of reasons. The other two ways, *starving*, and *punishment*, take away behavior which is already present. *Crowding* is the only way which adds behaviors, and sometimes new behaviors, at that.

I can't exaggerate how important this point is. If one way for a person to accumulate payoffs pleases others, he will choose it, especially if the other ways get people annoyed, or angry at him. In other words, he would not use his problem behaviors at all if he knew other ways of getting equal payoff that were just as reliable, and not too much extra trouble. Stated another way, *people have problem behaviors because they do not have enough alternative behaviors.* Either they do not know enough behaviors, or the good behaviors are not rewarded enough to make them strong. In some cases, other people will not allow the good behaviors to take place. For example, I mentioned in Chapter 6 that we had taught Louie to walk, only to find that the hospital staff kept him in his crib because he started getting into things.

For whatever reason, there are not enough behaviors to choose from. We call this situation a *behavioral deficit,* and the name means just what it says. It is my belief that *all* problem behaviors, except those resulting from a damaged nervous system, are the result of behavioral deficit. People wouldn't act conceited if they were getting enough praise, attention, and respect through their other behaviors. People wouldn't be violent, if violence was not the best way they had learned of dealing with others. People would not go through all sorts of attention-getting behaviors if they had other, more acceptable ways of getting attention. People would not rob filling stations if they had better ways of getting the same amount of money. People would not be wishy-washy if they knew how to be decisive and firm and confident. People would not wallow in self-pity if they knew better, more pleasing ways they could relate to other people and still get plenty of social payoffs. People would not drink "to escape," if they knew better ways to deal with their problems successfully. People would not rape if they knew how to seduce successfully. People would not frown if they could smile.

In short, people would not have nearly as many problem behaviors if they had better behaviors available that would be acceptable and pleasing to themselves and others. That is why I believe all problem behaviors result from behavioral deficit—behaviors a person has not yet learned, or behaviors he has learned, but which have died out from lack of payoff.

You should always try to build in acceptable and pleasing target behaviors to compete with and crowd out problem behaviors, because every new behavior means you have reduced the behavioral deficit that much. This alone is reason enough to recommend crowding, if you want to eliminate problem behaviors. You simply choose a target behavior incompatible with the problem behavior and then you pay off that behavior whenever it occurs. Sometimes, the learner has not yet acquired the target behavior you choose. How can you reward it then? Well, you certainly can't reward a behavior that does not take place, and you surely do not want to reward it on the promise that it will come—that would be backward conditioning, which you already know does not work very well. Fortunately, there are ways to get behaviors that have not yet been acquired, and I will show you how in Chapters 11 and 13. For the time being, all you need to remember is that if you want less of a problem behavior, reward and build up a competing behavior until it crowds out the behavior you do not like.

There are other reasons I recommend crowding out as the method of choice. First of all, when you get hung up trying to weaken problem behaviors, you forget that the "problem behavior" is not the real problem. The problem is actually behavioral deficit. A hyperactive child who disturbs an entire classroom by attention-getting behaviors is a good example. Most teachers and parents think of his running around, screaming, making faces, hitting the other children, and throwing books and pencils as the problem behaviors. That is not so.

The real problem is the large number of *missing* behaviors. He does *not* pay attention; does *not* remain seated; does *not* follow the teacher's instructions; and does *not* have study habits and/or academic skills that permit him to take part in the class and benefit from it. So he disrupts it instead.

When you look at the behaviors you don't like and think you are seeing the problem, the logical, "normal," or "natural" thing to do is to punish the learner, or at best, starve the problem behavior. Few arrangers ever think to replace the behaviors they eliminate. It is one of the most common errors made, and I have seen *everybody* do it, no matter how much better they knew. I still do it at times, and I have no excuse, for I know better. When a problem behavior has become annoying, we try to deal with the problem behavior, but hardly ever give enough thought to the fact that some other behavior will have to replace it.

Let's say that you counted the total time a learner spent in a particular problem behavior every day. Let's say it averaged one hour. Now, through the miracle of behavioral starvation, that problem behavior exists no more. But the hour still goes on, and you can't simply have a hole in the time once occupied by that behavior. The hole will be filled in by some kind of event—some replacement behavior, even if it is nothing more than standing, sitting, or lying still. Something will happen during that sixty minutes. That something could be a new behavior. Or it could be an old behavior, either one that happened rarely or one that happened often—in other words, an old low-rate behavior or an old high-rate behavior, although the high-rate would be more likely to occur. The replacement behavior might be one you like, in which case everyone is happy. Or it might be another problem behavior, new or old. Let us further suppose that a problem behavior occurred 40% of the time. This would mean that all incompatible behaviors could occur not more than 60% of the time. Suppose that you began to strengthen the competing behaviors by giving them more payoff, and now the competing behaviors occurred more often—say 75% of the time. This would mean the problem behavior could only take place a maximum of 25% of the time. You got a 15% decrease in the problem behavior without even working on it directly. The incompatible behaviors crowded it out.

Obviously, it would be to your benefit if you could replace the problem behavior with something useful, or at least pleasing to you. Well, it can be done. Try to imagine, for example, two adults talking together, while little Clifford interrupts every few minutes. The adults stop their conversation, turn to Clifford, and either answer him or fuss at him for interrupting. You can look upon the interruption as a problem behavior, because a problem behavior is anything someone does or says that somebody doesn't like.

You can eliminate the problem behavior if you will just ignore it (that is, tune it out, starve it, and let it die), as we did with Ricky's tantrums. But remember that his first tantrum lasted 52 minutes, and you might not wish to take this route. Instead, you could say, "The *real* problem is not Clifford's interrupting." The real problem is that Clifford does not know a more pleasing way to get our attention, just as we could have said—and did—"The real problem is that Ricky did not ask us nicely, and did not accept 'no' for an answer."

What would be a more pleasing way of being interrupted? Won't *any* interruption be annoying? Well, yes, perhaps, but not quite as much. One thing you can teach the child is how to wait patiently until there is a natural break in the conversation before interrupting. Another thing you can teach is a more polite way of doing it, such as saying, "I beg your pardon." Most people would feel, "If I must be interrupted, I would rather have the child do it in a way which shows that he is sensitive to my feelings and is not just walking all over me."

Of course, it would make no sense to try to teach the child a more acceptable way to get your attention if you continued to reward his interruption. For that reason, you would try to reward acceptable competing behaviors, but you would also starve the interruption as well. This combination of starving a problem and strengthening competing behaviors is a good plan to follow whenever possible. It is the method we used with Ricky's tantrums, although we waited until the tantrum had run its course before we asked for the competing behavior. Still, you must remember that we not only let the tantrum die, but we also taught him to ask nicely, saying, "Please."

Incidentally, I have sometimes run across critics who feel it is extremely rude and degrading not to respond to children when they ask for attention, even when they interrupt or repeatedly ask meaningless or irrelevant questions. Often, of course, people ask questions when they are not really interested in answers, but use the questions as a means of controlling other people in unacceptable ways. Rudeness is like any other problem behavior. It is rude if someone thinks it is rude. I cannot answer these objections, other than to say that if starving a problem behavior is really rude (and I have questions about this), then the rudeness is a small enough price to pay to teach someone something worthwhile. If Clifford resents our "rudeness," it is easy enough for him to stop it. Our program has only asked a very simple response from him. You should never design a program so difficult that the learner can't make easy choices. All Clifford must do is pay some attention to the feelings of other people. In the long run, he too will be much better off for it, but even if he were not, doesn't he have the same obligations to his society that other people have? If he is *unable* to meet our terms, it is then our responsibility to make the competing behaviors less difficult, so that at no time will it be impossible for Clifford to get his payoffs. I personally find it hard to justify the morality of rewarding obnoxious behavior that will cause Clifford punishment in the future, and guarantee punishment for people around him in the present— especially if these people had done nothing to deserve it.

Now turn back to Chapter 3 and read example number 4, which begins, "The children were bored." I did not complete the story then, but here is the rest of it:

When the mother finally asked me to help her, I explained how the parents were strengthening problem behaviors. I also told them something about rewarding alternatives. "Watch this," I said.

A few moments later, the children temporarily became quiet. That is, I observed a short break in their wild activities. When they had been quiet for a few minutes, I broke away from my conversation with the parents. I told the children, "That's very good! You're being nice and quiet. We like children to have fun, but we don't want them to bother other people, either. Here is a piece of cookie for you." (Fortunately, I had wrapped my dessert from the meal I had eaten on the plane. I would have to give Ricky a different treat when I got home).

I then went back to my conversation with the parents, but kept "tuned in" to the children. I didn't let too much time go by, because they were still quiet, and I wanted to be sure to capitalize on this fortunate state of affairs. As I said before, becoming quiet and remaining quiet are two separate processes. I could not know when they would suddenly change their minds and start a ruckus again.

Fortunately, I did not wait too long—perhaps another minute or two. It was long enough that the children had to wait awhile, but not so long that the honeymoon was over. I repeated the payoffs, each time saying, "That's good. You are being nice to us, and not running wild." When the children were quiet for a few minutes, the parents repeated what I had showed them. After a few more repetitions of this scene, we began to wait a bit longer to reward them. Soon, the children were able to stay quiet for fairly long periods of time, and the parents were able to converse longer. If the parents waited too long, there might then be a bit of commotion from the children, who had not yet learned to wait quite so long for their reward. I urged the parents to play it cool, for I knew any disruptions that did take place would not last forever. I urged them to tune out these disruptions and wait patiently for a break. This is not as hard to do once you understand that such a break is inevitable. It *must* come sooner or later, and you must be prepared to wait for it. So be on your toes, and capitalize on the golden moment when it finally does arrive.

There is still another reason why it is good to reward competing target behaviors: Because it is so much more pleasant to work that way. If you can get rid of a problem behavior by strengthening a different behavior frequently, you will find that the periods of starving (or punishment, if you go that route) are not quite as hard to live through. The person receiving the payoff will obviously like the program better, but so will the arranger giving him the reward. It is always more fun to give and please someone else than it is to punish, or to ignore, as you must do when you starve a behavior.

I might as well tell you of some of the drawbacks to crowding out. It is sometimes a bit slow, but so is starving, especially when the behavior is still strong. But crowding keeps you on your toes, and demands that the arranger be active and creative. Thus, there are more real demands made on the arranger than simply starving a behavior by mechanically ignoring it. The arranger must always be thinking about alternative behaviors, and it is easy to run out of things for the learner to do. The main drawback is that most arrangers sooner or later tend to forget to keep the payoffs coming often enough. At the beginning of the program, when the problem behavior is present and still annoying them a great deal, they are highly motivated to eliminate it. They start in and are very conscientious, and usually, they are soon successful, too. The good behaviors do crowd out the problem behaviors. But as the problem behavior occurs less frequently and starts to become a thing of the past, arrangers tend to forget about rewarding competing behaviors, and accidentally begin to starve them. The result may be a return of the problem behavior.

Another drawback is that crowding doesn't work quite as well with very low-rate behaviors. For example, if a problem behavior only occurs once every six weeks, you could pour on the rewards for more than a thousand hours. If the problem behavior is itself a reward, the learner can afford to miss a few of the other payoffs. More will be coming soon. But what if the behavior is something like setting fires?

One time in six weeks—or six years—could be a real danger. In cases like this we may be forced to rely on punishment. If so, however, we must realize that we are dealing with an emergency, and that an emergency forces us to do things which may not actually be the best choice in the long run. We must deal with crises in the best way we can, and our choices might be quite limited.

We should also remember that any punishment program will become more effective if it is combined with a deliberate effort to teach the learner a number of new and desirable alternative ways of getting what he wants, whether he sets fires for attention, anger, money, sexual gratification, or what have you. There exist better and more satisfying ways of getting attention, expressing anger, getting money, and sexual gratification. All of those problems have other and better solutions, so the arranger must teach the learner how to seek them out and then try to strengthen them until there is no longer any need to set fires. Incidentally, the consequences can be pretty serious if your program to decrease a dangerous problem behavior fails, so you might wish to seek some help or advice from a skilled, highly trained professional behavior therapist.

Another nice thing about the process of crowding: You might have set up a program to eliminate one specific problem behavior. Most of the time, however, your program calls for you to pour on the rewards for good behaviors. While you are weakening the problem behavior you wrote the program to deal with, any number of other problem behaviors will tend to be weakened at the same time. Thus, the method has economic advantages as well as therapeutic ones.

It is fortunate that when payoffs come often enough, the severe problems tend to drop out automatically. This is especially true if those rewards that do come do not follow immediately after problem behaviors. In just about every program I have seen where a severe but low-rate behavior continued, the reason was that the competing behaviors were not being rewarded often enough.

Problem behaviors of any sort are likely to be very rare in a situation where a lot of reward is given for socially acceptable behavior. And prevention is much better than trying to patch up an emergency. The very best time to deal with any emergency is *when it is not happening.* If you wait until a problem behavior appears, you may not be in a position to do anything sensible about it. If the problem behaviors are dangerous, like aggression or property damage, you may have to intervene, even though you may know the problem was an attention-getting behavior, and your intervention will be its payoff. In this way, you might stop the emergency this time, but actually cause it to happen more often. You sometimes have no choice. A crisis does not give you the luxury of time to think about it, and leisurely plan the best possible program. Therefore, the time to teach new, useful behaviors is when no problem behavior is occurring. The time to teach a person useful ways of getting attention, affection, or other social rewards is not when he is climbing over the railing of the Golden Gate Bridge. That is an emergency, and you are forced to do whatever you can to salvage the situation. When the forest fire is blazing all around you, it is not the best time to hold fire prevention classes and lecture about Smokey the Bear! You must first put out the fire, any way you can, and it might not be the best way in the long run.

Many people spend their entire lives putting out fires, living from crisis to crisis. Are you one of them? Then study this chapter well, and try to think of all the so-called "emotional crises" you have lived through, or expect to live through. I am not talking about physical crises, even though they are sometimes related to problem behaviors. For example, heart attacks can result from such problem behaviors as improper eating habits, smoking tobacco products, failure to exercise properly, or simply letting too much steam build up within you. All of these things can be dealt with by programs rewarding incompatible behavior patterns. You can learn proper eating habits, devise programs to help you stick with beneficial exercises (see Chapters 11 and 13). and learn to relate to other people in ways which will seldom put you in a position of such pent-up-rage and hostility that you not only blow your top but an artery as well.

The method of crowding out has still another advantage: It accentuates the positive (see Chapter 2). Problem behaviors are always negatives, and most people get so hung up on them that they fail to look at the other side. It is far better to accentuate the positive. So crowd out the bad with the good. That is the central message of this chapter.

Chapter 8

Punishment: What it Does
And What It Doesn't Do

Question: What is it that nobody likes to get, most people don't like to give, rarely works exactly the way you want, creates a lot of extra problems, makes life much less pleasant for everyone involved, is not as effective as most people think it is, and yet is used as much or more than other things which can do the job better in many ways?

If your answer was *punishment*, then you were right. Let me start by saying that there *might* be times when punishment could be the method of choice, but these are few and far between. At the end of this chapter I will discuss a limited use of punishment which I do recommend, as an exception to the general rule, which I give you now:

Avoid the use of punishment whenever possible.

Almost always, in practice, if you are forced to use punishment, you must understand that it means your other programs were not as effective as they should be. In short, you should be prepared to admit that you have failed whenever you rely on a program based on punishment.

The plain fact is that scientists do not know as much about punishment as they do about reward. Part of the reason is that it is not as easy to get people to let you study them when you are going to use punishment in your experiments, and use it on them. There are a lot of social pressures preventing the scientist from deliberately hurting someone just to find out what effect the punishment is going to have on his behavior. It is a good thing these restraints do exist, for we all remember the so-called experiments done by the Nazis in World War II. But meanwhile, the restraints leave the scientist high and dry. He is forced to carry out relevant studies on lower animals, and then hope the laws he discovers apply to humans as well. This is not as bad as it sounds, because most of what we know about reward in humans was also originally discovered from animal studies, and it was only learned later that human behavior is so similar to that of lower animals that the same studies are very often applicable to both. In other words, animal studies have been extremely useful in developing an understanding of human behavior. But scientists do not wish to punish animals any more than they have to either. The net result so far is that the scientist knows much less about punishment than he does about reward.

It really wouldn't matter very much to most people if the scientists didn't know the answers to the questions their experiments are set up to answer, except for one thing: Nearly every society on earth uses punishment very freely. Our own society is a major example. Since punishment is used so often, it is about time we began to understand what we are doing. Whole systems of law are built around the idea that if you punish a person for violation of the law, he will not violate the law as much. Nobody has challenged this idea seriously, but we now know enough about punishment to give us a good reason to raise the question of whether or not this is in fact correct. I will discuss this again in Chapter 9.

Every one of us punishes other people, and sometimes we punish ourselves as well. We might not do these things on purpose, and we might not even know we are doing it, but it makes no difference. It still happens. There is not a person living who does not use punishment, and even the dead ones used it while they were here. Since this is so, it is astonishing that we really know so little about the effects of punishment, how it should be used, when it should be used, and what are its side effects.

In this chapter I will summarize some of the things we know about punishment, and try to show you how these things affect our lives.

1. In some ways, *understanding reward helps us talk about punishment.* We know that the effect of a reward drops off quickly when there is a delay. The same is true of punishment. The longer you wait to punish, the less effective you can expect that punishment to be. If Shawn spilled his paints on the living room carpet in the morning, and his mother told him, "When Daddy gets home from work this evening he's going to spank you," it is not the most effective way to teach him, because the delay is too great. If the spanking was to be the consequence of his act, his mother should have done it at once. The main things she accomplished were to fill Shawn's day with fear (unless his mother bluffs so often that he doesn't believe her anyway), teach him that Daddy is the bully who spanks, and that Mother is incapable of dealing with the problem adequately.

2. Just as it takes longer to teach a behavior when it is given occasional payoff, so it is with punishment. *If you want maximum effectiveness–that is, the fastest possible learning–you must punish every time the problem behavior occurs.* The more times you skip, the less effective the punishment will be in suppressing the behavior you don't like. Every time you miss, you are weakening your results. If you are punishing at all, it is irresponsible to allow the program to last any longer than necessary. If you cannot be consistent and catch the problem behavior *every* time, you have no business using punishment in the first place.

Behavior which has been given occasional punishment also seems to die out less rapidly than behavior punished every time. I suspect that the reasons are different, but with the use of punishment—as is true of the use of rewards—behavior persists longer when the consequences are only happening occasionally.

3. If you pay a man 50¢ to cut your lawn, he will probably not come back again. If you pay him $500, you can be nearly positive he will be back. Somewhere between these extremes, you can perhaps decide on a price high enough to bring him back and low enough to make you willing to pay it. The value of the payoff to the learner will help determine its strength. Its value to the arranger is more or less irrelevant[9]. In a similar way, *a weak punisher will not be as effective as a strong punisher.* A light slap on the wrist will not have as much effect as a haymaker. Please don't interpret this to mean that I am recommending violence. I'm only saying that a lot of times, people use punishers that are not strong enough to do the trick, and for that reason they should not be used at all. Most people try to justify their use of punishment by such nonsense as, "It's really for your own good," or, "I'm just trying to teach you a lesson that will help you in the long run," or, "One of these days you'll thank me for this." While each of these statements may in fact be true, they are not usually the *real* reason the arranger has chosen punishment. Most often it is because he doesn't know any better way to deal with the problem behavior. The hidden messages in all of these statements say that the arranger feels guilty about using punishment, and wants to make his reasons for using it sound as good as he can. It is true that the learner may some day thank him for teaching certain lessons, but he is likely to thank him still more profusely if the method used had avoided the use of punishment.

The best reason to use punishment, and maybe the only good reason, is to stop a dangerous, destructive, or anti-social behavior before someone or something gets hurt. You might also justify it—maybe— if it is a good teaching device, and the lesson being taught is important enough. Under some conditions, maybe it is, but if you don't want to contradict yourself, you would then have to go all the way, and use really severe punishment. If you want a person to stop doing something, and you choose punishment as a means of teaching him not to do it, you have already learned three rules: Punish immediately—don't wait an extra second; punish every time it happens; and punish severely.

Don't like that so much, huh? Well, if you don't, then you have no right to use punishment at all, because it will not be as effective as you are pretending it will be.

One additional point: Immediate punishment means *immediate*, as I have mentioned. And if you are dishing out punishment within a second or two of the time a behavior occurs, there are bound to be times when the learner is punished, although innocent. He has not had the time to explain what happened, which might have been beyond his control. He is convicted and executed without benefit of a trial. Punishment under such conditions inevitably gives rise to resentment with the system of punishment itself. And rightly so.

4. *Just as starving becomes more effective when you strengthen alternative behaviors, so it is with punishment.* In fact, if a person has his choice of two ways to get a payoff and he happens to choose one which is punished, he will probably turn to the other next time. Even if the punisher was relatively mild, he will most likely choose the competing behavior instead of the mildly punished one, as long as it gets rewarded. So this should then become a rule:

Before you punish someone, including yourself, be sure that there is at least one alternative behavior which can give the learner payoff.

Animals trained to get food by pressing a lever will quickly learn to obtain food this way. If the lever is then rigged so that pressing it gives a shock, the animals often continue to press the lever, ignoring the shock, especially if it is mild[10]. But if pressing a second lever gives them food without shock, they will quickly learn to press the second lever, and abandon the first. Likewise, people need extra levers to press—that is, alternative ways to get their rewards. Having more alternatives permits a person to be less panicky in case one of his goals does not work out. This is true whether his goal is a certain job, a certain graduate school, a certain mate, a certain business deal, or a certain political office. I have already alluded to this fact when I mentioned that the bachelor who is more successful, and has many alternatives does not have to pursue any particular partner who turns out to be less available than he would prefer (see Chapter 4). He can be more "independent," (translation: He has more levers to press). The person with no alternatives is the desperate one, and being desperate is also more vulnerable. The person who is least desperate (that is, has more alternatives—more levers to press) controls the situation.

In your relationships with other people, there will come times when you must stand up for your rights. It is wise to do this in a way which does not punish your adversary. You must give him extra levers to press. That is, you must give him some way to save face and if possible, get a payoff out of the deal as well. In other words, you must maintain your rights, but you must do it in a way that insures that your opponent is not punished excessively, unless you are really more interested in revenge than results. If revenge is your game, forget about everything I'm telling you. Punish the hell out of him and then prepare to catch the flak he will try to shoot back at you—and he will. But if you really want to fix things so the person who has wronged you will be more fair to you next time, then leave him some way to escape intact, and if possible get rewarded for his dealing fairly with you.

5. *People tend to* **adapt** *to punishers, especially if the punishers start out mild, and their intensity is increased gradually.* That is, people "get used to" a punisher, and gradually accept it without even thinking much about it. When you first slip into a very hot tub, or a very cold shower, the water is a punisher. But as you stick with it, you find that you adjust to it and accept the temperature extremes a bit better. Still easier is to get into a warm tub and gradually add hot water. You will find you can stand water much hotter than you would care to expose yourself to suddenly.

A child who is spanked very often, especially when the spanking is relatively mild, tends to accept a spanking as just one of the facts of life, and may not even be bothered much by it. On the other hand, a child who is rarely spanked may really freak out the first time it happens. On a few occasions when I have been too lazy or preoccupied to do a good job of programming, I have blown up and given Ricky a swat. Although it is rare that I become that annoyed with him, being human, we both occasionally push beyond limits. It has happened before, and the effects on both of us, and on Susan and Emily, are always disruptive. On the other hand, I have seen one of the young boys in our neighborhood get really violent spankings, and I know it happens often. The neighbor's boy seems hardly to notice this treatment at all. At least, he ends up by repeating the punished behavior before very much time passes.

I have known adults who have had one major surgery after another. They have lived with pain so long that sometimes they can almost lead normal lives, and hardly stop to think that they never really stop hurting. On the other hand, I have been so healthy it is boring to hear me talk about it. When I have a very minor injury, or come down with a slight touch of flu, or my bursitis acts up, it becomes a big thing. I have never had the chance to learn how to live with pain, for which I am quite thankful. Nevertheless, I am sure other people must find me disgusting when I try to squeeze a bit of extra mileage out of some attention-getting behaviors every time I get a hangnail or run a slight temperature or stub my toe!

Punishment is the same way. To some people a parking ticket is a calamity. Others have been in and out of jail so many times that they are not upset to the extreme when the judge tells them, "Six months this time, Jake. Let this teach you a lesson." Jake didn't seem to mind too much, but would you? I think probably so.

The moral to this rule should be that if you're going to use punishment at all it should be used sparingly. You shouldn't overdo it. Very frequent punishment tends to become meaningless, and teaches a bunch of other things you'd probably prefer not to have learned. This does not mean you should not be consistent, but if you find you must punish very often, you should question how effective your program is, and consider re-designing it. You'll learn more about how this is done in Chapters 11 and 12. If you continue to punish frequently over a long period of time, you'll probably find that your program is losing whatever effectiveness it might have had at one time, and you'll find a lot of other problems cropping up that you never anticipated. As only one example, I should mention a program I once used to stop extremely violent self-injurious behavior. Some of the children struck themselves almost twenty thousand times per day, if permitted to do so. Although the punishment reduced the number down to a dozen or two—and it would seem the program was therefore very effective—in every case the self-injury gradually returned. But we relied too heavily on the use of punishment for the self-injury, and the staff began to forget how to reward alternative behaviors. What was more surprising, the staff began to punish each other as well. They had become so dependent upon the use of punishment that they no longer related to each other in ways as rewarding as they once did. This is what happens when people accentuate the negative!

6. *Punishment decreases behavior.* That is why you use it in the first place. You are well aware that if you do something which is followed

right away by a punishment, you are not quite as likely to do it again. A baby touches a hot stove and learns from the experience to stay away from hot stoves—we hope.

A young boy on his first date tries to kiss his girl, who refuses to let him, and then ridicules him for trying. He is less likely to try it on the second date. As a matter of fact, he is less likely to ask her for a second date, especially as he becomes more confident, develops good relationships with a number of other girls, and in short, gets more levers to press.

In the example I gave you in Chapter 3, I talked about a possible ending to example number 9. In this case, the boss would have punished me for honesty, which would have made me less eager to be honest with him next time. Right after that I described how parents often punish children for telling the truth. In both of these cases, and in many more, the presence of the punishment did decrease the behavior. That was why it was given. Sometimes, as with the boss punishing the employee for honesty, or the parent punishing the child for telling the truth, they were really trying to punish a different behavior, but honesty and truth were the casualties, simply because they happened at the same time. They were caught in the crossfire, so to speak. It is a case similar to superstitious behavior, except that instead of accidental reward, this is accidental punishment. But the wrong behavior is changed in both cases. Nevertheless, telling the truth is punished so often, and so rarely rewarded, that you can almost make a categorical statement: Where you find a person who frequently tells lies, you will nearly always find that he was punished often and rewarded seldom— and many of the rewards he did get were for undesirable behavior.

Punishment, like starving, tends to weaken behavior. Many of our problems arise from the fact that we already have too few behaviors to begin with, so why punish problem behaviors and reduce the pool of available behaviors still more? Of course, we would not want to hang on to some problem behaviors, even if we do have an excessive behavioral deficit. Sometimes, however, they might not even be problem behaviors in a different setting, or when they happen less often.

The eagerness to weaken an unwelcome behavior often overrides the much more important job of increasing the competing behaviors. As long as you are intent on punishing behavior you don't like, it becomes that much harder to see clearly the good behaviors you should be trying to strengthen in their place to crowd out the problems—that is, you will find it that much harder to give the learner extra levers to press.

7. *Punishment can strengthen behavior under certain circumstances.* After all I've said about punishment reducing behavior, such a statement may seem strange to you, but it sometimes happens. For example, some people want attention so badly that they are willing to accept punishment in order to get it. In the process, punishment and attention become so closely associated that the person may eventually work for the punishment, even when the attention is not there.

There are clinical cases of people who were punished so severely for childhood sexual responses that the punishment became strongly associated with sexual pleasure. These people are sometimes unable to have an orgasm unless someone inflicts pain on them. Clinical psychologists and psychiatrists have a heyday when cases like this come to their attention, and call them *masochistic*. Of course, as I made quite a point of telling you in Chapter 2, giving them such a title in no way helps treat the condition, which would have to involve an entirely new set of experiences involving pain and pleasure, and somehow separating the two. Much easier, of course, would have been the avoidance of the use of punishment in the first place.

Pain and pleasure are often closely related, especially when the pain is mild, or if it started out mild originally, and was gradually made stronger. If the pain is not too intense, it might help us understand why people inflict pain on themselves. The first time a person smokes a cigarette or cigar, his experience is usually one of distaste, and certainly not pleasure. But he soon may grow to *like* the mild pain the tobacco smoke inflicts upon him, although the same is not true of the intense pain caused by the emphysema, lung cancer, or angina that may be a delayed result of that first smoke. But soon after that first smoke, he becomes unaware that it is even painful any more. In fact, it stops *being* painful.

I once lived in the Land of Enchantment for three years. During that time I often inflicted intense pain upon myself by eating New Mexico green chili. Before long, I adapted to the pain, and soon grew to love the flavor, which surprised me by its subtleties. Today, I no longer feel much pain, unless I encounter an extra-hot one, and I have grown to love the taste so much that I have even grown New Mexico green chili in my California garden. A punisher became a payoff.

8. *Aggression begets counter-aggression.* If I hit you, I increase the odds you will want to hit me. You might be able to control yourself and not actually strike me physically, but the urge will still be there, and it might take some effort on your part to overcome it. The aggression does not have to be physical, either. Verbal aggression also begets counter-

aggression, which might or might not be verbal. In other words, if I make a hostile remark to you, you will want to attack me in return. Many a duel has been fought over verbal hits. A parent spanking a child should expect the child to long for retaliation in some way. It is as natural as breathing for him to want to square accounts, and it doesn't matter in the slightest that he "drove you to it." But he might learn at an early age that he is too weak to be able to spank such a giant successfully, so he will refrain from physical counter-aggression. Still, the urge will be there, and the child may then try verbal aggression. The parent often finds this unacceptable as well, and punishes the child again.

"You shouldn't *say* things like that."

But the parent can't stop the child from thinking hostile thoughts, and might be better off in the long run if he taught the child that there is a way to express hostility that is not as aggressive as simply blowing up. I already mentioned how an individual should leave his adversary a means to save face. It would certainly be unwise for the parent to follow up a punishment by telling the child, "I know what you're thinking! Shame on you. You're terrible for even thinking such nasty, horrible thoughts!" The child thus gets painted into a corner, with no exit. But the urge, or tendency, is still there, and it will come out in some way perhaps too subtle to recognize, such as "accidentally" spilling ink on the carpet, or leaving the car door slightly open so the dome light runs the battery down. Adults may be even more devious, and deliberately sabotage your efforts at success, but do so in ways which leave so much room for doubt that it is hard to prove who did what and with which and to whom.

In short, when a person is hit, he will want to hit back. Look back into Chapter 3, at example number 5. The husband made many attacks on his wife, and vice versa. Sometimes the attack was subtle, and only became clear when the hidden messages were examined. For example, Laurie said, "I suppose you think keeping house is all a bed of roses?"

That doesn't sound very bad, does it? But she is actually saying, "I work hard too, and you are ungrateful and stupid for not realizing that." But Jim felt the hit, as subtle as it was. He hit right back, saying, "But you're *supposed* to do that." He told her, in a hidden message, "Your feelings are unimportant. My work is important, and takes somebody extra-special, but *anybody* can keep house. So don't feel so important."

Now Laurie was hit, so it was her turn to hit back. "You smug male chauvinist! You're *supposed* to go to work and earn a living, too." She told him this message: "You're not so special. What you're doing is nothing more than any husband is supposed to do." So now he must hit her again, and she will try to return his volley, like a tennis player. Once the ball is in motion, it makes little difference who served. The name of the game is to overcome your opponent.

Read through the conversation and you will see exactly what I mean. Often, people find themselves in arguments and they really don't know how it all got started. "What are we arguing about, anyway?"

"Hell, I don't know—I forgot."

Usually, the original thing that started the argument was not very important, but the use of punishment made a mountain out of a molehill. Before long, it doesn't matter in the slightest who "started" the argument. Both parties keep it going, especially if they perceive an extra punishment in the loss of face they might suffer by "losing" the argument, or by terminating it. In reality, terminating the argument might very well be the only sensible thing to do. This is also true of wars between countries. Who is wise enough to say who starts a war? Both sides have gripes, and both sides feel their gripes are valid ones, and usually both sides are absolutely right, even when one side is righter than the other. But both sides also lack the proper behaviors to solve their disagreements in a more intelligent, or sane manner.

The moral to the story is that if you punish, you must expect some punishment in return.

9. *Punishment, perhaps even more than starvation, easily gets to be on cue.* I have been a bad boy. Father punishes me. Therefore, if I wish to repeat the punished behavior, I will try to do it when and where father cannot see me. Sometimes punishment may not teach us to stop a forbidden behavior, but instead, it might teach us to try harder not to get caught.

At times, every driver exceeds the speed limit, but we are much more likely to do so in situations where we feel certain we will not get caught—such as the wide, straight, level, open highways of West Texas or Nevada. We look for a highway patrol car, and slow down when we see one. And if we are caught, do we tell ourselves, "I should thank the officer for doing his job. It was for my own good."? No, we get angry at the law enforcement officer who just saved our lives.

Millions of people never meet a policeman personally, and their only contact is when they are caught violating a law and punished. Is it any wonder that so many policemen are killed needlessly? The person just arrested was punished, and punishment begets counter-aggression.

A behavior which is taboo in one place may be perfectly all right in another. But if it was punished while taboo, the behavior might be suppressed when it is desirable. In other words, we might get too much overlap (see Chapter 10). I recall a retarded girl in a state hospital who repeatedly soiled her pants on hot days so she could get a cool shower. The staff could not let her go dirty, so they did give her the shower, but tried to make it a punishment, by using water so cold that she would not want to repeat her behavior. The result was that the girl then refused to enter the shower room, whether or not she had become soiled. Her nightly showers became physical struggles, as the staff members carried her into the warm shower room, just incidentally giving her a lot of attention in the process. Was it any wonder that the girl created such disturbances? The staff not only rewarded the girl for her struggles, but got unwanted overlap when they would have preferred the behavior to be on cue.

10. *There is some question as to how permanent the effects of punishment really are,* as far as behavior suppression is concerned. Until a few years ago, most scientists thought that the main effects of punishment are temporary—in other words, that punishment quickly suppresses a behavior, but the suppression gradually wears off, so that in the long run, there has been little change in the strength of the punished behavior. More recent studies have shown that as we make a punisher stronger, the suppression comes more quickly and lasts longer. Eventually, a point is reached where the punisher is so intense that only one punishment stops the behavior for all time.

But even in scientific circles there is still disagreement. We just don't know the whole story yet.

My own studies, experiences, and observations have tended to agree more with the earlier studies, which found that punished behavior eventually returns. If this turns out to be a fact, the best we can expect from using punishment is to be able to buy time to strengthen competing targets. Once punishment has weakened the behavior enough that it is significantly less dangerous, we may then keep it low by crowding, with only occasional punishment necessary. But we could also have brought the rate of the behavior down by starving it and using crowding, without using the punishment at all. In other words, punishment might not even be necessary. The process might have taken a bit longer, but it probably would have gotten the same job done, without any of the problems associated with the use of punishment.

There may be times when we must use punishment because we have no choice, but these times should be recognized as emergencies, and not as models of good treatment. In emergencies, as I have already mentioned, you must put out the fire. Your baby is running into the street. You don't have time to set up a program to reward the child for staying on the sidewalk and weaken going into the street by starving it. So you punish going into the street. But the real time to deal with the problem is when the baby is *not* running into the street. It takes some foresight and some effort, but if you reward him often enough for staying on the sidewalk, you can simply pick him up and put him back on the sidewalk if he should wander off. It would accomplish the same thing. Staying on the sidewalk is incompatible with running into the street. He can't be both places at once. If we punish wandering into the street without giving a payoff for staying on the curb, we run a risk of putting running into the street on cue. In other words, he might learn to stay on the sidewalk when we are around, but run into the street when we are not. This is a very serious risk to take. It would almost be better if he ran into the street when we are there to stop him instead of waiting until there is nobody around to save him! I think you'll agree that rewarding the good behavior here is very important!

11. *Consistency is important in all programming, whether or not punishment is used, but especially so when it is.* People adjust their behaviors to fit into situations, but they learn how to do this when a consequence follows a behavior in a reliably predictable pattern. This predictability is often missing when people rely on punishment to get most of their control of other people's behavior. Most of the time, parental punishment, for example, comes so unsystematically and so inconsistently that children rarely learn to *expect* it as a consequence of their behavior. When the punishment does come, it is not firmly associated with their disruptive behavior (but instead becomes associated with the person doing the punishing). Punishment then tends to be used more often than necessary, and adaptation to it becomes more likely. That is why you so often see children tuning out threats made by their parents. Punishment becomes ignored, if used too often. The parent using it too unsystematically tends to use it more and more, with less and less success, very much like an addict who needs more and more narcotic as he gets less and less effect from it. As the parent fails to get satisfactory control of his children, he becomes increasingly frustrated, and this generates more aggression. The repeated failure of the parent renders him impotent, and he grows to resent his children more and more. This produces still more punishment, which the children must (or do) counter. Where will it all stop?

Usually, it stops with armed truce, the children ignoring parental command much of the time, and when they do respond it is after the parent has been pushed beyond his limit, resulting in his use of force. Much of the time, they do not respond at all, while the parent ineffectually tucks his tail between his legs and walks away.

12. At the beginning of this chapter I promised I would tell you the exception to my rule that punishment should be avoided whenever possible. I have left this exception to the last few pages of the chapter on purpose, so that you would first have time to learn some of the really compelling arguments against the use of punishment. Now that you know them, you can put this rule into proper perspective.

There are times when even a mild punisher can be highly effective, and just as humane as any other program. First of all, you must very clearly spell out the alternatives the learner may choose. The alternatives are the behaviors he can use to get payoffs—in other words, they are extra levers he can press. This is really nothing more than crowding out. But if the punishment is simply taking away a reward, and the learner is then allowed to earn it back with targets that are clear and accessible to him, the combination of consequences works very well. For example, if a child whines or throws a tantrum, there is nothing wrong with putting him into his room for "punishment," provided you do so calmly, in a way that does not reward him with excessive social payoff. In this case, the actual punishment is his removal from other people around him. (The assumption is made that he will be having more fun around the other people than he will in his room, even though the latter is filled with toys, etc.). But we have told only half the story. You must also tell him, "As soon as you stop whining and crying, you may come out and join us, but be sure to give us a big smile!" When he comes out smiling, you too can smile, saying, "We're really glad to have you back with us again!" Smiling is his extra lever, and he gets additional reward for re-entering the group. Another example might be telling a teen-age boy, "I must take the keys to the car away from you because you drove to town when you should have been doing your homework (the punishment is confiscation of the keys). But if you do the best job you can on your homework, then as soon as you finish, you may have the keys back." (His homework is the alternative behavior, and through it he can earn the keys again). This combination of mild punishment, crowding, and spelling out *how to remove the punishment* is more effective than punishment alone, which does not have much to recommend for its use. Notice also that it was not possible to starve his driving to town, first of all because its payoff had already taken place, and it is too late to do anything about the past. But it was not really the problem. The problem behavior was something he had *not* done. He did not do his homework. His payoff for doing his homework would be the use of the car.

13. *Last, but not least, we live in a world which is already too full of punishment.* We would all like to have less punishment directed toward us, but in order to have our wish, our entire society must first change, and changes in societies only come from changes in the behaviors of their members. We are told that these changes come about as a result of new technologies, changes in climate, or invasion by foreign troops, but still, before the society changes, the behavior of its members changes. Every time an adult punishes a child or another adult, he is modelling a behavior which other people might copy. Children of punishing parents may easily grow to adulthood accepting punishment as a way of life, and punish their own children in the next generation. Each time you punish a child, you are sending him a hidden message that violence is ok, because his parents endorse it and use it.

Parents often fail to see that punishing children makes them (the parents) bullies, even when they punish a child for bullying smaller children! If you punish children, but do not believe you are a bully, here is a simple test you can take. Think of the person you fear the most, and ask yourself, "Would I behave toward this person as I do toward my children?" If the answer is, "no," perhaps it is time you thought about changing your behavior. Any time a person tries to control another by using more force than his opponent can return, he is a bully. This is equally true of nations, and no jingo slogans can change this simple fact.

The more we punish others, or threaten punishment, the more we delay that day when we, our children, and all other people as well, will no longer have to fear punishment to the extent we do today. There will always be some around, of course. Nature alone will guarantee that. But why should we add to it unnecessarily when we now know better ways of getting the same things done? With the exception I have noted above, it is our responsibility to use punishment only as a last resort, and not a first one. Think about that the next time you say, "I've tried everything, and nothing works!"

Chapter 9

Escape and Avoidance:

Stopping or Postponing Punishment

If you have learned everything in the previous chapters, you now know the most basic facts about human behavior. The next two chapters will make you more sophisticated, and increase your depth of understanding of what makes people tick—and behave.

In Chapter 8, I repeatedly made the statement that punishment usually weakens behavior. That is true, of course, but there are two more exceptions to that rule, and this chapter will be about those exceptions. They are called *escape* and *avoidance*. Many people confuse the two, not only because the names are similar, but because both are situations in which punishment can play a role in strengthening behavior.

If you are uncomfortable, hurt, or frightened, whatever gives you relief will become a payoff. Suppose you have a headache. You take a tablet and the headache goes away. You are more likely to take a tablet next time you have a headache. Sometimes, the tablet contains a substance that actually stops the headache, but other times, the pain would have gone away without the tablet. Either way, the disappearance of the headache strengthened taking a tablet. You can see that a lot of superstitious behavior goes on when people want to get rid of pain, and that includes annoying problem behaviors. Physicians can give *placebos*–that is, capsules or tablets that look like a drug but aren't. They might contain nothing more than powdered milk, sugar, or some other inert substance. They know it will do no harm and many times, the patient just wants to take *something* . The fact that he believes it will take away pain may actually help reduce the pain, and in a safe way, too.

Physicians are also human, and can sometimes be fooled. They might prescribe medication needlessly because the patient's symptoms went away the last time they precribed that medication for one of their other patients. It is precisely for this reason that elaborate tests are devised to evaluate each drug before it is marketed. A good drug study will usually be done "double blind." That is, neither the people taking the drug nor those giving it will know which person is getting the drug and which is getting the placebo. Only third parties who have no contact with either will be able to decode the results.

For whatever reason, the headache goes away, and the patient escapes from the pain. Whatever he did to escape is more likely to be repeated next time he has a headache. Testing the true effect of any drug is further complicated by the fact that there might be a long delay between the time the patient swallows the capsule and the end of the symptom.

You "escape" from cold by leaving the room, or by turning up the heater, or by putting on more warm clothing. Excessive cold is a punisher, and the behavior which results in your escape from the cold is more likely to be repeated next time you feel cold. In other words, the behavior which reduces the punishment is rewarded by the punishment getting weaker.

It is this ability to escape from punishment, or to avoid it entirely, which explains why people have used punishment on other people since mankind first pressed his feet into the ancient sands, and why he will probably continue to use it until the human race becomes extinct—quite possibly as a direct result of his use of punishment. As the arranger punishes the learner's problem behavior, the learner stops, and the arranger feels relief. The relief is a strong payoff, so the arranger is more likely to repeat the act of punishment next time he is distressed by someone's behavior. Story number 4 in Chapter 3 was a good example. The parents shouted at the children because the shouts occasionally made the children get temporarily quiet, even though the long-range effect of the shouts tended toward the opposite effect. Here is another example:

You are trying to listen to a concert on FM radio, but your children are making noise which lessens your enjoyment of the music. That is, they are punishing you. Finally, after many warnings which go unheeded, you swat their buttocks. Their noise stops at once, and you have temporarily escaped from their punishment. You escaped by eliminating the source of the annoyance, which was the loud noise. In this example, your relief from their noise strengthened your behavior of swatting their buttocks, and made it more likely that you will swat them the next time they annoy you.

The things you try to escape from may be thought of as punishers, so that in this case, the use of a punisher does in fact strengthen behavior. But it is the *turning off* of the punisher which acts as the payoff. Your violent behavior was strengthened because the punisher (the noise) was already there, and your action, or behavior, stopped it and gave you relief. That behavior was therefore strengthened by the relief.

Seen from the child's eyes, however, your swatting them was a punisher. Why then didn't it increase their behavior, as it did yours? Well, it might actually have done that, if their noise was attention-getting behavior. But if not, the reason is simple. Your swat came after their noise. Therefore, their noise did not stop your swatting. Their getting quiet did, and so they escaped from more of your aggression by stopping their noise. If they would rather have been punished than ignored, swatting them would pay off their noise.

When the punishment—that is, some unpleasant or painful circumstance—is already there, and you do something that gets you away from it, you *escape*, by physical movement away from the punisher or reducing your discomfort by some other means. It happens all the time, and you should be prepared to recognize how it can contribute to some of your distress by strengthening problem behaviors. Remember example number 3 in Chapter 3, describing Bill's excessive drinking? He drank alcohol to reduce his tension, which was already present. His relief was his payoff, so drinking alcohol was strengthened. It became his most serious problem behavior.

Any time a person escapes from a punishment, that punishment has to be there already, or he would not have it to escape from. It must be on before he can turn it off, and whatever results in escape becomes a payoff. When we have a hard time trying to find a reward strong enough to strengthen some behavior, we might be tempted to start punishing someone so that we could then turn off the punisher, and reward by using the relief. This is tricky, at best, although some spectacular results with severely disturbed children have been obtained by turning off a punisher at the exact moment the children ran into the arms of the therapists. Within a short time, these children were making affectionate and warm responses toward their therapists—it was the first time such behavior had ever been observed in these children.

But this type of program is extremely tricky, and there are many ethical pitfalls. My advice would be to look more carefully, and you will probably find enough other payoffs you can use. If so, it should not be necessary to start punishment deliberately, for the sole purpose of turning it off later. One ethical question concerns the right of the arranger to make the learner deliberately uncomfortable just so that he can later make him feel better by escaping from the same discomfort. If the case were very serious it might be justified, but the odds are not with it, and such practice is not for beginners.

One reason is that when you first turn on the punisher, it will tend to suppress behavior taking place at the time the punisher is turned on. That behavior was probably acceptable behavior, since most behavior is. The result would be that perfectly good behavior is accidentally punished and weakened. Using rewards other than escape from punishment is certainly more pleasant, and avoids both the ethical and technical problems that you get into when you use punishment. Use of these alternative payoffs will make the programming process much more enjoyable all around, both for the learner and for the arranger.

For all practical purposes, then, escape behavior is something which will always go on, because the world is already full of punishers, and not all of them last forever. When distress occurs, it may eventually stop, and whatever stops or diminishes it will be a payoff; this is good, because it teaches people how to reduce the stresses and pains they will encounter all their lives. But my main reason for discussing escape is to help you understand, avoid, and get out of those situations in which escape is the main payoff.

There is a similar situation, called *avoidance* behavior, which is a lot more important. Avoidance behavior *postpones or prevents punishment from happening.* It is different from escape because the punishment has not yet occurred. Avoidance behavior prevents or postpones *future* punishment, while escape turns off punishment which is already present. You work at a job you hate in order to prevent or postpone the finance company from foreclosing on your house. You study for a test in order to prevent your failing the test. You drive carefully in order to prevent having a police office write a ticket, or to prevent a serious accident. You might sometimes stay at home wishing you had a date with a certain lady but not call her, in order to prevent her from telling you, "no." You might stay away from the water in order to prevent your drowning. You might back down and change the subject when you feel someone has insulted you, in order to prevent yourself from becoming a target for more of his aggression. You might hold off from asking the boss for a raise because you are afraid he might refuse, or because you are afraid you didn't do that last job quite to his satisfaction, or perhaps you are afraid he might mention your coming in late so often, and he might hold any of these things against you. In each case, anticipation of the punishment produces some distress, and by avoiding the source of the distress, you produce relief. The avoidance behavior is whatever you did to avoid the distress. All of these avoidance behaviors are strengthened by relief because the punishment does not come at all, or does not come until later. By then, the avoidance behavior has already been rewarded by the relief.

Avoidance behavior is one of the most important types of behavior. It can be good or bad. It can help you keep really bad things from happening, but it can also block any progress you might make in dealing with certain problem behaviors. If you ask a person why he does not stand up for his rights, you might get an answer like, "It really wasn't worth creating a scene for such a small thing." The hidden message is often quite different, however, and says, "I'm afraid to." Fear can be a strong force. But most of the time, fear is not the whole story. In the first place, most of the things people fear are really things which cannot hurt them anyway, or the fear is all out of proportion to the real danger. But in addition to fear, the person has probably learned a lot of ways to avoid the situation he fears. In some ways, these avoidance behaviors can be more damaging than the fear, because they can be strengthened by the payoff of avoiding the fear. But once they become strong habits they can be strengthened still more by other rewards which have nothing to do with fear. In fact, the avoidance behaviors often remain, many years after the fear or the source of the fear has disappeared.

Even when the fear remains, the avoidance behaviors prevent the learner from eliminating the fear, and here is why: If a person repeatedly goes near something he is afraid of when he is actually perfectly safe, his fear will gradually decrease, and eventually disappear altogether, very much like starvation. In other words, starving a fear requires repeated exposure to the feared object. But the exposure must be benign. That is, it must take place when the feeling of fear is absent, or at least relatively weak. If feelings incompatible with fear predominate, the fear can be starved by repeated exposure to the feared object. But repeated exposure is often prevented by the avoidance behaviors which have been learned. In fact, that is the purpose of the avoidance behaviors, and it is how they became strong in the first place. (A few competing emotions are relaxation, fun, physical well-being, sex, vigorous exercise, etc.). It is interesting that it works the other way around, too. When fear is strong, people cannot relax, have fun, feel well, or adequately perform sexually. Thus, people lose their fear of dogs when they spend a lot of time around *friendly* dogs. A child who is afraid of water will gradually lose his fear if he is allowed to wade as long as he wants, and to play in shallow water that he feels cannot hurt him, and furnishes fun. Fun is incompatible with fear.

The adult who refuses to go near water is not in a position to starve his fear of water. The adult who refuses to assert himself can never lose his fear of asserting himself. The person who is afraid of close relationships can never lose his fear of close relationships if he will never permit himself to get closer. And most of the times, the many avoidance behaviors we have learned are all that prevent us from the repeated benign exposures that are necessary in order for us to starve the fears. These behaviors supposedly protect us by not letting us get close to the things we fear. They also render us unable to approach them, even when we *know* they will not hurt us. That is why avoidance behaviors are so important. We must eliminate the avoidance behaviors if we ever hope to get close enough to let the fears starve. Our main strategy involving avoidance behaviors will be to deal with them as problem behaviors which compete with and prevent us from obtaining increases in target behaviors we need or want.

One of the most important things to know about avoidance behavior is that it too will die out if it is not rewarded. It was strengthened by protecting us from a punisher. If the punisher never comes, the avoidance behavior will starve, just like any other unrewarded behavior. If you stop to think about this for a few moments you'll see that it is extremely important, for reasons which are almost never recognized. It means that punishment is *necessary* to keep an avoidance behavior alive. It also means that you can never completely eliminate punishment by using avoidance behavior only, and the reason is that the more successfully you avoid the punishment, the more certain you make it that some time in the future the avoidance behavior will starve. When that happens, of course, there will be nothing to prevent the punishment from occurring, and it will return, just as if the avoidance had never been there in the first place.

As an example, turn back to story number 9, in Chapter 3. Here, the behavior we are interested in is "coming to work on time," which means entering the door before 8:00 AM. Most people are not fortunate enough to love their work, or look forward to it so eagerly that they don't want to lose an extra minute. Those who come early often do not do so because they are eager to be at work and eager to get started, although of course there are exceptions. In the example, coming to work early was only a means of avoiding punishment by the boss for being late. As long as the employee came early, he avoided, or postponed for another day, the chewing out the boss would have given him if he were late. Let us suppose this went on for many months or years, and everyone was consistently early. Nobody ever got punished for coming late. Now, suppose that one person arrived at 8:04 AM one morning. Perhaps the boss did not notice, or felt it was too trivial a violation to make a scene. At any rate, he overlooked it and did not punish his employee for coming late. A few days later, the same employee arrived at 8:20, another time at 8:12, then 8:02, 8:45, 8:18, etc. None of these times were punished. Gradually, you could expect the employee to become a ten o'clock scholar who used to come at 8:00 o'clock, but now he comes at noon. His coming late would be *shaped* (see Chapter 13), and coming on time would gradually die out. As I said, coming to work on time was only a means of avoiding punishment, and was not rewarded on its own merit.

But one fateful day, the boss was waiting for him and delivered a very stern and unpleasant lecture, accompanied by some threats to the security of his job. What was the result? The employee appeared before 8:00 the next morning, and came early every day for some time to come. Gradually, after a few weeks, he again slipped up and arrived at 8:12. The boss did not react, but the cycle had started again.

What can this teach you? Two things, I hope. First of all, if you are an employer who wishes his workers to come on time, you must not depend upon avoidance alone. Somehow, your employees should be rewarded for making it to work by 8:00 on the days when they did as you wished. The other thing you should learn is that avoidance behavior is just that. It *avoids punishment*. If the punishment is avoided without the avoidance behavior, that behavior will gradually disappear, or at least, change.

There is still another reason why knowledge of avoidance behavior should be very important to us, and that is because our entire legal system is designed as a series of hundreds of thousands of avoidance situations, called *laws*. When was the last time a Highway Patrol Officer pulled you over to the side of the road and told you, "You were obeying the speed laws of the State of California. Congratulations! I am going to write you a ticket. If you will send this ticket to Sacramento, you will receive in return a check for $25.00"? In all probability, it has never happened to you. In other words, the law does not concern itself with rewarding you for obedience. I am no lawyer, but I have read quite a few laws, and have never yet seen one which reads like this: "Driving more than 40 mph and less than 65 mph on this stretch of road is subject to an occasional reward of $25.00."

Instead, all the laws I have seen tell what happens to you if you violate them, and reward is used solely as an incentive for informers. Laws contain phrases such as, "Punishable by a fine of not more than $50.00 or not more than 10 days in jail." In other words, the law is written in the language of avoidance. You obey the law not to receive payoff for obeying the law, but in order to prevent punishment. That makes it avoidance behavior. Obedience is taken for granted, crime means only a violation of the law, and reward exists only for the stool pigeon. Do you realize what that means? It means that laws set up punishment to prevent crimes—that is, violation of the laws. Since we know that this makes obedience to law an avoidance behavior, it also means that if a person is obedient to the law all the time, he will never be punished for violation of the law, and therefore, the avoidance behavior (obeying the law) will eventually weaken and starve. What's more, it means that the punishment *must* take place from time to time, or the laws will not work.

For quite a few months after getting a ticket in a certain speed trap, I drove less than 25 mph in that particular place. But that was more than nine years ago. Now, I am back to driving at a speed which feels perfectly safe and comfortable to me, and happens also to be about 45 mph. That speed limit sign is no longer a signal to me that punishment happens here, and my behavior is no longer controlled by that cue. In other words, my avoidance behavior of obeying that sign has died out.

What this actually means is that in order for the laws to work at all, they must be violated from time to time, and preferably punished every time they are violated, since occasional punishment does not suppress as well as punishment on every occurrence of the behavior. Thus, *some crime is necessary in order to make crime prevention work!* It seems crazy, but once we know something about avoidance behavior, it is a conclusion we cannot escape—at least, as long as our entire crime prevention program is based upon avoidance of punishment.

Fortunately, there are some things operating in favor of the law, even though at present they seem to be operating on a deficit, just like nearly everything else. One of these things is the fact that people often respond to vicarious punishment. That is, they can learn of someone else being punished, and this might work as a temporary deterrent. Most of us have never killed another person, so we have never been punished for doing so. But we read or hear about others who have been punished. The extent to which this controls our behavior is unknown. We know that there are a large number of cases where vicarious punishment does not work. We have all read of the historical fact that when pickpockets were hung publicly as a program to prevent picking pockets, more pockets were picked at these hangings than anywhere else. We also know that the death penalty did not deter the majority of murderers, but on the other hand, we do not know how many murders were *not* committed because of the death penalty. Where capital punishment has been in effect and removed, or in cases where it has not been in effect and has then been adopted, there is almost no noticeable difference in the rate at which murders are committed, which suggests that we are just as well off without it as with it. Legalized murder by the state is clearly not the answer, and I don't know what is, for society must be protected too. On the other hand, the greatest number of murders are committed by people against members of their families, or their friends or acquaintances. A relatively small share of blood is spilled by the work of "hardened criminals." Perhaps life sentences without possibility of parole might afford a large measure of protection, but in all probability the greatest reduction of murders could be obtained simply by making possession of guns illegal.

One thing that helps the law operate even to the limited extent that it does is the fact that we do get some payoffs for obeying the law—we can feel good about ourselves, or self-righteous because of our obedience. But these feelings are all incidental to the way the law is written. The laws themselves will only guarantee that they can be partly, but never totally successful in preventing their own violation.

Since avoidance behavior requires punishment in order to remain effective, it means that an entire legal system is inherently unstable. That is undoubtedly one of the many reasons why there is so much lawlessness today. On the one hand, people say that the reason for so much crime is because judges are too lenient, and do not punish severely enough. That might be in some cases, but only as far as it goes. I've said that people can be punished vicariously by the knowledge that other people get punished for violating laws. They can surely grow to ignore the laws for a similar reason, when they learn that many others violate the laws and are never punished. What must it do when millions of people see both a president and vice president commit serious crimes and both go unpunished, and in fact rewarded substantially when a person of lesser status would have been jailed and broken for the remainder of his humiliated life, with no probable return to favor? Thus, avoidance behavior results in crime prevention which starts out with limitations, and unjust leniency merely erodes the remaining obedience to law a bit further. Justice is a word that only has meaning in a society which punishes, because it means that two people who commit identical crimes will receive identical punishment. If the society was not punishing violation of laws but was instead rewarding obedience to laws, we would seldom or never talk about justice, but of effectiveness, instead. Two people obeying the same laws should receive the same rewards. However, a society sophisticated enough to install such revisions of its legal code would also recognize that rewards are idiosyncratic and individual. If one person feels short-changed, his obedience would then begin to starve, and the result would be that he would not be as likely to repeat the target behavior. The same reward he rejected might be sufficient to maintain the target behaviors of a different individual.

Lenient sentences become a factor only when the law requires punishment in order to make it work. It is relevant only when we are thinking mostly of problem behaviors we want the laws to suppress. But there are more effective ways of controlling behaviors, and these ways do not depend upon, or even need punishment. You learned about them in Chapter 7. If we de-emphasize the problem behaviors by thinking of competing targets, and then reward the target behaviors, we will not need to punish problem behaviors nearly as much, or nearly as often. Doubtless, this kind of legal system is at least decades away, and it looks like we will still have to rely on laws written as avoidance of punishment for the present, and probably for the remainder of our lives. But if the laws are eventually re-written to reward desirable behaviors, punishment could then be used only for the emergency cases, or those cases where we failed to design and carry out a good enough program. This would then be a reflection of our own failures as arrangers. Punishment would be used only in cases where we had to put out fires (see Chapter 7).

We would probably find that such a system would be vastly more pleasant to live under. There is also evidence that it would be much less expensive than the present system, which costs us *billions* of dollars a year, to say nothing of the broken lives that might have been salvaged. Without a doubt, there would be far fewer law enforcement officers killed by people who have equated them with punishment, because they would then be equated with reward. People rarely hate or shoot Santa Claus, who brings them goodies, and represents reward to them.

Of course, these kinds of changes will take place slowly, if at all. But that does not mean that you cannot work toward such goals on an individual basis. If you wish to change societies, you must remember that violent overthrow seldom makes major changes in societies. It merely changes the faces of the leaders with the same kinds of problem behaviors. After all, people use aggression in order to overthrow anything violently, and there is surely nothing radical or new about one more dictator who has to get himself entrenched by means of violence.

Societies change primarily as the behaviors of their members change, for whatever reason. As you learn to rely less and less on punishment, and to accentuate the positive more and more, it will not only permit you to improve your own life, but your influence will be felt by those people around you, and you will become a model for others to follow. This will extend your own influence, and will happen even more times if others also see you are successfully dealing with problems by using rewards, when they use punishment on the same problems and fail.

Avoidance of punishment can be an important means of protection, but it should be used that way, and not as a way to do things poorly which are better done by other, more effective and pleasant means. Let me repeat: Accentuate the positive more and more. There are good, scientific reasons for doing so. The use of reward for target behaviors remains our most hopeful means of changing societies into organizations that serve the best interests of their individual members.

Chapter 10

Overlap: Alike But Different

We are always reacting to a bunch of different signals, along with whatever behaviors we have learned as a response to those signals. That is, we react in special ways to everything we see, hear, touch, smell, and experience through our senses. A famous man once said, "We never bathe twice in the same stream," meaning there are no two situations which are exactly alike in all respects. Knowing what you know already, how can you explain the fact that we don't have to learn everything we know hundreds, or even thousands of times every day—in short, each time a new situation arises? As you know, this is not the case. For example, you may learn to drive a car or fly an airplane with your instructor in the seat next to you, but when you fly solo, or drive with a different person next to you, you do not have to learn everything from scratch again. Although different, these situations are still alike. If you see the signal light on the corner of Van Ness and Lombard turn red, you stop. It is not necessary to learn separately to stop for every other red light in San Francisco. You might first learn to tell a joke because you enjoy your parents' laughter. But you do not need to learn all over again with everyone else in the world who will laugh. You may learn to ski using Head Standard skis, but that does not mean you must learn to ski completely from the beginning when you strap on a pair of Rossignols. For that matter, you will not have to learn from the beginning every time you ski on a different mountain, a different run, at a different time, with different lighting, different snow conditions, different physical condition, or you are wearing a different colored parka.

Each situation is just a bit different, or a great deal different, but you learn to alter your behaviors appropriately for each one. On ice you might use the edges of your skis a bit more, but in deep powder snow you would keep your weight back a bit. To accommodate the different and changing conditions, you make adjustments you have learned, and each adjustment is a behavior you will use in response to new signals which tell you that conditions have changed. But the basic skills of relaxation, unweighting the skis in turns, using the poles, using the edges, keeping your weight above the skis, keeping your knees slightly bent, and remaining responsive to the snow and slope conditions are pretty much the same, no matter where you ski. In other words, you have learned skills which you can use under a variety of conditions. I will use the term *overlap* to describe how we make the same response to slightly different signals. The skills of skiing, flying, playing bridge, riding a skateboard, or plowing a straight furrow overlap to a variety of different conditions.

You learn to walk when you live in one house. You do not have to learn to walk all over again in other places, unless conditions are very different, such as on very steep slopes, climbing up loose cinders, walking a beam of steel 65 stories above the street, walking on stilts, on skates, or on a rolling deck of a sailboat. Walking has overlapped so well that you rarely have to change it. So have a great many other skills, such as talking.

The more closely one situation resembles another (that is, the more identical the signals are from each situation), the more likely it will be that your behavior will be the same for both signals. Most people learn to identify a person by his voice, even when he can't be seen, and their conversations to this voice are the same as they might be to the person if he could also be seen. Not only that, but they can usually recognize the voice even when it has been distorted quite a bit. We still recognize voices over the telephone because despite the distortion, the telephone voice is still similar to the real voice. We continue to recognize voices of our friends even when they have colds, or when they are excited, and the pitch and speed of their voices have both been raised. We recognize them under a wide variety of conditions, but sooner or later, the voice may become too different, and we no longer respond the same way to it. "Oh, I didn't recognize you!"

Disguises work on this principle. Change the signals enough and you will change the behavior of the people who see or hear them. Add enough seasoning and you might get little Archibald to eat squash, even though he doesn't like squash.

We learn certain behaviors—that is, certain ways to respond to people—and these behaviors overlap quite a bit to situations which are not identical to the conditions present when we learned the behaviors. We first learn to relate to other people by learning to relate to our parents, or those people in our life who have taken the place of our parents. This early training forms behavior patterns that may last a lifetime. It is sometimes said that men marry women who resemble their (the men's) mother. That is pretty safe to say, since you should be able to find something about every woman which resembles your mother. Still, there is no doubt that some men react toward certain women about the same as they did toward their mother. I have often worked with men who are ordinarily confident, assertive, friendly, relaxed, and productive in their work, as long as their employer is male. But with female employers, female supervisors, female authority-figures, or even "just plain women," they begin acting like little boys (see the case of Mark, Chapter 11). Around their employer they act as they once did toward their mother—or father, for that matter. Often it is not just the official role of a person, but the behavior of the person in authority which sets off such behaviors in other people. When a person's behavior closely resembles that of your parents, you are more likely to treat them or behave toward them as you did toward your parents. The more different he is from parent, the less your behavior toward him will resemble your own childhood behavior. In other words, the greater the similarity of the signals, the more the responses to them will overlap. Many times, a particular behavior is called a problem behavior only because it happens in the wrong place, at the wrong time, or around the wrong person—that is, because of its setting. As I mentioned in Chapter 6, stripping is on cue. It is not a problem behavior in a shower room or dressing room, but it does become somewhat of a problem behavior when it is done in the lobby of a theatre, or in Golden Gate Park at noon on a summer day. In this case, there is too much overlap. In other cases, we might find that a child will be polite to strangers, but to his parents he is rude, inconsiderate, demanding, tyrannical, and obnoxious. His politeness is on cue. When one signal (the parents) appears so does his rudeness. When other signals (strangers) appear, his politeness returns. We want to overlap target behaviors such as generosity, consideration, or politeness (and this becomes easier after these terms have been translated into behavioral language such as we discussed in Chapter 2). We want to overlap those target behaviors because by doing so, they can compete with some of the rude behaviors toward his parents, and automatically crowd them out. What is left would be polite (or neutral) behaviors, and of course, they would now overlap into areas they had not appeared before.

You have already learned that there are situations in which our behavior will be different, depending upon the signal. This is what was meant in Chapter 6 when I talked about a behavior being *on cue*. Actually, for all practical purposes, such control by signal (behavior on cue) is the opposite of overlap. Where we have strong control by signal, we are really saying that the behavior has not overlapped to other situations. Where we have a great deal of overlap, the control by cues is weak.

At various times, you will want either strong or weak cues. That is, you will want weak or strong overlap, respectively. Which you want will depend upon the circumstances, and at times, your own preferences. You will probably find that as a rule you will have less overlap—that is, more control by cue, when you are using either starvation or punishment alone, without rewarding competing target behaviors. A good example would be punishing a baby for going into the street. In this case, you would not want his behavior on cue. You would not want the control of his behavior to depend on your being present. You would want overlap to be so complete that he would never go into the street alone—when nobody else is around to monitor and intervene. Of course, it is possible to overdo it, so that you could not even get him to cross the street when it was safe, but such situations are extreme. They happen rarely, and when they do they are relatively easy to deal with, and worth the risk.

Cues develop when a behavior has been rewarded in one setting and not in others. If starving always takes place in one location, or around a certain person, but the same behavior is rewarded by another person in a different place, you can expect that behavior to come under control of the signal present at the time of reward—that is the people and the places. One person will be a reward-signal and another will be a starve-signal; the behaviors they control will be appropriate to the consequences that had taken place in the past. People then become cues when one rewards the learner's behavior and the other starves the same behavior. Phyllis laughs at my jokes, so I drop by her office every time I hear a new one. Tom does not laugh at my jokes, so I rarely tell jokes to him. Each person rewards those behaviors which interest him, by paying attention at the time those behaviors occur. If he is bored he does not pay attention. This process of discrimination teaches the learner not to talk about that subject to the person he has learned is not interested. In this way, everybody learns to do different things, and talk about different things, around different people.

I have somehow paid attention when people told me their problems. My attention, interest, sympathy, and sometimes advice were the payoffs these people wanted. Other people become uneasy when friends talk about their problems. Psychologists are taught to listen to the problems of other people (at any rate, we *hope* they are taught), and so are ministers, social workers, and sometimes, bartenders and physicians. Every one of the people who become sounding boards for the troubles of the sufferer also rewards those victims by paying attention to their problems, so they end up hearing more of them. But often, the victim's mate will not listen, except perhaps during a commercial. Is it any wonder that talking about problems starves under such conditions? The victim no longer tells problems to his mate but unloads freely on friends, professionals, and sometimes complete strangers, like the Ancient Mariner cornering the wedding guest. Telling private facts about your life is a behavior on cue.

I repeat: When a person's behavior is rewarded under some conditions but is starved under other conditions, it is on cue. It is controlled by the signals which represent the conditions. This is why we often find that two people have completely different opinions of a third person. It is true that they may see the person from different viewpoints, but it may also be true that the person in question really *acts* differently around them. The college professor may be seen as a stuffed shirt by his students because he is so formal, seldom smiles, and tolerates no foolishness in the classroom. But what would his faculty friends say about him after that party last Saturday? "Did you see Dr. Frisbee drinking out of the punch bowl? It was hilarious. He is really the life of the party!"

The students would find it hard to visualize this other Dr. Frisbee, so different from the one they know. Most people find it impossible to imagine their parents copulating, even though they know it must have happened at least once. And who can conceptualize a matinee idol, president, Playmate of the Month, or Shakespearian scholar defecating? Drinking out of the punch bowl, copulation, and other behaviors may be rewarded in the presence of *some* people, but not others. Professor Frisbee's students pay him awe and respect for being so formal, which competes with drinking from punchbowls. These behaviors are incompatible, because they cannot occur simultaneously. Formality is starved at faculty parties, and there is no opportunity to drink out of punch bowls during Professor Frisbee's lectures.

When cues have become strong enough, some striking things happen. If one of the signals suddenly appears, the behavior it controls might start (or stop, as the case may be), just as though a switch was controlling the behavior. Of course, it does not always happen this clearly, but people often ask me, "What do you think triggered off that problem behavior?" When they think in terms of a signal that triggers a behavior, they are asking which cues appeared. Behavior that was rewarded in the presence of those signals then has a way of reappearing at the time the signal (cue) appears. Let me give you an example of what something like this might look like when it does happen.

When I was a teen-ager, I had a friend named Craig, who was very interested in magic tricks, although he was not very good at doing them. Still, he was fascinated by them, and above all loved to see them done by an expert. He talked about magic so much that some of his peers got tired of hearing about it, and tuned him out or punished him when he began to talk about it. They changed the subject at times, and at other times they even walked away. They starved talk about magic. By and by, Craig began to talk more about other things, and rarely mentioned magic around them.

One afternoon, Craig was visiting me at my house. My older brother had a visitor, Kenneth, who was one of his college buddies. Kenneth happened to be a semi-professional magician, and let this fact slip in front of Craig. Once Kenneth had done a few sleight-of-hand tricks, that was all it took! Craig poured on the questions and comments, and from that moment on, whenever Kenneth came to our house, Craig was sure to be there. Around Kenneth, Craig talked about magic. Around his school friends, he hardly ever mentioned it. Craig's talk of magic was on cue. Kenneth was the reward-signal and Craig's other friends were starve-signals. They were cues for him to talk of things other than magic.

Being on cue means that you do different things in different situations. This means that somehow you are able to tell different situations apart. There are times when someone may try to point out how two things are alike, but you might not see the resemblance. I sometimes turn on my FM radio and catch music in the middle of a composition I don't recognize. As I listen, I suddenly hear a part that makes me say, "Oh, that must be Brahms." Someone else who is equally familiar with Brahms might say, "I'm sorry, but I don't see what you mean." He doesn't hear the resemblance. Or has someone ever told you, "That baby looks just like his mother," and you answered, "I can't see it. They just don't look alike to me"? These are examples of borderline cases that overlapped for one person but not for the other. The person who saw the resemblance also recognized the overlap. The ability to see similarities in things which are different is called *abstraction*, and is commonly considered by psychologists involved in the construction of intelligence tests to be one of the marks of higher-level intellectual functioning.

I frequently hear people say, "Never punish when you're angry." Of course, after reading Chapter 8, you too might be tempted to say, "Never use punishment at all." But we should be realistic and recognize that there will be times when everyone becomes angry and punishes, even though he knows better. People often yell at their children and later feel guilty because they did so. Other times, they control their anger and try to punish the children calmly and deliberately. There might be strategic reasons for wanting to do things that way— in other words, the arranger might be deliberately following a program that asks him to be calm (in order to avoid giving social payoffs for attention-getting behavior). But most of the time I do not think it is advisable to punish without some signals that tell the learner you are displeased. Why not?

Well, first of all, it prevents you from getting their behavior on cue. If they do something you feel is wrong, and their consequence is seeing the same calm, unruffled parent they see when they have done something nice, how are they to learn that there is a difference between right and wrong, or more accurately, behavior that pleases and behavior that displeases? If you are trying to starve the behavior, especially if the behavior is attention-getting, of course, that is a different story, as I said. But you do want them to learn that there are limits to what other people will tolerate, and if they go beyond those limits, people everywhere will become angry and punish them. It is true that they can learn to stay within limits because they have been rewarded for doing the "good," and they will seldom stray into the problem behaviors. But there will always be times when *someone* will blow up at them, even if you have been crowding out their problem behaviors.

In addition, pretending to be calm when you are seething with anger is morally wrong, because it is just not honest. If you are angry, you surely have an obligation to other people who will be affected by your mood to tell them they have gone beyond your limit. You don't have to tell them in a nasty way, but anger can be expressed quite honestly without being either violent or hypocritical. By learning immediately that the limit has been crossed, our children, friends, family, or other learners are able to experience different consequences for problem behaviors than they would get for target behaviors, and thus learn to put them on cue.

There are times when people overlap too much. This means that they do not learn to recognize differences between things which may be alike in certain ways but are different in others. When carried to extremes, it is called *stereotyping,* which means that a person reacts to all members of a group of people or things as though they were identical. You have heard statements that show this stereotyping. Here are just a few examples: "All women want to have a husband and children." "Cops are pigs." "When you've seen one redwood you've seen them all." "All Niggers are stupid." "Girls are easier to raise than boys." "You

men are all alike." "He must be Scotch, because he's a lousy tipper."
"She is so compulsive—it must be because she's Gemini."

In each example, someone showed that he could not tell that there
are individual differences between members of any group. Of course
some blacks are stupid, but some whites are stupid too. For that matter,
some blacks are brilliant, and some are beautiful, but that is true of
whites and other colors as well. Some Scotch are tightwads, but some
are very generous. Some girls are less trouble than boys, but some boys
are less trouble than girls. Some policemen do act like "pigs," but others
are warm, sensitive, and human, just like great people in any other
group. And some people who are not policemen act like "pigs." Some
communists are atheists, but some are very devout. Some women—
maybe most of them—do want a husband and children, but men also
want a mate and family. But some people of each sex do not want these
things either. Some Geminis are not compulsive, and compulsive
people may have been born at any time of the year. And anyone
fortunate enough to have spent much time in the redwood forest will
surely know that when you have seen one *Sequoia Sempervirens* you have
not seen them all!

All of these examples show that people may think and behave toward
each member of a group the same as he would toward the other
members of the same group. A young child who has just been bitten by
a dog will probably fear all dogs. He will learn a lot of avoidance
behaviors that will keep him away from contact with those ferocious
beasts. It will take some time before he can learn that all dogs are not
alike. Some are docile, friendly, playful, loyal, protective, gentle, and
trusting, while others are aggressive, ill-tempered, dangerous creatures whose parents were also canine. It can take time for the child to
learn that Old Red has been in the family fifteen years, and couldn't
bite even if he wanted to, because he has no teeth. Some people never
starve their fears because their avoidance behaviors have prevented
them from learning that all dogs are different from each other, just as
humans are. They are the same way about other people. They rarely
get past their avoidance behaviors and meet people of unfamiliar
cultures, so they don't have much chance to destroy their stereotypes
and prejudices. Until you can meet lots of people of unfamiliar groups
in unthreatening situations, you will probably also overlap members of
those groups, which is perhaps the best possible testimonial for de-
segregation. Overlap is why many Orientals say, "All Americans look
alike." Americans—whatever that might mean—have had more experience with Americans, so they rarely have trouble picking out indi-

vidual differences between them. But they might still say the same thing about sub-cultures within America. Thus, they might believe all Jews are alike, or all Italians are alike, and they might be unable to tell a Zuni from an Apache from a Blackfoot from a Navajo from a Hupa from a Hopi. And they might have some trouble recognizing the difference between a Nigerian and an Ethiopian, or a Congolese and an Angolan, or even an Arab from an Asiatic Indian. The darker skins of these groups might so resemble the skins of the other groups that a "typical White Anglo-Saxon Protestant" may not recognize that they are really different in any significant way at all. And of course, I put my term in quotation marks, for not all White Anglo-Saxon Protestants are that much alike either.

There will be times when you teach your children, friends, mate, or self some new and useful skills. If you are going to take the trouble to teach the skill at all, you must have had a good reason. Teaching takes a lot of effort, and you would not go to that much trouble if you didn't feel it was worth it. Therefore, you should try to teach the person when and where he can behave the way you have taught him. The more times and places a person can repeat the behavior in the future, the greater will be the overlap, and the more situations he will find which will give him reward. It will be wise to work deliberately to overlap most of the target skills you will want to teach the learner. For example, if you are trying to teach someone to relate to other people without "hitting" so often (that is, you are trying to reduce their verbal aggression), this skill would be valuable no matter who the learner was relating to, and you would therefore want to overlap it. Some techniques for doing so will be found in Chapters 11 and 12.

Now you know the basic facts of human behavior. I have tried to avoid giving you detailed advice on how to program to get the change you want in someone's behavior. I wanted you to have some background first, so we could talk intelligently about it, and you would understand the reasons for advice given in the next two chapters. Even though the information has been non-technical, and not as deep as you might get if you took a doctor's degree in behavioral psychology, you now have enough to be of practical use to you. As I said much earlier, this is a book for beginners, and as such cannot cover everything. Those seriously interested in pursuing the topic will have little trouble obtaining good material from various libraries, especially in universities or some of the better training hospitals. But you now have covered the major points, and all of the information here should be compatible with the best clinical or behavioral advice available.

Now at last, we're ready to go. For the first time, we will try to change your behavior, or someone else's, according to the rules you have learned so far in this book. As we go about making deliberate changes, try to remember that you have been changing people's behavior as long as you have lived, whether you tried to do so or not. And remember also that changing behavior is a process of teaching and learning. How well the arranger follows the basic laws of human behavior outlined in the ten chapters you have read will be what makes him a good or a bad teacher, regardless of his credential or title. Attitude, of course, is said to be a big part of it, but it is by no means the most important part— except that a poor attitude may result in the arranger's failure to follow the laws with the precision he should. You will also find that your success will usually *result* in more positive attitudes, especially if you follow the important advice and de-emphasize the problem behaviors. Once you habitually deliver rewards and payoffs for targets and "cool it" on the problem behaviors, you will find that you have become much less tense and "up-tight," and others will also notice. Don't be surprised if someone tells you, "My goodness, you have become so much warmer than you used to be!" Nothing succeeds like success, and as you become more successful by using social rewards, such as praise, warmth, attention, and affection, more of the social rewards are likely to come your way too.

If there is anything you are not sure of, go back and study it until you feel you know the material very well. You now have a good background, even though there will be exceptions to some of the things I told you. But these will be rare enough that you can proceed with a good deal of confidence. And now, the fun (and the hard work) is about to begin.

Part Two:

Programming for Change

Chapter 11

The Basic Cookbook:

Recipes for Making Changes in Behavior

At this point, your work starts. Part One taught you the principles, laws, explanations, and background. Now you are going to learn some ways to use them. Part One is not complete. No book is, and surely not a book which is trying to present ideas as simply as possible, without getting technical. In addition, scientists are always looking for more facts and laws. If I went into more detail, or tried to describe every exception, you'd soon be plowing through an encyclopedia, and I want to keep it all simple. I hope I have. In this chapter I describe at least a half dozen programs in some detail. These are given as illustrations, and they are not the only possible solutions to their problems. But study them and learn them well. When you do, you should be able to devise new and creative methods of your own.

In case you forgot, let me repeat something I said in the first chapter of this book. A *program* is simply a *strategy, or plan we will invent for the purpose of changing a behavior.* Programming is teaching. Like all good teaching, it means arranging a person's environment to make it more likely that he will learn what we want him to learn.

The most important elements in any person's learning environment are the people around him and the things they do—that is the *consequences* of his own behaviors. The cues which are present, such as the room he is in, the textbooks or materials a classroom teacher uses in his work, and other incidental signals, are also important—but rarely as important as the consequences of the behaviors.

When we give someone a payoff, or punish him, we are changing his environment, and you already know that these consequences change his behavior. We give them deliberately when we want his behavior to change. Don't you pay someone to do a good job for you? Don't people punish other people to make them stop doing things?

We change the consequences, always with the hope that the changes in the learner's behavior will be the kind we want—usually increases in target behaviors or decreases in problem behaviors. But sometimes you might program to put a behavior on cue, or to get more overlap. We can also program to teach a completely new behavior. You will learn how in Chapter 13.

Sometimes programs are informal, but for the best possible results, you should write the program on paper. When you do, you make it easier to find crucial points you might have overlooked. Before you are able to write something down, you must think more clearly about it. Not only that, but you then have a good record, which is more important than most people realize. Programs often continue a number of weeks, and you can forget a lot of details along the way. It is not usually hard to change behavior, but it is something you should take seriously. Writing things down is not always fun, and it might be tempting to omit this step. But changes worth making at all will be worth working for. I can tell you how to do it, but understanding is hardly ever enough. It will take some effort, and that part will be up to you.

Our first step in any program is to answer five basic questions:

1. What behaviors do I wish to change? (Where am I starting?)

2. What do I want them changed to? (What are my goals? What desirable, target behaviors do I want?)

3. What lies between those two points? (What steps must I take in order to get from where I am now to the goal I have set for the future?) This step is sometimes called *task analysis,* because we must break the task down into smaller steps, to find exactly what we need to do.

4. How can I measure and record what is happening? (How can I make the record help and guide me in the program?)

5. What consequences must follow the behaviors in order to get the kind of changes I want? Programming for change takes place at this step. If you want to increase behaviors, you must deliberately follow them by a payoff. If you want to weaken behaviors, you must not permit a reward to follow those behaviors.

You also have other options. You can use a punisher or you can strengthen competing behavior you want, in order to crowd out the behavior you do not want.

And there it is. Everything up to this point—and beyond it— is based upon the need to increase your ability to perform this one step.

You know in advance whether you want the behavior to become stronger or weaker, and this tells you whether you will mostly be using the techniques in Chapters 3 and 4 to increase and strengthen the behaviors, or the methods of Chapters 5 through 8 to weaken, or decrease the behaviors.

Something happens after every behavior. We call that something a *consequence,* even where the "consequence" really has no connection with the cause of the behavior, as in superstitious learning. Cause or no cause, the consequence may still reward and strengthen the behavior. You must arrange consequences that will help you get the results you want. If you want to increase a target behavior, you must find a rewarding consequence, and make sure that it follows the behavior often enough to change it. If you want to decrease a problem behavior, you must again think of the consequences. You must somehow remove the rewarding consequences which already follow. That is, you must tune it out, or starve it. In those relatively rare programs where you use punishment as a consequence, you must arrange things so that the punishment follows the problem behavior immediately. You must also make sure that the consequences you wish to follow the competing target behaviors will be strong enough to do the job. You should write out the program and be sure you describe the behaviors and the consequences very clearly. Any stranger who can read and follow instructions should be able to carry out the program adequately. We have even used a retarded girl as a co-therapist in treating one of the most serious problem behaviors in California. Her results were just as good as those of the highly trained staff members who were supervising her. Why? Because we wrote out clear instructions, so simple she was able to follow them exactly. Unfortunately, the program steps were repetitive and boring. The brighter, often college-trained staff members made subtle changes, and their results became erratic when they did. But Nancy stuck to the letter of the instructions, and she carried it off with precision, and therefore got excellent results.

You should also indicate the relationship between *when* the behavior occurs and when the consequence occurs. Most of the time, you will probably want two or three consequences for each behavior, which you would write as a ratio of 1:2 or 1:3 (one behavior for each two—or three—consequences). If you want only one consequence, the ratio would be written as 1:1.

Here is an example of a simple program. Suppose you want to teach Julie to be nicer to other children, as part of a program to help eliminate constant bickering between them. When Julie says something respectful or kind to another child, you might give her 1) praise, 2) a hug, and 3) a bit of cookie or raisin. You would then have three consequences each time the target behavior occurred, and this would be recorded as 1:3. Later, when you have been successful, and Julie is respectful most of the time, you would then want to thin it out. That is, you would reduce the amount of payoff you are giving, to make her good behavior more persistent, as you learned in Chapter 6. You might then wish to change to a ratio of 2:3, so that every *second time* she made a good response you would give her the same three consequences. Still later, you might wish to get her off the cookies, but continue the hug and praise. The ratio would then be 2:2. You could go through a series of changes, such as praise only, given every fifth time (5:1). Each time the ratio is changed, you are really changing the consequences.

Eventually, you would want to use an *average ratio* (see Chapter 4), because that is the way things most often happen in a real world. You cannot afford to get stuck the rest of your life trying to reward the learner every time he performs the target behavior, even though it is something you would like to have continued. Even if you could keep it up indefinitely, other people won't. An average ratio is a form of occasional payoff that can result in very persistent behavior, especially as the ratio gets thinner. In other words, when rewards do not come very often, the thin average ratio can keep the behavior from starving.

I have designed some forms which work well for me in a wide variety of programs I have done. The form works because it spells out and organizes the desirable and undesirable behaviors, the consequences, and the ratios between them. This information is really just about everything we need to know about the basic program.

	Behaviors	Ratio	Consequences
Targets			
Problems			

Change level:

Figure 3. Sample form for recording behavioral change programs.

Writing a program thus consists of listing and describing the behaviors and their consequences in precise behavioral terms. It also helps to spell out the ratio between them, although this step is the least essential of the steps I have listed. The reason is that the ratio can usually be figured out from a careful study of the behaviors and their consequences, and thus may be redundant.

If we are dealing with both a target and a problem behavior, both should be listed. There will be times when you have only a target, but you should probably never have a program that has only a problem behavior. One or more target behaviors should compete with it. If you still do not understand why, please stop reading here and read Part One again.

We sometimes add two further items to the five basic questions. The first can be called a *success point,* and can be incorporated into the description of the behaviors. The success point tells you when a behavior is good enough to meet your standards. For example, you might have described your target as, *Child does not tease other children.* This is somewhat vague, because you do not know how long the child must go before you reward him. An improvement would be, *Child goes five minutes without teasing other children.* Now you have spelled out what the child must do (or must not do, in this case) before you know whether his behavior was "good." The description also tells you how long he must be good. The five-minute criterion is the success point.

The other item we sometimes add is what I am calling a *change level.* This is a "landmark" which tells you that it is now time to change your program. A change level is like a screening test. When a person has passed the test, it is time for him to be promoted to a more difficult task. Here is an example:

In working with so-called "aphasic" children (children who have reached the age when they should be talking, but for some reason they do not), we designed programs to teach certain speech skills, one at a time. The children were kept at each level until 90% of their responses during three consecutive sessions were correct. The change level was then written: *Three consecutive sessions of 90% or better.*

The change level is valuable, because it gives you an idea ahead of time what you will be doing. It is like a stage director's cue sheet. You won't have to guess what to do when the time comes, and you won't have to guess when to do it either. Moreover, just the process of articulating the change level helps to think the program through, and thus helps organize it better. And having the plan written out ahead of time, you will not have to make decisions on the spur of the moment nearly as often. This puts you under less pressure, and you will probably make fewer mistakes as a result. As a final bonus, if the program involves more than one arranger, it helps maintain more consistency between them. Thus, one arranger is less likely to undo what the others do, and vice versa.

As the program progresses, you might wish to change the success point from time to time. A new target behavior might be, *Child goes ten minutes without teasing other children,* and later, *Child goes fifteen minutes without teasing other children,* etc. The consequences might also change. For example, at the five-minute success point, perhaps the consequences were, 1) praise; 2) one gold star in his book; and 3) a penny every fifth time. Once the child has successfully gone ten minutes without teasing he gets all three consequences at once. When he repeatedly goes for the ten-minute periods without teasing, you might wish to eliminate the penny, and have the child work for praise and gold stars only. The ratio would then change from 1:3 to 1:2.

The purpose of the success point is to tell you whether or not the learner has earned the consequences. You need the change level to tell you when to advance the learner into new tasks. You don't want to keep a child reading out of a primer just because he has done such a good job on *Run, Spot, Run!* You must keep him moving to more difficult things. You should always try to keep a program paced so that the learner performs at peak efficiency. That means he is doing the most difficult level he is capable of doing effectively. You will know if it becomes too hard, because failures begin to appear. The learner is then likely to become frustrated and uncomfortable, and the program will become punishing to him. If it becomes too easy, his progress will be too slow, and he is likely to become bored with the program. His performance will then drop off, and again, the program will become punishing to him.

Any truly good teacher has known this all along. He tries to keep the student moving at his fastest reasonable speed. Your behavior programs must do the same thing. After all, programs are meant to be efficient schemes to set up conditions that will be best for maximizing learning.

You must change the programs as progress is made, because the earlier programs will no longer be suitable. The learner will "outgrow" them. Some arrangers get upset when it is time for a program to be changed (and this is equally true of politicians committed to the programs they become identified with). They liked the program so far, and they are sometimes afraid to take the risk of changing. Sometimes they feel that changing the program means they have failed. In reality, if the program is well designed, program change should occur often, and it should tell them when they are graduating from the earlier program. Your change level is an estimate of the requirements for graduation. Graduation day, on the other hand, will be flexible, because you do not know exactly how fast progress is going to be made. *You* set the change level. *When* it is reached will be determined by the learner's behavior. But remember: Successful teaching means successful learning. One cannot happen without the other. Although he almost never realizes it, whenever a teacher brags about how many students he flunked, he is actually confessing that he was not able to teach his failing students the minimum he expects of them, so it is the teacher's failure as well as the student's.

Now that you know most of the mechanics of setting up a program to to change behavior, let me summarize the process so far by making you a check list of the steps to take:

1) **Where am I now?** (What problem behaviors do I wish to weaken, or what target behaviors do I wish to strengthen?)

2) **What behavior do I want to replace the learner's present behaviors?**

3) **What steps lie between those two points?** (Do a task analysis).

4) **What data should I take, and how?**

5) **What consequences shall I arrange for each problem behavior and each target behavior?**

6) **What will be the ratio between the behavior and the consequences?**

7) **What is my success point for each behavior?**

8) **What will be my change level?**

Once you have filled out the forms you are ready to go. Now, let us try a few sample programs together. The first is an example used as an illustration in Chapter 3, and later in Chapter 6. Using the forms shown in Figure 3, Ricky's program reads as follows:

	Behaviors	Ratio	Consequences
Targets	Saying "Please," in a pleasant, non-demanding tone of voice	1:3	1. Give him his request 2. Compliment him for asking nicely 3. Stars in Blue Chip stamp book
Problems	Tantrum behavior (any or all of the following: *Screaming, hitting, biting, whining, etc.*)	1:4	Starve: 1. Ignore by turning head 2. No eye contact 3. Do not grant his request 4. Continue conversation as normally as possible

Change level: None listed

Figure 4. Ricky's program: Tantrum reduction and alternative method of earning rewards.

We measured how long each tantrum lasted, and added them together to get a total for each day. Duration of the tantrums was more meaningful than the number of cries, hits, or whines.

Here is another program, derived from Chapter 2:

The parents were quite upset because Clifford would not wait for a break in the conversation. "He constantly interrupts us when we talk to our friends."

Let us go through our check list.

1) What behavior does the learner now have that I want to change? That one should be easy. You want to eliminate Clifford's interrupting; am I correct?

Well, only partly correct. You are now focussing on the problem behavior, which is not the whole story. The real problem is seldom the problem behavior, but the lack of alternative target behaviors. The real problem is not interrupting—everyone must do that at times. Too frequent interrupting, or rude interrupting would be closer to the point, but the *real* problem is his lack of targets to substitute for rudeness. You need to teach him some good behaviors to crowd out the rude ones.

2) What are the goals? You could start by thinking of some useful, desirable behaviors we may use as targets to replace his problem behavior. What might some possibilities be?

I mentioned "polite" behavior, not because I want to make an old-fashioned conformist out of Clifford, but simply to give him a way to show other people that he is not trying to be rude, and is trying not to displease them. I would list two goals. First, teach him a nicer way to interrupt; and second, decrease rude interruptions to a tolerable level. Both behaviors can be defined in more detail. It is much easier to understand descriptions such as, *says, "Pardon me, please,"* for the first and *Waits for a natural break in the conversation,* as a suitable target for a later stage of the program. You should also decide in advance what is meant by "tolerable level," and use this as your change level. For example, you might define your change level as, *One interruption or less during a ten-minute conversation.*

3. The *steps* might consist of:

    a. Teaching Clifford to say, "Pardon me, please," even though he still breaks into the middle of the conversation;

    b. Teaching him to recognize a natural break in the conversation;

    c. Teaching him to use a polite phrase *and* to wait for the break;

    d. Decreasing the frequency of interruption still further, if necessary.

4. *Data for the target behavior:* Number of times Clifford asked, "Pardon me, please." *Data for the problem behavior:* Number of rude interruptions. *For both behaviors,* the time of the beginning and the end of the observation period should be recorded, so that you can compute the length of the conversation. You'll learn why in Chapter 12. Needless to say, the length will be the same for both the problem behavior and the target behavior.

If possible, you should begin taking your data some time before you actually start the consequences. This gives you a period of time called *baseline,* which you can use for comparison. Remember the ads in the pulp magazines? On the left is a photograph of a fat, sloppy woman, slouching in a 1946-style bathing suit. That picture is labelled, *BEFORE.* Then she took Vanishing Pounds Weight Reduction Pills, and on the right you have a beautiful, slim young lady right off a Playboy centerfold, wearing a microscopic bikini, standing with her abdomen held flat and her shoulders held back to accentuate her own positives. The picture on the right is labelled *AFTER.* Vanishing Pounds Weight Reduction Pills, it is implied, has accounted for the difference.

We take baseline data for the same reason—not to lose pounds, wear bikinis, nor get pictures on the Playboy centerfold, but rather, to show where we were when we began, and contrast that with wherever we happen to be later.

5. *Consequences for the target behavior:* Here are some choices. You might use one or more of them, or you might use all:

    a. Attentive listening to Clifford's request

    b. Permitting him to speak

    c. Favorable comment toward what he said

d. Social reward, such as, "Good boy; you're being so polite!"

e. Physical contact

f. Other payoff, such as a bit of pretzel, gold star, or something idiosyncratic (see Chapter 4).

Of course, you probably will not use every possible payoff every time, but these are typical examples used in many successful programs. The important thing you must remember is to give reward of *some* kind, and of a kind that is a reward to the learner, even though the arranger is not too fond of it. After all, the learner is always the boss. If he doesn't learn, then your program hasn't worked, and you have the responsibility of changing it to something else that does.

Consequences for the problem behavior: Starving. That is,

a. Continue the conversation. Do not permit his interruption to break up your conversation.

b. Turn away from Clifford when he is interrupting. Do not even look at him.

In short, starving means about the same thing as *tuning out,* or *actively ignoring* the learner.

You will of course choose your own consequences, especially for the target behaviors. The consequences I listed were some I have used, and they worked well for me, but of course, you know your learner better than I, and you will choose the rewards most relevant to him. In the great majority of times, however, starving is one of the best consequences for most problem behaviors, especially if there is no risk involved as a result of aggression or destructiveness.

6. Ratios: In the examples I gave above, the ratio for the target behavior was 1:6, assuming I used all the consequences I listed. The ratio for the problem behavior is 1:1 (that is, starve the problem behavior each time. If you want more detail, the ratio could be 1:2, as above, or 1:4, as in Figure 4).

7. Success point: Is the way he said, "Pardon me, please," acceptable to the arranger?

8. Change level: Move to step 2 (teaching Clifford to wait for a natural break in the conversation) when he asks for recognition politely 90% or more of the times he enters into your conversation.

At each step of the way, we will need some data to help us. When we ask the first two questions, we not only need to know the problem and target behaviors, but also how strong each of them are at the time. Even the worst interrupter must wait for the proper moment at least some of the time. If Clifford interrupted rudely only once out of fifty conversations, you would probably agree that there is not much of a problem there. On the other hand, if he asked nicely only once out of the next fifty times, that would be a different matter. Both cases involve average-ratio interruption, but it is the degree which is important, so we need to know the strength of both behaviors. We will learn more about keeping records in Chapter 12, but for the time being, let us suppose that we have kept a week of baseline records before we started the program. We got our data just by counting the number of times Clifford interrupted every day. A simple count like this has some serious drawbacks that would keep me from using it altogether, but I will use it for demonstration, as it is easier to understand. Here are our baseline data[11]:

	Day 1 (Sun.)	Day 2 (Mon.)	Day 3 (Tues.)	Day 4 (Wed.)	Day 5 (Thurs.)	Day 6 (Fri.)	Learner: Clifford Day 7 (Sat.)
Targets	0	0	0	0	0	0	0
Problems	12	3	1	0	5	17	14

Figure 5. Week 1 (Baseline data): *Target behavior:* Asking nicely for permission to speak. *Problem behavior:* Interrupting conversations. (Week 2 will be found in Figure 6).

You will notice that the target behavior did not appear at all during the week. "Pardon me, please," was one of Clifford's behavioral deficits. On the other hand, the problem behavior appeared a number of times. Between Monday and Thursday the count was fairly low. Clifford stayed after school on Wednesday for a scout meeting, and the parents were gone that evening, so there were few opportunities for them to observe his behaviors, or for the interruptions to take place. The weekend rates were higher than mid-week, because there were adult visitors spending those evenings with them, giving more opportunities for the problem behavior to occur. One of the drawbacks of the use of the simple count is the fact that more of the behaviors are likely to occur on the days which have more time available for the behavior to happen. There is a way around that drawback, and you'll learn it in Chapter 12.

The parents thought there were at least fifty interruptions every day, and were surprised how few there were, even on the worst day (Friday). Their data proved to them that people exaggerate the extent of some problem behaviors. They just *seem* to happen more often than they really do.

Now that we know where we stand, we can design a program to change the situation. Our forms and check list tell us that we must choose some consequences for each behavior. We already know that we can starve or punish problem behaviors, and it makes no sense to keep rewarding them. Thus, weakening the problem behaviors must be a part of every program which contains a problem behavior. As you now know, punishment creates so many problems most of the time that I advise you against its use.

You can see that the program, as most of them, will consist of two parts, conducted simultaneously. You wish to decrease a problem behavior and increase a target behavior. Every time the child asks nicely, we should immediately give him the payoffs, and every time he interrupts we should tune him out. When we are starving a behavior, we do not need to explain, apologize, reason, nor give any payoff for attention-getting ploys by the learner. If you feel an explanation is required, by all means, be my guest and explain to him. But don't do so at this time. Do it before you start the program, or else wait until no problem behavior will be strengthened by the explanation. In other words, don't sabotage the benefits you'd be getting from the starving by giving simultaneous payoff for problem behavior.

"But how can we reward his asking nicely when it doesn't ever happen?" you might protest. "Our data showed zeroes all that week. We'd wait forever before we could strengthen his target behavior at that rate!"

And you would be right. Your strategy should always be to reward target behaviors immediately. But you can't pay off behavior that isn't there, so you must somehow get that behavior—or at least a part of it—to occur. One way to do this is to use a process called *prompting*, because it resembles the way a stage director "prompts" the actor who has forgotten his lines. He gives help which, everyone hopes, will result in the correct behavior. We do the same thing in programming. We prompt the learner to make the correct move. There are a number of ways to do this, including physically moving his muscles, if necessary. Much of the time, all we need to do is explain what we would like the learner to do. Such a *verbal prompt* could be given before you start the program, and might sound like this: "We want you to ask nicely and not interrupt us. If you say, 'Pardon me, please,' we will listen to you, but if you do not, we will pay no attention to you. We won't answer you and we will not even look at you."

Let me digress a moment, and talk a bit about explanations. I often observe parents trying to "reason" with young children who are not being very reasonable in return. Parents often feed and nurture attention-getting behavior in this way. Explanations should never be given when the child is hammering away trying to get you to recognize his rudeness with questions like, "Why?" This is not the time to get into a debate with him. He probably does not want answers to his questions anyway, for he already knows why! He also knows the answer to questions like, "Why won't you let me talk? Why won't you listen to me? Don't you love me?" He also knows he can make you feel guilty and cheap with coercive talk. He might make statements like, "You hate me, I know you do!" How many people can resist denying assertions like that? He is not after information, and not even assurance. Rather, he is after control. Some of the efforts are designed to produce guilt. Don't let them suck you into their trap! It is true that they might make you feel terribly evil if you do not answer them, but remember that the evil and the guilt will all be in your imagination. You do not need to feel guilty when you are teaching him something worthwhile. You do not need to feel guilty when you are doing something that will help him, even though he might take a dim view of it at the moment. Does a dentist feel guilty because he gives his client a bit of pain in order to save a tooth? If you cannot resist the pressure and you do give in to his manipulations, you should then ask yourself, "Aren't I proud of the little monster I'm helping to create?"

If starving his interruptions makes you feel guilty, starve them anyway. You have an obligation to your child and you cannot escape it just because you have let yourself become his victim.

If you are not asking for too big a step, a verbal (or physical) prompt is enough to do the trick most of the time. If it is, you will save a lot of trial and error. If not, there is another way, called *shaping*, which can even build up a brand new behavior. You'll read about shaping in Chapter 13.

Sometimes, especially when the relationship between a child and parents, or between quarreling mates, has become very strained, the learner may intentionally hold off, refusing to accept the payoffs his opponent starts to give him. Strained relationships are those which have been characterized by a high rate of punishing behaviors. Since you know that punishment will generate counter-measures, you can recognize that such tricks are hostile devices, and they are usually temporary. But after you have given a verbal prompt, the learner at least knows what is expected of him. It should not be necessary for him to be reminded again each time. The only time you should repeat instructions is when you have good reason to think the learner might have forgotten what you want, or when he is confused and does not understand the instructions. Maybe they were too complicated for him to grasp completely. In this case, you should simplify them, or break them into further steps, working on only one step at a time. You'll learn more about how to do this in Chapter 13.

Incidentally, one of the most common errors made by arrangers is to repeat commands many times. You should make it a rule:

Give commands clearly, but only give them once.

If you give a command twice you teach the learner to ignore your first command. If you give the command five times you teach him to ignore the first four. If you give the command twenty five times, you teach him to ignore the first twenty four. If you give a command and the learner does not listen, or obey, do not repeat the command right then. Be cool about it. Don't beg and don't nag. Wait a minute or two and then give the command a second time, quietly, with the confidence that comes when you expect your command to be respected. Be prepared to prompt, if necessary. You must teach that you are serious, and that you do not *expect* your command to be overlooked, and that it is not all right with you for your wishes to be ignored. If you are not successful at this time, think about it. Perhaps you have made the request too big, or too complicated. When you are just beginning to teach compliance to commands, always try to **give commands which have high odds of being obeyed.** For example, if you give a simple command, "Come to me, please," don't do it the first time when the learner is a block away, involved in his favorite activity. If necessary, come to him most of the way and then ask. The odds that he will comply from three feet are much higher than from three hundred yards. And wait for opportune moments. If the learner is clearly engrossed in his favorite activity, wait for evidence of a lapse of attention, or some other clue that his activity has for a moment become less involving to him—for example, if your husband is watching the Super Bowl game with his team 5 points behind, they've got the ball on their one-yard line and there are 30 seconds left in the game, at least wait for a commercial before you ask him to carry out the garbage.

Of course, once the learner has obeyed your command, give him payoffs. Do it consistently, so that every time he obeys your command you do something nice for him too. Give simple commands you feel certain will be obeyed, and then reward them liberally when they have indeed been obeyed. If necessary, prompt. We taught retarded children to follow the command, "Sit down, please," by guiding the child to the chair so that he stood immediately in front of it. Then we pushed the chair gently into the back of his knees, giving him a slight nudge backward at the same time. When he was almost off balance, it was nearly inevitable that he would continue his downward motion and end up sitting in the chair. We gave him the command at that instant. We did not really give him the chance to disobey. Then, when we got the behavior we wanted, we gave him his payoff immediately, just as though he had done it all by himself. Don't let it bother you that he got the reward even though he didn't completely deserve it. When you have a low rate of compliance to commands, worries like that are a luxury you can't afford. Count your blessings instead. You wanted him to sit down and he sat down, so reward him for it. Repeat this a number of times, and you will soon find that he will sit on your command alone, without the prompt. As you will learn in Chapter 13, there will be times when you might have to settle for less than you would like at first, on your way to the goal of getting more.

Once you have made it clear that you do not expect to play games, the learner will quickly do what is expected of him. He will usually do what you ask, if you arrange suitable consequences. You should then aim for a rate of compliance of about 90% or more.

Now let us get back to Clifford. After you have your baseline data and you have given him clear instructions once, you will proceed the way Susan and I did with Ricky. You must starve his whining and interrupting, but you must also reward the target behaviors. You might get a record for the second week that looks like this sample:

Learner: Clifford

	Day 8 (Sun.)	Day 9 (Mon.)	Day 10 (Tues.)	Day 11 (Wed.)	Day 12 (Thurs.)	Day 13 (Fri.)	Day 14 (Sat.)
Targets	9	11	4	12	—	18	6
Problems	8	3	0	1	—	2	0

Figure 6. Week 2 (First week of program): *Target behavior:* Asking nicely for permission to speak. *Problem Behavior:* Interrupting conversations. (Baseline data [Week 1] are found in Figure 5).

This week, let's say, everyone was gone Thursday, but there were plenty of people around the other days. In general, the problem behavior has decreased, following a curve more or less like those of Figures 1 and 2 (Chapter 6). The strength of the problem dropped off rapidly the first day. Remember that on the last day of baseline it was up around 14. Then its descent began to slow down, but the behavior continued to occur at a low rate before it disappeared entirely. Notice that the target behavior is gradually becoming stronger all the time the problem behavior is on its way out.

You will see that I only worked with one of the target behaviors (saying "Pardon me, please."). As you will understand when you read Chapter 13, learning is faster when you work on only one behavior at a time. Once Clifford learns the target behavior, you can add some conditions to it. There is no point in teaching *when*, if he still does not know *what* to do at that time. You have to accept something less than perfect at first. If you try teaching two target behaviors at once, there will be times when their programs will conflict. For example, Clifford may barge into the middle of a sentence, saying, "Pardon me, please." You would not know whether to reward what he says or tune him out because of his poor timing. That is why you should get one behavior under good control before you tackle a second. Once he reaches the change level, then you can move to the next phase, which would be to teach him to use the phrase only when the disruption of his asking would be minimal. Any changes in results which start at that point are probably the result of changes you made in the program, such as moving to the next level, so make a note when you make a change. If you want a change and do not see one in your data, you should then revise your program until your data begin to change in the direction you want. Suppose Clifford was doing well just before the change level was reached, and you would like him to continue just as well at the more difficult level. You should then change the program, but keep your eye on the data, to be alert for any signs of unfavorable change. You would not want him to start interrupting rudely again, and you would not want his target ("Pardon me, please") to weaken either, simply because you are now asking for two conditions instead of just one. In other words, keeping your eye on the data will help you keep on top of your programs.

You should be able to use this basic plan with the majority of your problems. It capitalizes on some of the rules you have already learned. For example, the Payoff Rule is the most important law of human behavior: *If a behavior is followed by a payoff, that behavior will become stronger under similar conditions in the future.* Once a behavior has happened, of course, you can't change history. But you can work for future control of that behavior. You can stack the deck so that you will be able to deal aces when they are needed. If you want a child (or adult) to say, "Please," you repeatedly give a payoff each time he says, "Please," and not otherwise. If you want your husband to listen to your suggestions more often, you should be sure he gets a payoff when he does, and not when he ignores them. You have not done anything to things which have happened in the past, but if you are consistent, you will be teaching the learner that the behavior you have just rewarded is more likely to pay again in the future. In other words, you have arranged to make it more likely these targets will happen again under similar conditions.

And what do we mean by similar conditions? Here is where overlap and cues enter the picture. He has learned only to do it around certain signals, and will not usually do it when these signals are not present. Some are obvious. The learner will not say, "Please," if nobody else is around. He will not say it if he doesn't want something. He will not say it to someone else who had perhaps teased him about being a sissy if he said, "Please." He would be more likely to say it to people who had already given him a social payoff when he spoke with respect toward them. The husband would be more likely to listen to suggestions from someone who rewards when he follows the suggestions, but not when he ignores them.

In my work with patients in state hospitals, there have been times I made programs to eliminate some rather serious problem behaviors, such as self-injury. Our baseline observations showed that some children hit themselves more than twenty thousand times per day! Not all hits were hard ones, but still, that was a lot of activity. Our observations also left little doubt that most of the self-injury was related to attention-getting, and that well-meaning staff, parents, or visitors often rewarded it with attention, sympathy, or giving in to the demands the children made. One program we used is shown in Figure 7. Using this

| Targets | 1. Hands held below waist
2. Other, competing behaviors, lasting a full _____ seconds (gradually lengthened to _____ minutes). | 2:3 | 1. Praise
2. Token
3. Food snack |
| Problems | Any of the following:
1. Hand striking head
2. Head striking wall or floor
3. Snapping jaw against shoulder bone | 1:1 | 1. Starve
(Note: If desired, this consequence may be broken into its parts, as in Figure 4) |

Figure 7. Controlling self-injurious behavior by crowding out the problem behaviors. *Target behavior:* Hands below waist. *Problem behaviors:* Self-injury.

program, we had some very serious self-injury under control very quickly, but only for a few seconds at a time between payoffs. Over the next few days we gradually lengthened the time between payoffs. We were very careful not to make the increase too big, so perhaps we took longer than we should have. Still, within a few days the children were doing almost no hitting while in the training room. We then found that we had accidentally gotten self-injury on cue. As long as they were in the training room, with the same arranger who had given the consequences recommended by the program, there was hardly ever any attempt to hit, and any hits within the room were such light taps they could not have been injurious. But as soon as we brought a different arranger into the room, the children started hitting again, and harder. The new arranger then had to go through the same program with the children until there was no longer any hitting in his presence. We also got the problem behavior again when we added a third, and then a fourth arranger, but each time we got smaller increases. We were able to eliminate it more quickly each time. After the children had been through the program with four arrangers, they did not usually start to hit when someone new came into the room. Even groups of strangers could enter, and there was no increase in the problem behavior. We had gotten enough overlap in the room that the hitting was no longer on cue for different persons.

Still, when we led the children out of the door, their hitting began at once! Depending on whether we moved them into or out of the training room, we could start or stop their hitting, almost as though we had turned a switch on or off. One boy hit himself two hundred twenty five times as much in the hall as he did in the training room, and the hits in the hall were hard ones, too. They could have caused serious injury if we had allowed prolonged episodes to take place.

This was one of the most remarkable examples I have ever seen of behavior on cue. We could turn the behavior on or off with ease, and all we needed to do to flip the switch was to move the child a foot or two. That was why it was so important to get overlap. Just as we had to repeat the program with new arrangers, so we had to repeat the program in new rooms. Each time we repeated the program, we aimed for a change level of three consecutive no-hit sessions. Then we repeated the program in another room. I don't think you will ever run across cases as extreme as the one I just described, and I surely hope that neither of us ever do again. But the behavior was on cue to an extreme degree, and taught us some things I will pass on to you. We had never anticipated anything to this degree. We thought we were successful after the first session, and were all set to cash in on some of the warm glow and glory. When we saw the children start all over just because we added a new arranger, our first thought was that we had failed miserably. We didn't know we had not failed. We had succeeded, up to a point. We had arrived at the place to make a change. But even if we had failed, it was still better to have one room without their self-injury than none at all. Last, but not least, it was an excellent training period for the staff. We learned about overlap and behavior on cue in a way which could not have been more vivid!

What can you learn from this? Simply that there may be times—especially when you are concentrating on eliminating problem behaviors—when you might find that you will have to repeat a program a number of times in different settings, so that you can get a wider range of overlap. In most cases, you will find some overlap when the program has been repeated two or three times. By the time the program has been repeated ten times the overlap from then on will become more and more automatic. You will also see that it takes less and less time to reach the change level as the program is repeated, so that repeating a program ten times would not necessarily take ten times as long. It is not possible to say exactly how much longer it would take, because the length of programming time will depend on how tough the problem is, how long it has been a problem, what alternative rewards the person has available, and many other many other factors as well, including how consistently the program is carried out. The only thing you know with near certainty is that the more times you reward a behavior the more likely it will be repeated, and the more different signals which are present, the more likely it will overlap to settings where those signals are prominent features.

Notice that I did not guarantee that a behavior will always be repeated. I was careful to state that it is *more likely* to appear. It becomes stronger. I was careful not to say, "The behavior will occur 100% of the time." It doesn't. But if you get less than 100% it doesn't mean you are not getting satisfactory results, either. It is important to understand that each time someone rewards a behavior, it becomes just a bit stronger. It becomes a secure habit only after it has been rewarded many times. Learning takes place in small steps. It may take a lot of these small steps to get the job done.

Any new behavior will be weak at first. It will become stronger only after it is followed by payoffs many times. Weak behavior dies out quickly when there is no payoff to keep it alive. What if we had ignored Ricky when he asked, "Please, may I have some donuts?" What if, a few minutes later, he had asked, "Could I please go to the park?" and we had said, "No, it's getting too dark and cold," or worse, "Damnit! You have just spoiled our afternoon and now you're expecting us to do you favors. Do you think we're crazy?" One or two such experiences *at that time* would have taught him that saying, "Please" just doesn't work. "Ah, but I know what does," he could have thought, and turned back to the strong behavior we had just starved. We would have had to face the tantrum problem all over again, even though it would have been weakened by its previous starvation. We would have made the common mistake of trying to eliminate a problem behavior without giving the learner any alternative ways to get his payoffs.

We would be in no such danger today, because that target has been given thousands of payoffs. Unless I miss my guess, saying, "Please" is a behavior he'll have for the rest of his life, even though we can expect its strength to fluctuate as he encounters situations in which it is starved or rewarded.

Many people overlook their own obligation to reward good behavior. Then they say, "Don't tell me about teaching him competing behaviors! We tried getting him to say, 'Please,' but it didn't work."

The reason it did not work is usually because the program was not followed consistently. The learner had no chance to find from his own experience that a rewarding consequence could be expected reliably, after the target behavior.

The most common cause of failure is inconsistency. Consistency is important, because it teaches the learner that the consequences of his behavior will not be changing unpredictably. Consistency teaches him to expect the same consequence next time for a behavior that he got last time for the same behavior. If you write a good program and consistently follow your own instructions, you can look forward to the same kinds of favorable changes we got with Ricky when we consistently withdrew payoff for his tantrums and conscientiously rewarded saying, "Please."

The results do not usually come instantly. You can see from Figure 2 that the biggest drop in Ricky's tantrums took place between the first and second days, although they did not disappear instantly. By the fourth day, however, there were few tantrums left, although very minor problems continued for a number of days, so we had to continue with the program. Inconsistency can wreck any program. What if, on the seventh day, we had said, "Well, it looks like it's not working? Two days ago he didn't have any tantrums at all, and now look. It's getting worse." Suppose that at that point we had abandoned the program and started giving in to his tantrums, the way we had done before? We could have expected the tantrums to get longer and stronger. Of course, they would not have gone as high as they did on our first day, because nobody would have waited an hour and a half to give in to him! There would have been fewer, and possibly shorter tantrums, because tantrums stop when they have accomplished their goal. But he would have become worse in other ways—more demanding, more controlling, and less of a delight to be around.

Incidentally, just as an item of interest, Ricky's saying, "Please" overlapped easily to most other situations in which he wished to ask something from an adult. On the other hand, we have not had as much luck teaching him to say it to his peers. They do not always accept behavior which shows respect, and seldom reward it. Moreover, they often punish it. We are unable to guarantee consistent payoff for his behavior toward them, partly because much of his contact with the other children comes when we are not around. Our neighborhood is a bit unusual in the degree to which parents (mostly professional, fairly affluent, young, and abnormally conservative, successful people on their way up) overlook their responsibility to reward target behaviors such as respect, responsibility, cooperation, and simple courtesy. Most of the parental training seems sporadic, and a lot of punishment is used. These children are often bored, and spend a lot of their play time arguing with other children. They are often rewarded for tattling, or getting their friends in trouble. Sometimes they compel other children to do mischief, while they enjoy the show, safe on the sidelines. These boys are more prone to reward highly competitive behavior instead of cooperative behavior, or to give other children what they want when they demand it disrespectfully, without saying, "Please." There are ways to deal with such a situation, and I will talk about just one possibility in Chapter 14.

One more thing about consistency: People usually adjust relatively easily to bad situations, if they are consistently bad. They know what to expect. That is why so many people can survive experiences such as prison, boot camp, many schools, or extremely harsh parents. The rules have been spelled out clearly. But if the rules change all the time, the learner will get punished one time for doing something that gave him a payoff before. He never knows just what to expect, and the result is an especially disturbing emotional state called *conflict* (see footnote 10). More people "crack up" over conflicts than over strong punishment. Parents who are wishy-washy and inconsistent do not help their children become confident and secure people. *Confidence* can be translated to mean that a person is pretty sure he will be successful when he tries something. If he is never sure of the consequences, he can never be sure of his odds of success, and thus, he can never be very secure. Incidentally, the "nice" parent is also more likely to be inconsistent, if he lets the child plead and whine and get him to change his mind on important decisions. A tyrant may be consistent—not always for the best reasons, however. He often draws the line and makes no exceptions. That is why children of these parents, although perhaps stunted emotionally in other ways, at least manage to deal with the world with more security than might be expected under the circumstances. But it should not be necessary to choose from these two extremes. It is possible to be kind, gentle, loving, and still firm. You must realize that firmness can be kindness. Firmness takes courage, especially if the learner is manipulating you with guilt or threat. If giving in means teaching the kinds of behaviors that will hurt him in the long run, then firmness is the kindest thing you can do for him—and probably yourself as well.

Now let us return to Chapter 3 for another example. Go back and read the fourth story. You will recall that I ended the tale shortly after explaining how the parents were giving payoffs for the wrong kind of behaviors. I pointed out the payoffs when the children misbehaved, and said, "Now watch this." I continued to talk to the parents while I waited a few moments for a break in the wild activities of the children. Soon, there was a brief quiet spell, so I broke away from my conversation and told the children, "That's very good! You're being quiet and not disturbing anyone. Here is something for you." I gave them a piece of cookie, which was left over from my meal on the plane. I had carefully wrapped it in a paper napkin, as a surprise for Ricky. The bits of cookie immediately made the children interested in what I had to say. "Stay quiet and I'll give you more later." (Later, I would have to square accounts with my son!)

I went back to my conversation with the parents, but stayed "tuned in" to the children. I was careful not to wait too long to come back to them; as I said before, becoming quiet and remaining quiet are two separate processes. I had completed the first. Now I had to work on the more difficult, second task.

After less than a minute, I turned to them again and said, "That was fine. Here is another piece. I'll give you more if you stay quiet. You can talk if you want, but don't yell or run around."

Gradually, I made them wait a bit longer—but still not too long. I did not want their quiet behavior to die out. I could never know ahead of time when they might change their minds and start a ruckus again.

Fortunately, I did not wait too long—perhaps another minute or two. It was long enough that the children had to wait awhile, but not so long that the honeymoon was over. I repeated the payoffs, each time saying, "That's good. You are being nice to us, and not running wild." When the children were quiet for a few minutes, the parents repeated what I had showed them. After a few more repetitions of this scene, we began to wait a bit longer to reward them. Soon, the children were able to stay quiet for fairly long periods of time, and the parents were able to converse longer periods of time. If the parents waited too long, there might then be a bit of commotion from the children, who had not yet learned to wait quite so long for their reward. I urged the parents to play it cool, for I knew any disruptions that did take place would not last forever. I urged them to tune out these disruptions and wait patiently for a break. This is not as hard to do once you understand that such a break is inevitable. It *must* come sooner or later, and you must be prepared to wait for it. So be on your toes, and capitalize on the golden moment when it finally does arrive.

The use of food as reward brings up several problems. Giving bits of cookie has its drawbacks. It was before dinner, their dentist (or any sensible nutritionist) might not have approved of so many sweets, I was running out of cookie, and I had a pocket full of crumbs. So I thought, "What else can I use for a payoff?"

Fortunately, I remembered something I have not yet mentioned to you. There is a way to find payoffs which will often work, but which you might not have thought about. You simply watch the learners to see what they do spontaneously, when they have the choice. What did the children at the airport do when left on their own in this situation?

You guessed it! When we had left them alone before, they ran.

Running might be a payoff for them, so I pulled the following stunt. When they had learned to wait quietly about three or four minutes, I told them, "Next time, let's see who can be the quieter of the two of you. Whoever wins will get to run as fast as she can, over to that candy machine and back. Just wait until there is nobody in the hallway, so you won't annoy anyone."

This is an unusual kind of program, because it used the problem behavior as an arranged consequence. How is that possible? Isn't it like using a martini to reward an alcoholic for not drinking?

The answer is that running is not a problem behavior. If nobody is being disturbed, there is no reason the children should not run. It is beneficial exercise, as millions of joggers can testify. It only becomes a problem when someone is annoyed by the commotion. So we crossed our fingers and tried it. The children loved it, and were very quiet between runs. They did not try to run wild when they were not sup- posed to. Even the parents didn't seem to mind, because the children were doing it under different conditions. Many times, it is not the problem behavior that bothers people most, but the hidden message that the problem behavior conveys to them. These parents were disturbed by a number of such messages. The children would have made the parents responsible in case someone objected to the commotion. Another message was, "When I decide I want to run wild, I can do so. I can embarrass you and you are powerless to stop me. You are a weak leader. You are completely at my mercy. You are inadequate, and not very smart, either." But I changed the meaning of the running. It was now a part of the scheme in which the parents were in control. Running wasn't so bad, now. "After all," said the father, "This is kind of fun, and we are telling them whether they can do it or not. Besides, who knows? With enough practice, one of them might grow up to be another Babe Didrikson Zaharias!" Thus, it was clear that the issue was not the running, nor even the noise, but rather, who was in control of the situation.

Actually, the children could have still continued to run wild, and they would have, had they wanted to. We did not force them to be quiet. We only changed the consequences of their running. Most children, even rowdy ones, are reasonable, and don't always do those annoying things with the intention of making other people get upset. (Exception: As a hostile reaction to a situation characterized by a great deal of punishment. As I mentioned a number of times before, aggression begets counter-aggression). I repeat. We did not force them to behave, but we stopped paying them for misbehaving, and we made them *want* to please us, because it was to their benefit to do so. Isn't that what everyone really wants—to please others?

The program would have been written as follows:

Targets	Talking quietly @ 60″/5′	1:2	1. Praise 2. Cookie
Problems	Running wild	1:1	1. Starve

Figure 8. Crowding out noisy running. *Target behaviors:* Talking quietly. *Problem behaviors:* Noisy running.

Later, "Praise and cookie" was changed to "Praise and a vigorous run to the candy machine and back."

You will notice that I indicated approximately how long the children would have to talk quietly. During the course of the program, we gradually changed our success point from about sixty seconds to about five minutes.

Classroom teachers, babysitters, or parents with a number of children at home might find the kind of program I improvised at the airport to be ideally suited to their needs. Parents can reward a child repeatedly when he is quiet, and gradually stretch the success point. In this way, they can soon teach their child to be orderly through an entire church service or concert. If the child is hugged, rocked, or given candy in order to make him get quiet, the results are apt to be exactly the opposite of what the parents want. The same is true of what are called *distractions*. These are nothing more than payoffs given when the child's behavior is unacceptable. They are given in hopes of luring the child from a problem behavior to a less annoying behavior. No one ever tries to distract a child from a behavior that both of them like. People who want children to remain in their seats throughout a wedding, movie, or funeral should not reward them when they begin stirring around, getting up, crying, or fussing, and then wonder why they sit such short times. The reward should come while they are sitting[12]. Remember that most children who are called "hyperactive" are those whose payoffs come when they get up and move, and not when they are sitting quietly. The next time you have the chance to observe a child who has been called hyperactive, remember that the term does not have anything to do with the cause of his more-than-average movement, but rather is a description of the fact that he does move around more than most children. You will almost always see the child sit for long periods of time—sometimes hours—while he does things which interest him, such as drawing or coloring, playing with cars, dolls, or other favorite toys. So-called hyperactive children are often bored with the things adults demand they do, but they have not learned to sit still despite their boredom. Slowing hyperactive children can usually be done rather easily, if they are rewarded for being quiet. And while you are at it, try to remember to give them something to hold their interest, so that they are not just learning to be vegetables. There are many ways they can learn to sit quietly and still do something that is not annoying. But it does take a degree of committment from the arranger, who is usually too busy or preoccupied to spend the time in what is essentially a boring kind of pastime.

Every time I visit a typical classroom, I find most of the children are doing at least some of their work. Others might be finished. Still others cannot figure out how to do the assignment, or perhaps they're bored, so they look around, and find some way to attract the attention of their peers. Eventually they are likely to attract the attention of the teacher as well. The teacher stops what he is doing to say something like, "All right, now. Get quiet," like the teacher I described in Chapter 4. His behavior is escape behavior, and so is that of the child. The behaviors of both the teacher and the child get strengthened, because both get payoffs. The child's disruptive behavior bothers the teacher, who tries to stop the annoyance. Usually, he is at least temporarily successful, and that is his payoff—the class temporarily quiets down. On the other hand, the children in the class sometimes enjoy seeing the teacher lose his cool, and might even enjoy seeing the problem child catch hell for his shenanigans. Some might even admire him for getting under the teacher's skin. The child gets extra attention from both his peers and teacher. That attention can be a very strong payoff. So the child temporarily stops this round of attention-getting behavior, but is more likely to start again a bit sooner. After all, he was paid for it, wasn't he?

A teacher who really knows what he is doing will realize that boredom—in addition to being a strong punisher—is a signal, and will put behavior on cue. Boredom means the learner is not getting enough reward. The behavior the teacher wants to see him doing has begun to starve. The teacher might handle the situation in a way something like this: "Boys and girls, please turn to page 23 in your workbooks. You will find twenty math problems on that page. You should find most of them are fun, so look them over quickly to see if you understand exactly what you are being asked to do. [Pause]. Any questions? [Pause]. OK, then. Start working, please. I'll set this timer for twenty minutes. When you have finished, raise your hand. I'll come back and check your work. If you have done every one correctly, you can listen to some records through these headphones. If you have finished before the timer rings, you get an extra reward. You may also run completely around the room when everyone else finishes. If you miss any problems, I'll try to help you figure out what you did wrong, and you can work them again. When you have them all correct, you can also listen to the records until recess."

The room might become a bit noisy for a few minutes, but so what? It is often noisy already because of the uncontrolled rowdiness. The teacher should be less concerned with how noisy the class is than with the benefits the children will get from a reward-based classroom. Some possible advantages are:

1. The children learn to work their problems correctly.
2. If they do not understand how to work them at first, they will try harder to figure out how to work them, on their own.
3. The children will concentrate on their work.
4. The children will enjoy their math class.

5. Because they enjoy their math class, they will like their teacher, and may even learn to love mathematics in the process.

6. Because they like their teacher, there will be no problem behavior designed to get under the teacher's skin. That kind of problem only comes about when the children associate the teacher with punishment.

7. The teacher will not spend so much time rewarding the wrong kinds of behavior.

8. Everyone will get substantially more work done; more and better learning will take place.

9. Because the learning process was made so enjoyable, they will eagerly look forward to school each day. There will be less absenteeism, less dawdling in the morning, and a more positive, favorable attitude toward the entire learning process. This attitude could and should last a lifetime.

Unfortunately, even when you find a classroom run according to the laws of reward, you will rarely find the other classes the child attends to be equally rewarding, so to some extent his attitudes toward learning are being changed toward the negative by his other experiences. Almost every day, hundreds of thousands of schools are now teaching millions of children and young adults to associate learning and study and intellectual pursuit of all kinds with punishment. It is small wonder children play hookie, teen-agers drop out of school, adults vote against school improvement bonds, teachers and school administrators keep a child after school *for punishment,* instead of permitting him to stay longer as a privilege and reward! It is small wonder that a president of the United States, largely at the urging of his wife, appoints a "Minister of Culture," and then refuses to listen to his (or the First Lady's) recommendations. It is not surprising that teachers spend a large part of their time acting as disciplinarians or policemen instead of spending their time constructively, doing what they were supposedly hired to do—teach useful skills. It is no wonder that an entire nation developed anti-intellectual attitudes, using derogatory names like *egghead* to describe scholars who devote their lives to the pursuit of learning. Why should people be ashamed of learning, or of their intelligence? Why should astrology, the occult, and other current versions of fairy tales, including a lot of professional psychological practice, all be so much more popular than approaches which use reasoning and careful, scientific observations?

When people enjoy learning, they will learn. At first, the children in the class I just described go along with the running game only because they find it fun to run around, and because it gives them a break from their work, which is often seen as a mild punisher. The math problems might just be an annoying price they have to pay for the privilege of doing what they want to do. But little by little, having tasted the success of working their math problems correctly, they also begin to enjoy the subject they are learning, for people learn to enjoy those things which reward them with success. Mathematics, they suddenly find, can be fun, but think of the millions of unfortunate people who do not know this! The same can be said of English literature, social studies, science, Latin, physical education, pencil drawing, auto mechanics, needle point, golf, general psychology, practicing the piano, wood carving, or even baseball! Why? It doesn't have to be that way. Maybe the people who dislike things are those who have never had the chance to learn that they can be fun. Maybe their teachers were frustrated by their own failure to make the subject meaningful to the students. And something is *meaningful,* or *relevant* only if it somehow results in payoffs which are related to the learner's success. Maybe the teacher's inability to keep "discipline" in his bored class (translation: To make the students obey him) made him angry and hostile toward them, and hence more likely to deliver punishers. Or maybe the teacher simply did not reward success in the students. Here, the *teacher* lacked necessary target behaviors. This lack starved the children's desirable behaviors, and caused them to die out. The competing problem behaviors then won out, and were further strengthened because both the teacher and the peers rewarded them.

No, you can bet that when the teacher's target behaviors happen at a high rate, the children will learn almost everything the teacher is trying to teach, provided only that the steps are small enough and well-organized according to their progressing levels of difficulty (see Chapter 13). Moreover, they will learn as quickly as their mental limitations will allow. The teacher who is rewarding rowdy behavior could use the same amount of reward he is now giving for problem behavior, and get much better results if he gives them only when the children are working at the things he wants them to learn.

The teacher could write a program such as this:

Targets:	Work fifteen problems correctly	15:1	Play 1 rock record with head phones
Problems:	All other competing behaviors, especially attention-getting behaviors	1:1	Starve

Figure 9. Maintaining classroom order. *Target behaviors:* Working assignments correctly. *Problem behaviors:* Competing behaviors.

Many teachers who are unfamiliar with these basic principles of good teaching, even though they might have had twenty five years of experience standing in front of a classroom punishing children, might argue, "But I don't have the time to do all that. I have twenty five little monsters in my class, and it takes all my time just to get them quiet and started with their work."

Perhaps they do have twenty five rowdy children, but whether or not their teaching is adequate, those twenty five children will still be there in the classroom, and must be dealt with. With good teaching, these twenty five children will no longer be rowdy. The first job of any teacher is to get command of the class. He will get little else taught until he does, and actually, this job takes relatively little time, especially when all the resulting gains are considered. The traditional teacher gets control of the class by being firm, strong, authoritarian, and by teaching that any violation of the rules will be punished.

That never worked as well as once thought, and it is no longer necessary. Firmness, yes. You can get good behavior because the children like the teacher well enough that they don't want him to be unhappy, or you can keep the children "in their places" through fear of the teachers. But in this day of switchblade knives in the classroom, maybe the shoe is on the other foot.

My wife once taught in a black ghetto school in Oakland, California. The children in her class were so accustomed to punishment they hardly noticed it any more. Some had been arrested by the time they were in the third grade. What could a young, white, female teacher do to them that could be worse than what they had been through already?

As an experiment, she read stories to these teen-age delinquents. Gradually the disturbance disappeared. First, she taught them to enjoy the class, making very few demands on them. She gave the students things they could do easily, and she poured on the social payoffs. For the first time, many of these children found a teacher they could be loyal to, even though her skin was the wrong color. When she left the school, one of the toughest boys in the school cried. You seldom get that kind of response when you control a group of people by force. Those youngsters showed her far more respect than most people get from some of the affluent, bored children of the professionals in the elite neighborhood where we have lived for the past four years.

Whether it is in a classroom, a family, a marriage, or on the job, two preliminary steps are necessary for good results in programming. You must first get the learner's attention. You must also get a reasonable rate of compliance to your commands. I have said that 90% should be a good minimum. This does not mean the learner becomes your slave. Once he learns that your commands are reasonable, easy, and result in payoff, he will usually obey at least 90% of your requests. Most people will do so anyway, under ordinary circumstances. But there are some exceptions. When a relationship has gotten completely out of control, the learner may resist as a means of counter-aggression against punishment in the past. The arranger must first get attention and obedience before there is any point in going ahead to teach more complicated things, including academic skills. Some institutionalized mentally ill or mentally retarded people must first be rewarded for acceptable behaviors, until they become more "normal," and can pay attention to the arranger's requests. It is becoming more clear every day that institutions commonly reward bizarre and undesirable problem behaviors. These people must have time to learn that sane behavior will be rewarded. They are no different from other people. Their behavior follows the same laws, and they will act "normal" when such behavior gets payoff. They will act "retarded," or "mentally ill" when those behaviors are rewarded, and rational, sane behavior is starved.

Once an arranger has the learner's attention and a 90% rate of command compliance for periods of twenty minutes or more, he is ready to start programming in earnest. And once he has the attention of all twenty five children in a classroom, or all twenty five residents of an institution, or all twenty five boys in a scout troop, or all twenty five employees on a job, there is really no good reason why one arranger cannot program that many learners at one time, or for that matter, one hundred twenty five. It is true, of course, that he will spend much less time on each one, but that is often a minor drawback. Most of the questions which are asked can be handled just as well by less trained assistants, and assistants are very easy to come by, as a rule. In a world dying of overpopulation, the one thing nobody has a right to complain about is too few people!

Assistants do need to be trained, of course, but the instruction may be, and should be kept simple. We did it with Nancy, the retarded girl I mentioned earlier in this chapter. We trained her to be an arranger for a single step of a program. Every child in the classroom is a potential helper. It takes a lot of planning and organization, but any bright teacher can show a number of children how to "monitor" a class, checking answers against a scoring sheet, or in other ways reducing the teacher's work load. There are other benefits as well. The monitors learn from this too, and the learner finds how he did on his work within just a few minutes. It is not necessary for him to wait a day or more for the teacher to finish her drudgery of scoring dozens of papers. The more often the feedback, the better the teaching, because, as you have learned, rewards are most powerful if given immediately after the behavior.

Each child could and should have his turn at being monitor, for he is doing teaching at such times. There are few things that help a person learn quite as rapidly as teaching someone else. Sometimes, the role of monitor can be used as a reward for doing some of his own work better than usual. And the monitors should share in the rewards of the rest of the class. If each monitor is assigned five peers to watch, their good behavior should mean that they get a payoff, but so should their monitor. He will then have a vested interest in their success. And if the entire class is taught how to reward targets and weaken problem behaviors, look at all the help you will have then! Help would come from peers as well as from the teacher, and peer payoffs are among the most effective of all.

Most of you are not classroom teachers, and may wonder why I have dwelled on this situation at such length. But what I have just described in such detail as a classroom problem might also apply to your own life. You might be a parent, scoutmaster, foreman, president of your lodge, or employer. All of those roles require getting some target behaviors from *groups* of people. The principles are everywhere the same. Keep the payoffs coming for target behaviors, and reduce or eliminate those payoffs that would ordinarily come after problem behaviors. The better you do those things, the more successful you will be in commanding those individuals.

People tend to give more payoffs to those people who give them rewards. You do more favors for people you like, don't you? You try to be around those who make you feel good, don't you? This is why some people who are not confident of their own ability to be successful with other people try to "buy" friends by using too many gifts, too many favors, or ask too little in return from them. There is a word people use to describe those individuals who are good at rewarding targets in other people, to such an extent that these learners spontaneously want to do what this arranger wishes: The word is *leadership*. When people do what you want them to do because they are afraid of you, you might acquire power, of sorts, but you will always have to be on the alert to keep your subjects in line, and to keep them from trying to assert their independence, which they will always try to do as a counter-aggression to your own force. But when people do what you ask solely because they want to please you, then you have real power! Just as aggression begets counter-aggression, you may also find that those people who reward other people more often are also the people most likely to receive payoffs more often. Unfortunately, this process is not quite as automatic as is the case with aggression, because rewarding target behaviors is a common behavioral deficit in our society. We are just not trained to counter-reward, as we are trained to counter-aggress, and in some extreme cases, the learner has been so punished for his counter-aggression that he is no longer able to defend himself. Even counter-aggression is one of his deficits. But the push toward counter-aggression is still present. The spirit is willing, but the flesh may be weak. Hence, counter-aggression appears in a passive, rather than a direct, open, honest form.

Now let us return to the newlyweds we met in Chapter 3. As you recall, we later studied them in Chapter 8. What were their crucial behaviors?

The most obvious were the problem behaviors of each partner. Both the husband and the wife had a high rate of hits—that is, hostile statements—and each hit stimulated the spouse to return the hit. It would not be hard for an observer to get a rough count, provided he could specify what was meant by a hit. Most observers, however, would have agreed on what was a hit in the example listed. The sample in Chapter 3 was taken from the middle of an argument, when you would expect the hits to come more often. That is why I recommended taking a full day's record, if possible. Those small samples will tend to be absorbed in the full day's data. A more lengthy period might have resulted in data much like the following:

	S	M	T	W	T	F	S	S	M	T	W	T	F	S
Hits by Jim	38	19	46	77	53	62	81	75	14	38	44	21	49	62
Jim's supportive statements	1	0	0	0	1	0	2	3	0	0	1	6	1	0

Learner: Jim (above, right)

Learner: Laurie

	S	M	T	W	T	F	S	S	M	T	W	T	F	S
Hits by Laurie	24	17	48	80	29	58	74	92	8	36	47	18	53	58
Laurie's supportive statements	0	0	0	0	0	1	0	4	0	1	0	8	0	1

Figure 10. Baseline data: Hits and supportive statements by husband and wife.

When you have that many hits, your relationship is in trouble. Notice that on the days there are a lot of hits by the husband, there are also a large number of hits by the wife. This is not only true because each person tends to return hits, but also because those were days when they spent more time together. If things are going right, you should also expect more targets on those days, but we didn't find them in our data above, which is more evidence that something in their marriage was seriously ailing.

In the second sample of the conversation, there were far fewer hits. The entire tone had become more positive and reassuring, even though both were still rewarding some serious problem behaviors, such as manipulation, game playing, etc. In spite of their other problems, the hits probably have priority, and it is best to work on one problem at a time. We should work to decrease hits and increase supportive statements, for they are two of the most crucial behaviors in any relationship.

Hits are usually pretty obvious, but sometimes there are hidden messages. When Laurie asked, "You wouldn't pair off with Barbara if you had the chance?" there was one message which read, "I'll bet you did pair off with Barbara, you sneaking sonofabitch," and another which pleaded, "Say you didn't, because I want to believe I have you all to myself." Recording accurate data will be one of your biggest problems. Do you count the hidden messages? How? They could be important, but two people might be less certain to agree whether to count some messages as hits. We will talk about these problems in Chapter 12, but for the time being, it should be enough to warn you to be aware of the problem, and urge you to try to be as consistent as possible. That is, if you decide not to count hidden messages during the baseline observations, don't suddenly start counting them when you start the program, for it would appear that there were suddenly more hits than there were before. If you decide you will count them, try to be as consistent as you can in the criteria that you use to judge whether a hit is hidden in a statement. Scientists studying behavior usually have more than one observer, whose observations are compared, in order to come up with more reliable data, but most of you will probably not be able to have a team of observers, and you probably will not be running statistical analyses of these observations to find your inter-rater reliability. Just do the best you can. Even if the data are not as accurate as a scientist might prefer, they are usually accurate enough to help you, and there is probably little doubt about what they mean. A glance at Figure 10 tells you that there were many hits and few supportive statements. That alone tells you a lot about how the two people related.

I have worked with a number of marriages or other relationships which seemed on the verge of collapse. Andrew and Sophie had been married sixteen years, but to judge from what I saw, the only reason they stayed married was to hurt each other. They were both gluttons for punishment, and I remember thinking that I could not recall ever meeting two more hostile people. "They deserve each other," I thought! During the first session in my office, I tallied their behaviors during a fifteen-minute period. Their scores: Andrew, 77 hits; Sophie, 75 hits. Each person gave out at least five hits per minute, or one hit on an average of every twelve seconds! Supportive statements during the same period were zero. Although people tend to act on their best behavior around strangers, they both agreed that their behavior in the sample was typical. I cannot see how they *could* have had more hits, because they surely had to stop for breath some time! Whether the numbers are exact is almost beside the point. It would have made little difference if there had been 85 hits or 65 hits during a similar period of time. Even one hit per week seems to me to be more than necessary, and one per day is undesirably high. This is especially true when there are no supportive statements to balance them out.

This couple denied they were hitting at all. When I showed them my tally, they would not believe me, until I played back a tape I had just made, and asked them to count the hits for themselves. I then gave them simple instructions. "Your assignment will be to talk to each other for the next fifteen minutes. I want to see how many supportive statements you can make, and how much you can cut down your hits."

The instructions were simple, but the assignment was tough. At first they couldn't think of things to say. It was new to them, and they were self-conscious. They had so much trouble they repeatedly turned to me to bail them out, but I did not participate. They were on their own, and I did not answer a single word. I did, however, permit myself to reward supportive statements—at first, by saying, "That's good. You are getting the idea," and later, simply by nodding my head in approval.

Soon they began to catch on. At the end of the fifteen minutes, I counted 36 hits by Andrew and 32 by Sophie—a reduction of nearly half. They did much better on the supportive statements, too. He came up with 14 and she gave him 18. At the end of the quarter-hour, I discussed the results with them and gave them more encouragement—payoff for their target behaviors, given to people who were unaccustomed to receiving much social payoff at any time.

Then we tried for another quarter of an hour. This time Andrew only hit his wife 8 times and she hit him 12. But he also said 37 nice things to her and she said 36 nice things to him. It was becoming easier, more natural, and much more spontaneous than the first awkward attempts, only a half hour before. The entire process took us less than an hour, but it might have been one of the most important hours of their lives.

In the early stages it seemed more like a game. Andrew objected, "But this is all so artificial."

"I know," I told him. "But do it anyway."

Sophie protested, "I can't do it. It doesn't feel sincere."

"If you can't be sincere, then be insincere, but just *do* it!"

They both argued, "This is all a big game."

"I know that too, but do it anyway. It will become easier and more natural once you know how. You cannot give a payoff to behavior that never happens, so we've got to get together and make the good things happen first. Then, once these targets are strong, you can have the luxury of worrying about whether it is natural or sincere."

Artificial, insincere, or not, it still worked, and before long, they felt more at home using rewards. They found that what started as a game eventually became sincere, and at times, even warm and affectionate. Even if they are clumsy and unconvincing, supportive statements have to be made before they can be rewarded and strengthened. It should be of some value to the warring partners that their opponent is trying— that he is making an attempt in the right direction, even if that attempt is only 10% successful. Why throw out that 10% just because it is not 100%? Why knock Mount Tamalpais because it is not Mount Everest?

I hardly recognized them when they came back a week later. During the entire hour Sophie said 66 nice things to Andrew and he said 60 nice things to her. He hit her only twice and she hit him only four times. All hits were mild. Their nonverbal behaviors showed me that they were beginning to like each other again. For example, she often smiled and placed her hand on his arm in an affectionate way, while he sometimes put his hand on her shoulder, looked into her eyes, or ran his hand through her hair, all in a very positive and warm manner.

I only saw that couple a few more times, mostly to keep on top of things and help them with a bit of encouragement. Three years later I was invited to a Christmas party at their home, and I did not hear a single hit. They were affectionate and warm toward each other, and it was not hard to see that they were still in love. They had felt their marriage was worth saving, and they both worked hard to do it. I'm sure they still have arguments at times, and must also hit each other from time to time, but these conditions are no longer chronic. They learned how to reward the kinds of targets they wanted, and how to tune out and starve the hits. These are good lessons to learn, and not at all hard to grasp, even though they are not always easy. But I never promised you that these changes would be easy to make. You can't take sixteen years of mutual punishment and wipe out all aftereffects in just fifteen post-war minutes. Still, it is possible to make a significant beginning during that time, as I have showed you.

Andrew's program to change Sophie looked something like this:

Learner: Sophie
Arranger: Andrew

Targets	Sophie says or does something nice to me.	1:3	1. Say, "Thank you, Sweetheart." 2. Say or do something nice in return 3. Count and record
Problems	Hits by Sophie	1:2	1. Starve hits 2. Count and record

Change level: Put a stamp into Sophie's book for each 100 targets.
Goal: Two pages filled with stamps.
Reward: Tickets for a three-week vacation for two in Hawaii.

Figure 11. *Target behaviors:* Supportive statements. *Problem behaviors:* Hits.

Sophie's program to change Andrew was similar in most respects. When Andrew had earned three pages of stamps, she bought him the hunting rifle he had wanted. She had been afraid to have it around the house, but she is not afraid any more.

Both Andrew and Sophie had agreed on their goals, and how many stamps they would need. Every detail was part of an agreement that I witnessed. Andrew's program was written when she was still afraid to have a gun in the house. That was why he had to earn three pages of stamps, while she only needed two before she was able to take the trip to Hawaii.

Hits are the most common problem behavior in ailing relationships, and supportive statements among the least common targets. Somehow, when people are angry at each other, they refuse to find anything good at all about their antagonist, and that is precisely the best time to be objective. But once these two behaviors (hits and supportive statements) were under control, we worked on other targets and problems too. They had to learn to talk to each other about how the hits (and supportive statements) had made them feel. This was not just to "ventilate feelings," but to teach them some of the cues and consequences of their behaviors which they might have overlooked, or been unable to perceive in the smoke of battle. We also discussed the little games they were playing, such as competing to be boss, and some of their mama-and-little-boy-type behaviors.

But the big project in saving their marriage, as it is in most other sick relationships, was to cut down the hits and increase the goodies, and that was just what they did. When you have been hit, you want to hit back, or at the least, defend yourself. Whether you just *want* to hit back or actually do so, it still makes sensible, intelligent, and objective problem solving that much harder. Once this couple had learned how to observe, count, and program for change, they could become more responsible for their behaviors, as well as the behaviors of their mate. They could take care of other problems after they had solved their big one.

Other problems can be solved in a similar manner. For example, I once had a client named Mark, who had attempted suicide by swallowing a bizarre combination of drugs, including mescaline, Valium, speed, alcohol, and LSD. While the speed and alcohol were perhaps the most dangerous of the drugs he took, none were taken in a quantity that could have killed him. Still, he was "out of it" for two or three days.

He had just broken up with his girl, Joyce, and said he did it to show her how miserable she had made him when she left. Apparently this incident frightened her enough that she came back to him. Although Mark had suggested to her that he seek professional help, it was Joyce who made the initial contact with me.

Joyce and Mark had many common interests, such as hiking, photography, political work, and other things, but she found some of his behaviors intolerable. The problem behaviors were of two related kinds: The first was statements soliciting pity, which I called, "Poor little me." The other was "Little Boy" behaviors, such as excessive dependency, and looking to Joyce for more support than the situation warranted. Joyce later told me, "When he acts like that it disgusts me. I want a man I can respect. I don't want to be a mother to him."

I asked to see both Mark and Joyce together. I began their session by telling Mark, "I think you should both understand that even though you are still alive, this little suicide attempt was really successful, at least, temporarily. Joyce, you agreed to give the romance another try. So he got a whale of a payoff in return for a hangover, don't you think?"

"But I couldn't just let him die, could I?" Joyce protested.

"No, of course not. He forced you into paying him off, but he still got the payoff. As things now stand, he would be more likely to use the same kind of pressure if you should ever try to leave him again. But I don't think he'll try another time. You'll understand why before you leave tonight. Together, we are going to teach Mark some new behaviors to replace his problem behaviors."

If it seems strange to talk about a thwarted suicide attempt as being "successful" when the victim is still alive, you must understand that Mark didn't really want to die. He was not after Death, but the Maiden. And he got her back, but not entirely. What he really wanted was her love, and people never get that through tricks.

Turning to Mark, I said, "Joyce's coming back to you was just avoidance behavior, to postpone another suicide attempt. But avoidance behavior dies out if there is never any punisher. Sooner or later you can expect her to try to leave you again. You can't keep her forever by pulling those stunts. Sooner or later she's bound to decide to let you go through with it. She needs to get enough payoff to want to stay with you. Those camera hikes were good, but not enough to cancel out the punishers that drove you apart. The games you play are your way of controlling her, to get her to do things she really doesn't want to do. It is just not honest. I want to change all that, and I think we can, if we all work together, and you do exactly what I tell you.

"First, I want the two of you to talk together for the next fifteen minutes. Talk about anything you want, but relate it somehow to your present situation. I'll just sit back and take notes."

There were few hits, but many "Poor little me's," "Little Boy" statements, and nonverbal behavior which I lumped together and called simply *negatives*. I counted 38, including his begging her to stay with him, talking in a whining voice, and statements which played down his strong points. Apparently, he hoped for a contradiction. In other words, it appeared to me that he was fishing for compliments. During the same fifteen minutes, I counted only one *positive*—that is, optimistic, assertive, or confident response.

Instead of showing the disgust she actually felt, Joyce's face would sometimes cloud over with sympathy. These looks would come after some of Mark's negatives. It was a good example of how she strengthened a behavior she did not like.

At this point, I talked things over with them and showed them my program:

Behaviors		Ratio	Learner: Mark Consequences
Targets	Positives (confident or assertive statements; smiles)	1:2	1. Social payoff 2. Record with right counter
Problems	Negatives (Poor little me; Little boy behaviors)	1:2	2. Record with left counter

Change level: None

Figure 12. *Target behaviors:* Positive statements and assertive behaviors. *Problem behaviors:* Negatives ("Poor little me"; "Little boy").

I tallied Mark's problem behaviors with a counter in my left hand and his target behaviors with a counter in my right. Mark quickly became self-conscious when I clicked the left counter. This is not an uncommon response, for most people are not accustomed to minute examination of their problem behaviors in quite such a public way. At times, he even asserted himself enough to argue, "That wasn't a 'Little boy'. I didn't mean it to sound like that!" Since assertiveness was a target, I counted his protest as a positive, holding the right counter high as I did so.

Gradually, the right-hand count grew larger, and when he made optimistic statements, he sometimes smiled or laughed self-consciously. For smiling, I told him, "That's good," clicking the right counter. "You are doing the right thing now." Clicking the right counter became part of an amusing game to him, but why not? What is wrong with someone enjoying his treatment? Isn't it the same as a child enjoying school? I have always felt that it is a trifle sadistic of therapists to claim that their clients must always find their self-examination so painful. Less progress can be expected when the learning is made into a punishing experience. Lord knows that their problems alone will cause them enough suffering without our adding more to it than is necessary!

Within the next half hour, Mark became skilled at recognizing his negatives—that is, his problem behaviors, which had formerly slipped by without his being particularly conscious of what he was doing. Sometimes, Mark even began to catch himself in the middle of a sentence, as he realized he had started another negative. He would stop and laugh, and of course, receive payment on the right counter.

The counters began to serve two purposes. They kept our data, and they delivered the consequences of Mark's behavior as well. Holding up the right counter began to mean social payoff for him, and holding up the left counter became a punisher, because it symbolized Mark's failure. By the time the couple left that evening, most of Mark's statements were positive. He was smiling, and much more optimistic about his prospects for the future. I also trained Joyce to reward his positives and starve his negatives. They both understood why I had said, "I don't think he'll try another time," when I referred to his suicide attempt. It was clear to Mark that he had acted like a spoiled child, and that adults who do so rarely emerge with the social payoffs they want most.

I saw him two more times, once with his brother and once alone. By the end of the third session, most of his immature (*i.e.,* negative) behaviors had disappeared, and he spoke with much more confidence. Two weeks before, his assertive, confident, or positive statements were artificial, hesitant, and self-conscious. But he had practiced them, received payoff when he did, and they became stronger behaviors as a result. Now he actually *felt* confidence and hope, and his positives were no longer faltering. During his two weeks of treatment, he and Joyce began to talk frankly, openly, and with assertiveness, even if they disagreed. He was able to mend some long-standing bridges with his brother, one of his aggrieved friends, and his employer, as well. Joyce admitted that he had become much more attractive to her since he had changed his behaviors, but she still didn't love him. After a long talk with him, she left him, still a friend.

He handled her loss very bravely. He did not try another suicide attempt, nor did he torture his friends with impassioned outpourings of self-pity. He learned that there is a big difference between disappointment, which is natural, and hopeless catastrophe, which is usually a product of a vivid imagination plus much social payoff for this problem behavior. He now recognized that he should not behave the same way toward a disappointment as he would a catastrophe.

We both agreed it was unfortunate that Joyce had left. Obviously, the change in his behavior had come too late. However, Mark could now replace her with someone new, just as he was replacing his problem behaviors with new, competing target behaviors. It is often easier to build a new house from the foundations up to the roof ridge than it is to remodel an old home, especially while it is still being lived in. With new relationships, he could build them soundly from the ground up, without finding it necessary to make repairs on old ones which had become soured. It was clear that Mark had clung to Joyce because she was the only attractive woman who had shown much interest in him. Once his behaviors became more positive, more women became attracted to him. For the first time in his life, he was able to make a choice, and his resulting confidence was reflected in a relaxed and comfortable way of dealing with other people, male or female. This made him even more attractive to women.

All of this took place nearly six years ago. I still hear from Mark from time to time, and he has done very well. He returned to school and finished his degree, working nights all the while. He found a new and more rewarding job, in a different county. He soon met another girl, and this time it did work out for him. He is now the proud father of a baby girl he named Natalie—after me.

Mark's experience was not unique. Success begets confidence, because it is a reward, usually for the right kinds of behaviors. As alternative behaviors become available, no single choice is so urgent that death is the only way out. The person who is least involved (that is, least committed to a single alternative) controls the situation. Any desperate person is at the mercy of those less desperate. A man is not very attractive to a woman who sees him as desperate for a woman, and no woman is as attractive to men who see them as desperate. When a man learns the right kinds of behaviors, he will become so attractive he will be able to build a harem. But he will probably be surprised to find that he no longer really wants one. Much more important, he will know how to relate to women, so that instead of their being regarded as conquests or potential conquests, they become friends he can enjoy, one of whom he will usually come to prefer over all the others. The same experience should also be true of women as well, and of either sex, whether they are trying to collect a lot of mates or whether they are looking for only one. It is probably even more true for those trying to find the "one right person" for them. Their process becomes much less frustrating and probably shorter as well, if certain things are kept in mind:

First and foremost, there is never a person so unique that there is only one other person in the world suitable for him. If there is, you can be positive that something about him is so seriously wrong that sooner or later the relationship will suffer, just as happened to Mark and Joyce. Second, relating to other people takes specific skills, just like everything else in the world. The more practice, the better the skills are learned. With each relationship, a person learns a good deal about how to relate, and when the relationships break up, he learns that there is a difference between catastrophe and disappointment. He learns that he will survive once more, although he felt it was not possible. This gives him the strength to ride out future crises.

And be assured, most "serious" relationships do break up, or at least, become less serious, for our society trains us very poorly for such an important job. The result is that our early relationships, as teen-agers and pre-teens, are pretty clumsy. I'm not saying such relationships never survive, but it is a rare thing if they do, and in large cities, or in more mobile populations, where people rarely see those they grew up with, it is even less common. Survival of these early relationships often means that both parties learn a lot about relating while they are in the relationship, and the odds of that happening to the degree necessary are pretty slim. How many of your childhood friends, and especially childhood crushes, are you still able to count among your best friends? If you are an adult, most have been forgotten many years ago.

The fact remains that the more choices a person has, whether we mean potential mates, potential jobs, or potential behaviors, the less dependent a person becomes on any one, and the less catastrophic the loss of that person becomes. In other words, the less "involved" he has become, and the more he is in control of the situation. With any loss there will be disappointment and sadness, of course, but with a lot of choices, such disappointment is much easier to cope with, and most of the pain will be gone within a few days. In general, the longer it takes to get over a loss, the more likely it is that the person has too few alternatives. Desperate people are people with few alternatives. As a matter of fact, desperate people are usually less successful than others in holding on to relationships they might form before their mate learns how desperate they are. This is why Mark and Joyce had their problems. Neither had enough alternatives.

I am not trying to knock monogamy, for there is certainly nothing wrong with it, as long as both parties understand that once the contract has been made, that is the beginning, not the end. Both parties should understand two things: 1) The mate needs just as frequent payoff after marriage as before; and 2) Successful monagamies are very difficult without those behaviors which are the result of success in many other relationships, which means many other partners, a lot of getting serious, a lot of falling in love, a lot of being in love, and unfortunately, a lot of disappointment when those temporary romances break up. But with each disappointment comes the knowledge that you survived the crisis, and actually found another relationship. You might have even been glad the old one broke up, because the new one was better. With each crisis survived, you have added one crisis mastered, and this tends to build more and more confidence in your ability to master present and future relationships.

Not all cases work out quite as quickly as Mark's or that of Andrew and Sophie, but if I have not seen some marked changes in the clients' crucial behaviors within a half-dozen sessions, I do not try to continue seeing them. Either they are not following my instructions, or else my instructions have not been appropriate. Usually, it is the former, but if

not, I must then ask myself the same questions you must always ask when your programs do not work out to your satisfaction:
"Were the program steps too big? Were the payoffs insufficient to keep them going? Were the data accurate enough? Did the learner get payoffs for problem behaviors? Were the target behaviors unrealistic? Were competing avoidance behaviors being rewarded? Why would a person who is suffering refuse to carry out simple tasks which could help end his distress and give him the relief he is paying me for? Are his payoffs for his problem behaviors so strong that he does not want them eliminated? Were the problem behaviors he first presented to me only a mask to hide or disguise other problem behaviors that were never openly recognized, or that the learner was unwilling to accept?"

This last question is often asked by psychoanalysts. At times I have concentrated on a problem which was different from the one presented to me at first. But these cases are somewhat of a minority, and almost always I can home in on the real problem in the first session or two, simply by analyzing the consequences of the client's behaviors, and looking for their payoffs and punishers. Months or years of lying on the couch were just not necessary in any of the cases I have ever worked with in more than a dozen years of practice—and I have always taken on all comers.

Another important point is demonstrated by Mark's case. We often hear professional psychologists and psychiatrists insist that before a person can change the way he behaves, he must first change his underlying feelings. In other words, Mark would never be able to act confident unless he first worked through his feelings of inadequacy, and increased his self-esteem. Clinical tradition insists that any show of confidence will be transparent, and unconvincing. Of course, this is certainly true, at first. But in the case of Mark, and of Andrew and Sophie, I showed how simply changing a few behaviors quickly changed feelings. As the ratio between problem behaviors and target behaviors began to change, the feelings began to change too. Mark *became* confident because he was making confident responses and they were rewarded and strengthened. You will recall my definition of a behavior as something somebody does, says, or thinks, and to this, I may add, *feels*. Feelings are also strengthened by rewarding consequences and weakened by starvation. Andrew and Sophie started out by playing a game of saying nice things to each other and not hitting. What started out in a very hostile atmosphere as a clumsy, artificial, insincere bit of play-acting quickly changed the entire outlook of these people . The notion that feelings must change before you can change the behavior effectively is simply nonsense, and professional therapists who take this route may be guilty of prolonging a process that could take a few days or weeks into one which sometimes drags out for months, or even years. To those people who can afford the $35 to $150 per hour fees once or twice each week for six months or five years, and whose problems are not so intense as to cause undue suffering, or who just have an intellectual interest in the process of exploring their own inner processes (and the financial ability to fund it), be my guest. It's your time and your money. But for a poor person overwhelmed with his problems, who has to scratch to pay his telephone bill, perhaps it is time to look more closely at how it will meet his needs.

As you can see, taking data was a vitally important part of Mark's treatment. Without the counts of his problems and targets, who knows how long it would have taken to teach him something he began to learn within fifteen minutes? How many suicide attempts might he have made in the meantime? Just recording his behaviors on the counter gave Mark feedback that made him aware of his problem behaviors, punished them mildly, and gave him a payoff for competing target behaviors that were absent when he began treatment. Feedback permits correction, and if it is perceived as punishment, it will be one of those cases described at the end of Chapter 8, in which I pointed out that even a mild punisher, such as clicking a counter, can be effective when alternative behaviors are being rewarded and strengthened. The counters played a therapeutic role in this and many other cases.

I am thinking of another case in which just the act of recording data helped the learner reach his goal, as was the case with Mark. One of my friends, named Ralph, knew that there are many ways to lose weight, and he desperately needed at least one of them. He is a very bright fellow, and realized that in most cases, after a person loses a lot of weight, he begins to gain it back again later. Ralph thought—correctly, I believe—that one reason for this is that while people may go on crash diets, or other instant-weight-loss regimes, they do not usually change the problem behaviors which led them to obesity. Half-jokingly, Ralph told me, "When I put food into my mouth, I have to bend my elbow to do it. If I can just cut down the number of times I bend my elbow every day, I should lose weight."

Now we all know, of course, and so did Ralph, that elbow-bending has nothing to do with weight, but we had fun calling eating by a new name, *elbow-bending*, or simply, *bending*. As a stunt, Ralph set out to reduce the number of times he bent his elbow every day. That is, he tried to lower the number of times he put food into his mouth.

When he started, he had no idea of his daily count, which is not surprising. You too have put food into your mouth nearly every day in your life. You'd be amazed how few people know how many times a day they do something as important to their survival as that! Do you?

Ralph used a mechanical counter. He was not too surprised to find that he bent his elbow about 208 times on the first day he counted.

Ralph then wrote a program designed to reduce his bites by about 5% each week, until his weight came down to the desired point. He began by trying to get baseline data.

As it turned out, however, two things took place nearly at once. The first was that his daily count of bends began to drop automatically, simply because he knew he was counting each one, and didn't want to make a poor showing. The other was that he quickly stopped snacking between meals. The counter became his conscience, reminding him that he really didn't want the snacks very much anyway. Within two weeks, all of his eating was done at the table during his meals. This made counting his bends more convenient, and also permitted his family to take part in his program.

Let me explain that no two bites were identical. One bend might bring a heaping spoonful of ice cream with whipped cream, while the next might be just a few of the sesame seeds which fell off his hamburger bun. He reasoned that the size of his bites, and the number of calories they contained, would tend to average out to a fairly steady value over a period of time, and the long run is what is really important anyway. I have since made observations which support his theory.

At first there was a temptation to pile his spoon higher, but this was not a serious problem. People who are after a certain result are not quite as likely to cheat on their programs, although it will happen, for the same reasons as those which control any other crazy behavior (see Chapter 4). But there was a built-in safeguard. His bends decreased from 208 per day down to 35, which is only one sixth of their original number. He could not take bites six times larger, for the spoon would not hold that much.

The program actually began as a gag to demonstrate counting to a class of students, and Ralph chose a ridiculous example just to make the demonstration more interesting. To everyone's surprise, Ralph began to lose weight rapidly. In the first five weeks he lost twenty six pounds, as well as eight inches of waistline. He also began to get additional social payoffs, as friends began to compliment him on his appearance.

I would not recommend this program for everyone, because weight loss is a result of a lot of things, such as exercise, caloric intake, carbohydrate intake, and bends, too. Besides, weight loss that rapid could be harmful, for it could result in organ damage. Weight loss of any significant size should always be monitored by skilled medical observers, to be sure that no harm is inadvertently being done. And a program such as this one, even if it worked consistently, would also have the drawbacks of not taking exercise or other important factors into account. Still, I know of at least six people who have tried this program, and it worked with all of them. I tried it too, although I only wanted to lose about eight pounds. Nothing at all happened during my baseline. After I continued about a month without results, I did what Ralph had intended to do at first. I set a limit to the number of bites I would take every day. I will spare myself the embarrassment of sharing my baseline data with you, but I chose 100 bites per day as my upper limit. Even though Ralph, who outweighed me by at least fifty pounds, did not feel hunger on 35 bites per day, I was hungry for a week or two on 100. But I did lose weight, got to my goal, and stayed there for a number of years. I no longer count bites, but if I begin to gain again I can always start back. The reason this method worked was because it made me change my eating behaviors.

    None of us gave up any of our favorite foods—another reason why medical monitoring might be desirable. We just ate less of everything, which made it easier to stick to our programs. We Americans eat more than we really need anyway—that is why we grow fat, and it is the only reason we grow fat. We take in too much food or burn off too little, or both. By counting bites to eat less, we did not give up the foods we loved. Most dieters can give up favorite foods for a short time, but not for the rest of their lives. All our program did was to organize a simple way to reduce the number of bites, and to let us know when we went over our limit. The number on the counter told us when it was time to stop for that day, and it did so in a polite, non-threatening way. Presumably we could have used the same technique to increase bites, if gaining weight was our goal.

    You would have to say I'm cockeyed if I ever said that Ralph's stunt is the best way to reduce. It did not measure any important blood chemistry, such as cholesterol or triglycerides. However, most physicians agree that cholesterol deposits take place more readily when people are overweight, and simply reducing the body weight could conceivably make even the cholesterol problem less serious.

    Ralph's way was one way, but it was not the only way. It showed the value of keeping good data. Although not as accurate as counting calories, it was simpler and did not force us to give up the foods we liked the most. Have you noticed that these are usually forbidden? The reason, of course, is that fats and carbohydrates just happen to taste better, and most favorite foods are probably to be found in one of the two groups. High-caloric foods are the ones a calorie counter is most likely to try to give up first, but being his favorites, he is going to be tempted for the rest of his life to "break training."

Our experiment showed something else. The careful scientist always tries to eliminate errors from his data. A person measuring his own behavior knows the way he wants it to turn out, and is always going to be tempted to cheat in that direction. He is on display, and wants to make a good showing. In Ralph's case, error turned into advantage, because it meant fewer bends. The only thing that changed was that he suddenly knew how many bends he made every day.

Later, I deliberately asked Ralph to stop counting. His family would count, without letting him know his daily totals, since they were present at his meals, which were the only occasions he ate. It would come as no surprise that fewer bites mean fewer pounds, but we wanted to test whether *the knowledge of the data* would produce fewer bites, and hence fewer pounds. At meals he was asked to repeat numbers, add large numbers in his head, spell the names of his friends, or their telephone numbers or addresses, but backward, and read math tables aloud, from right to left. Everyone had fun, and he lost count hopelessly. But his count was still recorded by his family, who used mechanical counters. He then began to gain his weight back again. When he had gained five pounds, I told him to start counting again. Almost the same day, his count began to drop. Within a week his weight was back down again.

This process is called *reversal*, because we change what we are doing to something just the opposite. From counting, he stopped counting; then he began counting again. The purpose of the reversal is to test our program. If his bends begin to change at the point of reversal, or re-reversal, we can be more sure that the changes are caused by the program. How else could we know that he didn't lose weight because of illness, drugs, worry, phases of the moon, the hot weather, inflation, a change in the stock market, or a good fairy? All of these things might explain a change in behavior, if you wish to believe in them. But they would probably not change the behavior just at the times we changed the program. If there remains any doubt, reversal can be done a number of times, and with each one, we become a bit more certain that *we* are the change agents, and not something else. Of course, reversal is not always done. Some behaviors can't be reversed. You can't un-read, un-talk, un-walk, un-ski, un-swim, un-memorize a Beethoven Sonata, or un-learn a maze, although you might "forget" any of them. But re-learning them will take much less time than original learning, which indicates that a trace of the learning was still present. Moreover, many arrangers are reluctant to increase problem behaviors deliberately. You must think about the ethics. Do you have the right to make someone's problem behavior worse? On the other hand, there is also an obligation to know the truth, and do you have a right to proceed with a program, knowing that you might be fooling yourself, thinking that what you did caused the changes, when they were actually due to a change in the Dow-Jones index? Your own program may have been irrelevant. You might continue your program, thinking it was successful, and later be faced with the same problem, when the weatherman or the good fairy changes his mind. I will talk more about ethics in the final chapter. In the meantime, you must decide which is worse, to go ahead without being informed or to make the problem behavior worse on purpose, even though you can change it back again in a short time. I tend to prefer the latter course, although it is not always possible or practical.

I have given you examples of a number of programs, along with some lengthy and (I hope) interesting digressions. Now let me try to summarize and generalize some rules to follow. I already gave you eight guidlines at the beginning of this chapter. Each program should: should:

1. Define the behaviors you wish to change
2. Define the goals you want them changed to
3. Analyze the steps you'll need to go through in order to get from the first to the final step
4. Measure and record what is happening
5. Deliver certain consequences after each behavior.

In addition, we also decide upon a ratio between the behavior and the consequence; determine a *success point*, which should be incorporated into the definition of the behavior (step 1) and, decide upon a *change level*, at which point you will wish the program to advance to the next phase.

Defining the behaviors means writing an objective description of the problem behaviors and those targets you would like to use to replace them. Each description should be in language clear enough that a stranger reading it will be able to carry out the program exactly as you desire, without much further instructions. An exception to this rule might be a program you are doing on yourself. You might have a problem or target behavior which only you can feel, and might not be visible to someone else, such as *sudden feelings of anxiety*, or *happy thoughts*, or *nightmares*. You should still try to make your descriptions clear, brief, and to the point, so that your own programs will be consistent, and you will not be changing your programs accidentally. Of course, you should change the program when your progress, or lack of progress, makes the present program inappropriate. The change is then made to deal with the new situations you face.

Another reason for keeping good data is to help you see when your program is *not* successful. Eventually, of course, you'd know anyway, just as you would with a successful one. But with good data you might find out much sooner. Even the most sensitive, intelligent, well-trained and conscientious observer will have trouble detecting minute changes in the rate of behavior until they are far larger than good data would have revealed. This means that data help you come to grips with situations in more complete confidence, much earlier in the game, and before tiny changes have become well-established trends. Most people will probably be unable to notice small changes, because day-to-day variations are often much greater, as you will see in Chapter 12 (Figures 16 and 17). By the time it becomes obvious to someone without data, a minor problem might have escalated into a major crisis, and everyone would say, "It all happened so suddenly!" But it might not have been so sudden after all. It only became visible suddenly.

People forget even important things. Can you remember the exact problems you were dealing with a few weeks ago? Can you remember how strong they were? Do you remember your weight a month ago? The amount of time you practiced on your French lesson six days ago? Your number of typing errors last March? Recording data permits us to keep information so that we can make comparisons we might need to assist us in being successful at changing those behaviors we want changed.

Once you have outlined the steps I listed, set the success points and the change levels, and written out the programs, you are all set to go. Get your baseline data, and good luck!

Chapter 12

Keeping Records That Will Help You Get
The Kind of Changes You Want

All science is based on measurement of some kind, because it is the best way we know to keep track of what we are doing. But keeping records is usually boring work. Most people don't like to count or make observations. They often skip this important step. It is the weakest part of most programs. While it is possible to go overboard and get bogged down with too many records, I suppose it is also possible to have too much money. But these are both rare problems. For most people, the problem is too little of both. Sometimes people are successful without keeping any records. People have also landed airplanes with their eyes closed, but it is not a recommended practice.

Programs (including businesses and governments) succeed or fail for a variety of reasons, but in nearly every failure we can be sure there is a lack of good, properly organized data. The kind of program doesn't matter. All need good data to give best results. This is true for a program to help you accomplish more work around your house or office; to teach Emily to pick up her toys; to keep a classroom interested and/or well-behaved; to reduce the number of spells of depression you go through each year; to reduce the number of cigarettes you light up; increase the time you spend in calisthenics; or a program by a major government to end a war, crime, poverty, drug abuse, inflation, or similar problem. People fail in all these areas either because they do not know what they are doing (that is, have inadequate or inaccurate data), do not follow their program consistently, or fail to change a program when it should be changed. All of these conditions can be remedied, but all remedies depend upon good data, usually information about someone's behavior. Large companies spend millions of dollars for programs called advertising campaigns, to change the behavior of the public so it will buy more of the product being advertised. Many advertising agencies would prefer their clients not have accurate data on the effectiveness of their services. It is interesting to note that when federal law banned advertising of cigarettes on television, cigarette sales increased. Maybe it was coincidence, but maybe the TV commercials were not as effective as the alternatives the tobacco companies were forced to use more heavily. I do not know of any cases where advertisers did reversals, for example. Who deliberately stops all advertising in magazines and puts all of his ads on radio, then stops all radio ads and puts his plugs into newspapers, then stops all newspaper advertising and uses nothing but television, or skywriters, or promotional balloons, or still other media? Only the direct mail businesses, which rely on coded coupons, can tell which ads *really* pull in their sales. Other businesses have to guess what caused any changes in sales, for the better or for the worse. These changes could also have been more the result of the state of the economy, beginning or ending a war or election campaign, the discovery that cigarette smoking increases the odds of cancer, the availability of alternative tension-reducing devices, or an accidental lining up of the planets than they were to the advertising.

Before we get too self-righteous and call the advertising agencies all sorts of bad names, let us also ask ourselves how many of us welcome an objective look at our own professional results! Those in professions such as law, teaching, or the so-called "healing arts," (which include medicine, psychiatry, and clinical psychology), or still others in manufacturing, plumbing, automobile repair, or baby sitting, have always resented being looked at critically by outsiders. Of course, the reason is that outsiders seldom look at us unless they are preparing to punish us in some way. Some professions use "confidentiality" as a defense, which makes them more immune to criticism. While it is true that we should honor the trust when our clients tell us important things they do not want made public, that same confidentiality protects the professional person as well, and prevents any kind of accountability. It protects the quack as well as the competent and conscientious practitioner. The public has no way to shop around, and to compare the services, the fees, the competence, or the bedside manner of various physicians, psychotherapists, lawyers, nurses, teachers, carpenters, or any other protected group. Nobody publishes complete, accurate data on all his successes and failures. To do so would take a full-time staff, and most people are just not that interested in the results. Many times it would not even be possible to do so if we wanted to, because it is a hard job to prove which of the many things happening made a person get better—or worse. You will recall my talk about superstitious behavior in Chapter 4. We often buy pills—and physicians prescribe pills—because we took them before and the pain went away. The pills might have had nothing to do with it. Sometimes the pain would have gone away if we had done nothing.

Let me tell you about something mathematicians call *regression to the mean*. A *mean,* as you know, is an average. *Regression* means that extremes to either side of the mean tend to move toward an average. Extra high rates tend to become lower and extra low rates tend to get higher. I believe it was Ogden Nash who shrewdly observed that he didn't know whether it was better to feel good, knowing that it could not last, and he would soon feel worse, or to feel bad, knowing that he'd soon feel better. He recognized that unusually good or bad conditions are usually abnormal, and in the long run they tend to settle, or regress, toward an average level that we become accustomed to. If we feel especially good, we know, just as Nash knew, that it won't last forever. "Eat, drink, and be merry, for tomorrow we die." We will soon feel more "normal," which in this case means not quite as happy. Except in cases of serious physical illness, if we feel especially bad for awhile, it doesn't last forever either, and we'll soon feel more "normal." That is, we'll soon feel better. If we go to a physician or psychologist or faith healer or astrologer or pastor when we are feeling worst, the odds are that no matter what he does we will still feel better by and by. If we don't even get to see him, we'll still feel better before long. It is well known that approximately 65% of the patients on waiting lists for psychotherapy "recover" on their own, which compares rather favorably to the 65% on the list of those who were able to get professional help[13]. The treatment often gets credit for improvement which would have happened anyway. But by keeping good data, and by using reversals and other checks, you will be better able to track down the cause of the change. Your defective program will not get credit for causing an improvement that was really a naturally occurring regression to the mean. If your program did not work, change it, or junk it. But don't fool yourself into claiming credit for something that would have happened without your intervention.

That is one of the most important reasons you should learn how to keep data. As I told you in the previous chapter, there are ways in which you can keep better tabs on how successful—or unsuccessful—your program has been. The technique of reversal was one way, and there are others.

I hope that I have convinced you how necessary it is to keep good records. They can help you, if only by calling your attention to things you might not have noticed. Using all the principles I've talked about in Chapters 2 through 10, you can often get results "on the spot" without bothering to take data. If so, more power to you. This is what happened to me in the case of my friends at the airport. We had no time to get organized, and as a demonstration it worked quite well. We were lucky. But if you are really serious, and want to get the best possible results over a longer period of time, you'll keep good records.

Now let's talk about data. First of all, many people do not realize that the word *data* is actually a plural form of the word *datum*. Look it up if you don't believe me. These words have been used incorrectly for so many years that I am expecting a gradual change in the accepted usage, but until then, we should speak of a single *datum,* or more than one *data.* "The data *tell* us," or "The data *say,*" "*These* data are very precise"(not "*This* data *is* very precise.") No particular reason for my burdening you with grammar at this time, other than to keep some readers from becoming confused when I talk about "they," meaning data, when they might have expected me to say "it."

The most common forms of data are: 1) number; 2) duration; 3)rate; 4) time-fix; 5) percentage; and 6) rating scales. Let me talk about each one in turn.

Number

You have already met the first kind of data, namely *number.* Any time you count how many times something happens, you are using total number as your datum. When Ralph recorded the number of bends each day, he was using that day's *number* as his datum. When we counted the times Ricky said, "Please," our datum each day was the total number. Many things happen so rarely that a person can easily recall how many times they happened, without using any mechanical help. But most people will have a bit of trouble remembering things that happen more than once a day, unless they keep a written record at the time they occur, and that means that some equipment will be necessary.

One of the simplest devices is a pencil and a small pad of paper that can be carried in a shirt pocket or purse. I have used something still simpler, in a pinch: A strip of masking tape stuck on the back of my hand. This gave me something to write on, and in a true emergency I could have even written on my skin, as I have done a few times when it was necessary. For the first kind of data (number), you need nothing more than a simple tally. For convenience, we usually arrange the marks in groups of five, like the count of 23 shown in Figure 13.

Figure 13. Sample of tally, showing grouping by fives. Tally shows a count of 23 behaviors.

All other devices are refinements, so you will not have to remember a changing number when there are more important things to think about. Pool players use buttons on a wire to keep track of points. Other simple and inexpensive counting gadgets are buttons, coins, pebbles, marbles, or poker chips, which can be moved from one pile or pocket to the other, one at a time. Some gamblers secretly keep track of crucial cards, such as aces, by stacking a certain number of chips, and casually removing one after each ace has been played. I know one psychiatrist who gives his clients books of matches to help them count their behaviors. He knows there are twenty matches in each book, and the client tears off one match after each behavior he counts. The number missing will be the number of times the behavior was observed. These are ways of keeping data without attracting a lot of attention, which is why they are used. They can be very useful to people who are shy or reluctant to explain what they are writing down. This way there is no writing down. People often "fiddle" with a book of matches, and "nervous mannerisms" are so common and acceptable they seldom attract attention, and almost never require explanations.

There are also mechanical counters which are available commercially, such as golf counters worn on the wrist, and slightly more elaborate four-digit gadgets. You have seen these being used at doors to auditoriums, cafeterias, stadiums, etc., to count the number of people who come through.

Any way you get them, your data are only numbers—the number of times something has happened, or the number of minutes something lasts. You might be counting hits by Andrew or Sophie, Mark's "poor-little-me" statements, the number of toys Billy left lying around, the number of times Clifford interrupted a conversation, the number of checks you wrote on the same day the statement arrived, the number of situps you did each morning, the number of times Emily dropped food off her plate, the number of spelling words Ricky learned correctly, the number of fights Shawn instigated, the number of suggestions the wife offered her husband, the number of times the husband ignored his wife's suggestions, or the number of times the husband acted upon his wife's suggestions. When you describe a problem behavior or a target behavior, you need to know the number of times something happened. Let me repeat what I said back in Chapter 2. Some behaviors are all right when they happen only occasionally, but if there are too many of them, they are seen as problem behaviors. One example might be Clifford's interruptions. Everyone interrupts once in awhile, but too often becomes a problem. Another example might be coming late to meetings. If it happens too often, someone is likely to call it a problem. Mild hits are not really problems unless they come too often, or become harder hits. An adult asking for advice from his parents is not doing a bad thing, and it can even be a sign of respect and friendship, until it happens five or ten times every day. Then, it may be a problem if it is evidence that the adult is so dependent upon his parent that he cannot make a decision on his own[14]. A single person staying home on a Saturday night has no special problem, unless it happens every Saturday night.

In each of these cases, the *number* of times—that is, how often, or how much it happens—determines whether it is a problem behavior. If you want to work up a program to deal with any problem such as this (that is, a behavior which you do not find annoying if it happens rarely) you should start off by counting the number of times it happens, to see just how strong the behavior is when you begin.

Rate

I said before that a simple count, such as a tally, has some drawbacks which are serious enough to limit its use drastically. I almost never make a simple count and leave it at that. Rather, I will add something to it, and that something is a measure of time. If I made fifty sarcastic comments, it would sound serious, unless you also knew that this was my total for all of 1973, 1974, 1975, and 1976. But if I made fifty sarcastic comments each day, that would be a problem for someone! So we usually convert the simple count to a measure of *rate*, and we do that by **dividing the total** *number* **by the amount of** *time* **we observed the behavior.**

In my opinion, rate is the most sensitive and meaningful measurement we can get, and it should be the most commonly used type of data, although for some reason it is not. I always try to use rate as a preferred form of data unless there are special reasons not to, and I will talk of those reasons in a few moments.

Rate is sometimes called *frequency,* and both words mean the same thing. Since rate (or frequency) is defined as the number of times a behavior occurs within the total length of the observation period, it is expressed as a number per time. Most people are familiar with terms like *miles per hour,* or *miles per gallon.* If you remember that *per* means the same thing as *divided by,* you'll never have any trouble remembering how to work problems using those data again. The term *per* is also indicated by a slash (/), so that *miles per hour* can also be written as *miles/hour.*

On the first day of Ralph's program, he got a simple numerical count of 208 bends. When we speak of it as *208 bends per day,* it becomes a rate. On the day Ricky said "Please," 125 times, we wrote the *number* (125) that night. We later talked about his *rate* being 125 per day (125/day). Rate is always expressed as number per time. On the day we counted 125 responses, Ricky was awake about fourteen hours. We could have also said that his average rate that day (sometimes called a *mean rate*) was 125 ÷ 14 = 8.93 "Pleases" per hour, even though it is obvious that there is no such thing as a fraction of a "Please." We could even divide this by 60, and thus obtain his mean rate of 0.1488 "Pleases" per minute.

Whenever we find an average rate, we are pretending that in each hour, or each minute, the number is exactly the same as it is in every other hour or minute. In other words, we are pretending that the rate of response throughout the day is uniform, or homogeneous. In practice, this is almost never true. If Ricky said "Please" 125 times the first day, we could expect nearly nine each hour. If you will recall, the first tantrum lasted nearly all of the first hour (*i.e.,* fifty two minutes), and there were no "Pleases" until the very end of the hour. The rate increased during the day, almost like a mirror image of the curve in Figure 1. We still talk about a mean rate of 0.1488/minute when we compare the first day to other days, and we act as if the behaviors were equally distributed throughout the entire day. Most of the time it doesn't matter, because we are looking for changes over a period of days or weeks. Averages are only conveniences we often use. If we say that the *average* person is right handed, or heterosexual, or less than sixty years of age, we do not mean that there are no twenty-five year old left-handed homosexuals. When we say that the *average* American woman is 5'4½" tall, we do not mean there are no American women who are 6'2" or 4'8" tall. We hardly ever run into any serious problems because of our little convenient verbal device.

The use of *mean rate per day* allows us to compare a behavior one day to the same behavior on other days, even though the days are actually different in length. In this way, we can take care of situations such as that of Jim and Laurie, who were together a shorter time on Mondays, giving rise to less behavior than on adjacent days (Figure 10). The use of a simple number, or tally, would lead us to believe that their behavior was "better" on that day (*i.e.*, we would believe they were not hitting each other as often). Now look at Figure 14. Rows 1 through 4 are

Learners: Jim
Laurie

Week 1–2	S	M	T	W	T	F	S	S	M	T	W	T	F	S
Jim: Hits	38	19	46	77	53	62	81	75	14	38	44	21	49	62
Supportive	1	0	0	0	1	0	2	3	0	0	1	6	1	0
Laurie: Hits	24	17	48	80	29	58	74	92	8	36	47	18	53	58
Supportive	0	0	0	0	0	1	0	4	0	1	0	8	0	1
Minutes together	272	46	238	317	116	209	333	291	48	115	188	70	117	443
Rates														
Jim: Hits/minute	.14	.41	.19	.24	.46	.30	.24	.26	.29	.33	.23	.30	.41	.14
Supportive/min.	.004	0	0	0	.009	0	.006	.01	0	0	.005	.09	.009	0
Laurie: Hits/minute	.09	.37	.20	.25	.25	.28	.22	.32	.17	.31	.25	.26	.45	.13
Supportive/min.	0	0	0	0	0	.005	0	.014	0	.009	0	.11	0	.002

Figure 14. Data used in Figure 10, with the addition of length of time spent together each day. Division by length of time converts the numbers of hits and supportive statements by each person into rate of hits or supportive statements made per minute.

identical to Figure 10, but I have added some additional rows. Row 5 shows the total time they spent together each day, and Rows 6 through 9 show their mean rate of hits and of supportive statements. You can check the figures, because the rates were computed by dividing each row of Figure 10 by Row 5.

I find that the most convenient way to talk about rate is in the number of behaviors per minute, even though this often results in fractions. It is convenient to me because I deal with behaviors which include some that happen over a wide range of rate values, and can use one kind of chart for all of them. Some behaviors happen less than once per day, but I also deal with severe problem behaviors in mental hospitals as well as those in the home and community. I have worked with clients who hit themselves more than 200 times each minute for long periods of time. You will probably never find that kind of behavior, and I certainly hope you don't. Still, you will probably find rate /minute a comfortable time period to use, as I do.

You will often find data written as behaviors per day. I wrote some in that form in Chapter 11. If possible, try to convert to number per minute, for the sake of uniformity, and learn to live with the fact that rates may sometimes be expressed in fractions of a behavior. After all, you have learned to accept the surveys which show that one out of every 2.4 marriages go on the rocks, even though you know there can not be four tenths of a marriage. And there cannot be 0.0167 hits, either. But there *can* be an average of one hit per hour, and that converts to 0.0167 hits/minute. You can easily perform the operation with the new pocket calculators which everyone seems to have now, but in case you don't have one, Appendix B converts some of the more commonly used rates to behaviors per minute.

Changes in rate are often very sensitive indicators of how a behavior is progressing. I won't burden you with other good reasons to use rate. Some of them are too technical to include here.

When you use rate, you will have to write down two things: The total number of behaviors which occurred, and the number of minutes your observation lasted. This is best obtained by recording the time at the beginning and at the end of the observation period. Then, dividing the number of behaviors by the number of minutes will give you the rate for that session of observation (usually a day).

It is best to get a complete count. For example, Ralph counted every bend during the entire day. And we counted every "Please" from the time Ricky awoke to the time he went to bed. It is much easier to do that when we are the learners, or with our young children, than with adults, who are much more mobile, and not around us as much. But complete counts are not often possible or practical. It is plain that I could not count every hit by Andrew or Sophie, or every "Little Boy" by Mark, because I was only with them a fraction of the day. Although they could have taken the complete data, I could not. I had to be content with what is called a *sample*. A cook tastes a few drops of soup, decides it needs more salt, adds a pinch or so, stirs it well, and then tastes again. Finally, he is satisfied and adds no more. He takes it for granted that every spoonful of soup in the pot will be equally salty. In other words, he tries to get a *representative sample*—that is, his spoonful will taste about the same as those in the remainder of the pot. If this were not an acceptable procedure, he would have to taste all the soup, and of course, that is rarely necessary. We "taste" a sample of behavior and do our best to choose a sample that is a good representation of the rest of the pot.

We usually have to deal with samples of behavior instead of all of it, and the samples are often of different lengths of time. Using the common denominator of rate permits us to compare one session to another, despite their differences in length.

Duration

I repeat. Use rate of behavior (number of behaviors/number of minutes) if at all possible. But there will be times when rate of behavior doesn't make as much sense as some other measurement. This happens with certain behaviors which can take a long time. For example, suppose you are interested in teaching an over-active child to relax, although at times I have known adults, and even geriatric clients, who were equally hyperactive, and what I say here about children will apply equally well to them. By *relax*, I mean that he must be able to sit quietly for more than just a few seconds. This is the type of a goal you might choose if you plan to take your child to church, a movie, concert, or to your adult education class with you. You could, of course, count the number of times he sits down. But what if he only sits briefly each time, then gets up, wanders around, and sits again for a short time? You may find, after an hour's time, that he sat three times, about five minutes each time. Now suppose you worked up a program, and after using the program you found that in the next hour he sat twenty two times, but each time he remained seated only about two and a half seconds. Looking at your data for rate, it would look like you got some improvement, wouldn't it? From a baseline of 3/hour (0.05/minute) to 22/hour (0.37/minute), is an increase of more than seven times. That doesn't look bad, does it? But even though he is now sitting more times, he is staying put a much shorter time. You are not really interested in how many times he sits, if he gets up right away. A jumping jack can do it a lot of times too. You want to know how much *time* he is spending in the chair.

We did something like this for Ricky's tantrums. We were more interested in the amount of time spent in tantrum than in how many tantrums he threw. Data of this type are called *duration* data. You might use duration data for programs such as the following: Increasing the amount of time spent studying; increasing the amount of time spent exercising; decreasing the amount of time spent watching television shows you didn't want to see; increasing attention span; increasing time spent working on your income tax in months before April; increasing the amount of time spent relaxing with your family; increasing the time you spent practicing French lessons; decreasing the time spent doing favors you felt pressured into doing; or increasing the amount of time spent practicing the piano.

You can see that rate might not be a very meaningful measure in any of those situations. You might just sit down once to talk with your family— a rate of 1/hour (0.0166/minute). But it would be of far more interest to your program that you spent an hour today, while a few weeks ago you never spent more than four or five minutes.

Time-fix

Another kind of measurement of behavior is sometimes called a *time-fix*. Frankly, I don't think much of this form of data, but there are times when it might be the best you can do. You can't always sit around and watch somebody to see how long a behavior is lasting. Time-fix is merely a sample of duration data, and is often used by nurses or other people who will be in a certain place at a certain time. Every hour (for example) they simply look at a certain patient to see what he is doing, and they mark their data sheets with a + or a 0, depending on whether he is involved in the behavior they are interested in changing. For example, John Blow may be a "pacer" who has been under physician's orders to get more bed rest and stay off his feet. When the timer rings, the nurse looks into the ward and finds Mr. Blow. "Ah," he says. "Mr. Blow is in bed." The nurse then marks his data sheet with a +. On the other hand, if Mr. Blow was pacing, the data sheet would be marked with a 0 (some people prefer to use − instead of 0). At the end of the shift, there will be eight observations made on the hour, or perhaps sixteen on the half hour, or thirty two on the quarter hour. Whichever scheme the nurse was using, all he had to do was to look and see if Mr. Blow was pacing *at the time of the observation*. That is why time-fix is so much easier than other forms of data keeping. It is self-evident why the information isn't as good as you would get with other forms of data collection, primarily because it can not get observations of rate. Time-fix, being a sample of duration data, is best expressed as a percentage of the observations observed. It is not a very large sample, either, so our data will only be approximate. Any time you have a small sample, you must understand that you are increasing the risk that the sample will not be representative. If you are able to get hundreds, or even thousands of observations, you could trust your sample a lot more. You could rely on it better. But our sample is a small one, taken only at certain times, and the data ignore everything that happens between those times.

You will end up with a sheet that looks something like Figure 15.

Learner: Mr. Blow

											Count	Percent
May 5	+	+	0	0	+	0	+	+	0	+	6	60%
May 6	0	+	0	+	+	0	+	+	+	0	6	60%
May 7	+	+	+	+	0	+	0	+	+	0	7	70%

Figure 15. Sample of time-fix data, with ten observations each day for three days. The last two columns count the number of pluses, and the percentage of the total observation which was plus. If desired, the same treatment could have been done with the minuses as well as/or instead of the pluses.

You can see that out of ten observations on May 5, Mr. Blow was seen lying in bed six times. From what the nurse could see, he was spending 60% of his time in bed, or 40% of his time out of bed, presumably pacing. Of course, as I mentioned, the data tell us nothing of what happened between times. More observations closer together will help remedy that somewhat, but when you start getting observations every five minutes, you have disrupted the nurse's routine, and you have defeated the purpose of using time-fix, which is economy. Mr. Blow might have been pacing most of the time between the + observations, but for that matter, he might have slept between sessions marked 0 or −, as well. With enough observations (that is, a large enough sample) errors such as these tend to average out—we hope.

Per Cent

Time-fix is expressed as a percentage of total duration. There are a number of other times when we can advantageously convert our data to per cent. For example, teachers have graded tests in percentage for many years. How long, or how fast you worked at the problems was probably not as important as how well you did them—that is, how many, or what per cent of the problems you worked correctly.

Rating Scales

Last and least are those types of data called rating scales, which require someone to state an opinion, with options such as, "Very often, pretty often, about average, not very often, very rarely," or some similar set of choices. While the rating scale may have its place in certain types of research (*e.g.*, studies of attitudes), for the purposes of changing behavior they are just about worthless, so don't bother with them. As far as I'm concerned, they serve two purposes: They waste time; and they fool people into thinking they know something they really don't know. They are of much more use to a politician than to a serious scientist, or to someone else who wants the best and most effective results. In other words, if your goal is to snow someone, use them. But if you want to change behavior in the quickest, easiest way you can find, leave them alone, and put your efforts into getting data that will help you obtain the kind of changes you want.

Regardless of the type of data you choose, you will need to convert those data to some form of table and from there to a graph, or plot. The purpose of the plot is to make it easier to visualize what is happening. In fact, the word *visualize* means just that—to make visual. You will usually notice that there will be a certain amount of fluctuation from day to day, for you will rarely find data that plot into a line or curve as smooth as the one I drew in Figure 1. The day-to-day fluctuations can confuse you when you see them written out as numbers. What could you say, for example, about the progress of a program whose data were as follows?

Learner: Bobby

Baseline

Days 1–11	12	13	9	14	11	12	10	13	11	14	12

Program

Days 12–22	13	10	12	11	10	7	11	9	10	8	10
Days 23–29	7	9	7	11	6	8	6				

Figure 16. Clothes left lying around. Days 1–11 are baseline data. Program begins on Day 12.

If you saw these rates of Bobby's behavior listed, you might not realize that the problem behavior was actually decreasing at a fairly steady rate. The change was slow, and had some high and low spots, both during baseline and later, but the dotted line shows you about where things are going. Here is what Figure 16 looks like when the data are plotted:

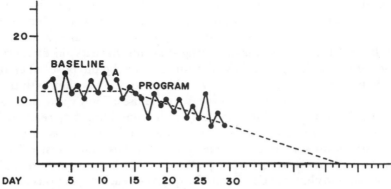

Figure 17. Clothes left lying around. The data of Figure 16 have been plotted on a graph. Dotted lines represent the lines of best fit. Note the steady decrease, starting at the beginning of the program at A (Day 12); since this plot represents a problem behavior, a decrease indicates improvement. Note that we can expect the problem behavior to be gone by Day 47 if the line continues down at the same rate. Note also the day-to-day fluctuations, including a rate of 9 on Day 3, and a rate of 11 on Day 27. Both of these extremes would have suggested the program was not actually succeeding (*i.e.*, there was no difference between the baseline and program data). But seeing the data plotted tends to put the results into a more realistic perspective that can be grasped more quickly.

The rate of 11 on day 26 might fool an arranger into thinking his program had failed, because 11 is within the range of his baseline data, which happened to contain rates as low as 9, on day 3. Rates of 9 could have fooled us into thinking the average during that time was lower than it actually was. But once you see it plotted this way, you are less inclined to jump to wrong conclusions, and possibly terminate a program which was really working.

The dotted line, called the *line of best fit*, can be calculated by a complex mathematical formula, but we can do it just as well by a process called *eyeballing*. You look at the plot and let your eyeball tell you which way it is going. Most of the time that is good enough, especially after you have had some practice at it.

Sometimes, if the line of best fit seems to be going down (or up) at a fairly steady pace, you may *project* the line beyond your present data to help you predict where it will probably be at some time in the future. In Figure 17, you could expect the rate of the behavior to be down to zero in just about eighteen days—by day 47, to be more exact. Of course, this assumes that the rate of decrease remains the same all that time. This is not always the case. The line of best fit is not always exactly a straight line. If you will look back at Figure 2, you will recall that Ricky's decrease was fairly rapid at first, then slowed down some near the end. The line of best fit was a curve, or at least, a number of short lines. If your program is short, however, you are probably dealing with a portion of a curve which is not too different from a straight line.

Suppose that your line of best fit for a certain problem behavior was going down steadily, as you saw in the past example, but you felt you wanted results somewhat faster. You decided to change the program slightly, by changing one or more of the consequences, the cues, the ratio, or for that matter, the nature of the behaviors you were working with—that is, you decided to choose slightly different goal behaviors as your targets. You might have also tried a different change level, which might have caused a more rapid increase or decrease. You can make intelligent plans to change the rate of decrease, but you still do not know what the results will be until you try out your plan. Up to this point, all you have done is to make up a theory, such as, "I think that if I start complimenting him on the way his room is still clean, and give him five points every half hour that it remains clean, I can get a faster decrease in the number of times he leaves his clothes on the floor." The decrease or increase is likely to start where you made the change in the consequences. This point is marked B in Figure 18. It is plain that the

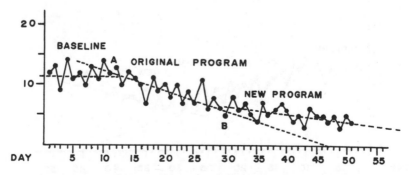

Figure 18. In an effort to speed up the results, the program was changed at B (Day 30). The rate of decrease slowed. The new program was thus shown to be less effective than the original program it replaced.

behavior is still decreasing, but not as rapidly as it was before. In this particular program, the change that was supposed to make the decrease come faster did not do the job, and in fact, slowed the progress of the learner considerably. You have tested your theory and found that it was not valid. Here is one of the strongest recommendations I could give you for keeping good data. You will be able to prove whether or not you were right. Your theory sounded reasonable enough, and in fact, for someone else it might have worked fine, but for Bobby, five points were not enough. There are thousands of theories people believe to be true. But how many of them will stand the simple test of observation? A little bit of data has been responsible for the junking of many promising theories, but it is unfortunate that so few theories are actually put to test.

Now that you know your very reasonable guess was in fact in error somehow, because of something you must have failed to take into account, you must now change back; or you might try an entirely different payoff; a different amount of the payoff; a different competing behavior; or reward the competing behavior on a different ratio; or add a mild punisher; or make still other changes. Only your imagination can limit the kinds of changes you could conceivably make in your program. Nobody can try them all, but make *some* kind of change and then give it a try. Your data will tell you whether you'll get something like Figure 17, at A, where the line begins to go down, possibly to your complete satisfaction, or Figure 18, at B, where your change caused the line of best fit to do down less rapidly, or like Figure 19, where the change made at B caused the line of best fit to rise, or perhaps it might

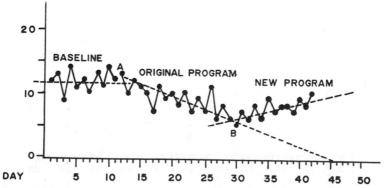

Figure 19. At B (Day 30), the new program resulted in an increase in problem behavior, thus demonstrating that the change had given the opposite of the intended results.

be like Figure 20, which suggests that your new program didn't make much difference, since the line of best fit did not change much after Point B, where the program was changed[15].

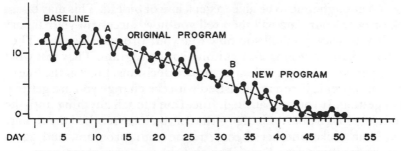

Figure 20. Change at B resulted in no detectable change in the line of best fit, begun at A. This indicated that whatever was changed at B was not related to the cause of the decrease in behavior at A. The original and new programs are shown to be equally effective. Factors other than effectiveness will determine which program should be chosen. Some of these might be how enjoyable or easy the program is to administer.

I won't repeat all the reasons why data are so important, but I should point out that lack of recorded data, or data which are not accurate, consistently recorded, and well-chosen, is one of the most common causes of program failure.

Let me summarize the ideas I gave you in this chapter:

Data are of different types. You must use the kind most meaningful for your particular program. You should write down the number of times something happens, how long you observe, or how long the behaviors last when they do occur. Record both the number of the behaviors and the length of observation time, so that you can compute the rate. It is an easy calculation to do, and in today's age of the pocket calculator, almost anybody can make the simple division which is necessary. Rate is the preferred datum, although there will be times when measure of rate will be meaningless or just plain silly. These exceptions are nearly always found when you are more interested in how long behaviors last than in how many times they appear.

Your choice might also be a matter of economics. Taking data is expensive in terms of time. This makes people cut corners. Thus, time-fix is sometimes used instead of more complete duration data, but in saving time, some advantages are sacrificed as well. Still, these data are often better than no data at all.

Using the data as your guide, you make a guess, based on what you know about the laws of behavior (Part One). Your educated guess predicts how to increase or decrease the behavior you want to change—to strengthen it or weaken it. This *theory* becomes the basis for your writing a program which must be followed consistently. Give the program enough time to be able to get a line of best fit. This may take a week or two. Your data will then tell you how successful your theory was. That is, your data tell you how well your program worked. They are your means of testing and guiding your program. They test what has happened and they guide your future decisions. Look at the line of best fit and decide if you are satisfied with the change you are getting, or not getting. If you are satisfied, fine. Don't touch anything until the data show you it is time to change—that is, you have reached the change level. Then make another theory, revise your program, and again check the resulting data. Keep changing the program as you progress, and check your line of best fit, until you have the results you want. There is some trial and error involved, until you finally stabilize the program at a level that is successful and comfortable. But remember to give yourself enough time between changes to get a *good* line of best fit. If you change too often, what you are doing is making inconsistency official. So change, but don't overdo it. Incidentally, your changes can include reversals, in order to check yourself. This technique was done in Figure 21. At point A, baseline observations ended and the program

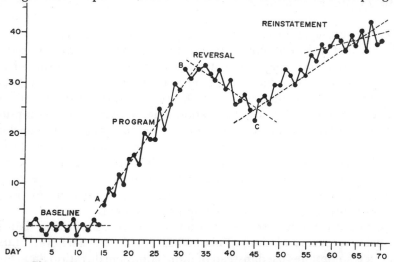

Figure 21. Will power and self-control of thoughts. Starting at A, the learner-arranger gave himself points for each happy thought. At B, he reversed the program by giving himself no points. At C, he reinstated the program, once more giving himself points for happy thoughts. Note that the curve begins to level off near Day 56. This often happens when a limit has been reached.

began. Points were given each time the learner had happy thoughts. Starting at point B, no points were given for happy thoughts, and at point C, the program was reinstated, so that the learner/arranger once more gave himself points for his happy thoughts. The change in the direction of the line of best fit tells the story. Give points and the happy thoughts increase. Stop giving points and they begin to decrease. Give them again and their frequency once more rises. If the changes take place at the time the program is changed, the arranger can be more certain that the change is actually due to the program and not some accidental thing which happens at the same time.

The sky's the limit, and you can keep changing programs until you find one that makes the line go where *you want it to go*. Remember, you can be the master. Let your data work for you. When you get the right kind of behavior changes in you or someone else, you will have power. Your life will be improved. It is to be hoped that you will have chosen your targets wisely and responsibly, so that the changes you are after will also improve and enrich the lives of others as well as your own life.

Chapter 13

Behavior Shaping: Or How to Carve an Elephant

I have said before that you can't reward or strengthen behavior which isn't there, and I promised I would tell you how to make an entirely new behavior happen. I have already mentioned *prompting* as one way, but there is another, which is called *behavior shaping*. We can mold, or *shape* a present behavior into a *goal behavior*—that is, the kind of behavior we want it to be.

How can we do it? Actually, the technical term is *the reinforcement of successive approximations,* and that tells it all, if you can decode the fancy technical jargon. It works something like this:

There is a story of a sculptor who was asked, "How do you go about carving a statue of an elephant?"

"Oh, that's very simple," she replied cheerfully. "You start with a big hunk of marble, and all you do is chip away everything that *doesn't look like an elephant!*"

Well, that is what we do. We "chip away" behavior that doesn't look like the goal behavior. Every moment we are working on a part of the final goal behavior, and we have a bunch of smaller goals along the way. Each of these smaller goals becomes a temporary target behavior. We eliminate the behaviors that do not look like the goal behavior by withdrawing their payoffs. Thus, the unrewarded behaviors die out, while the new targets are strengthened. Let me give you an example.

I once kept a pet rat named Hobart. I used him to show my students how easy it is to teach by consequences alone. I built a training box with a glass front. Each time a button was pressed, a small dipper on one wall gave Hobart a drop of water and also operated a buzzer. A coathanger wire was stretched from one end of the box to the other, about a foot above the floor. A piece of white paper tape could be moved along the wire. One end of the wire was above the water dipper.

Each day after training time, Hobart was given all the water he wanted to drink, for about an hour. By training time, however, he was pretty thirsty, so a drop of water was a strong payoff for Hobart.

When I placed him in the training box, he soon began a strange ritual. He stood on his hind legs, facing the dipper, walked backward the length of the cage, reached up to the coathanger, placed both paws precisely on the white paper tape, pulled himself up, chinned a few times, climbed the wire, and turned a somersault. I then pressed the button. When Hobart heard the buzzer, he dropped to the floor of the box and ran back to the dipper for the drop of water which was waiting for him.

How did he learn such a complicated ritual? I taught him. Obviously, I could not give him verbal instructions, and prompting was almost as impractical. Well, then, how *did* I teach him?

I taught him an entire sequence of behaviors, called a *chain*, but I did so bit by bit. First, I taught him to drink out of the dipper. He soon learned to come to the dipper when he heard the buzzer. Next, I kept him near the dipper, because that was his starting point. I did so by pressing the button only when he was near the dipper.

He spent about 75% of his time near the dipper, doing various things rats do, such as sniffing into corners, preening, and sometimes standing on his hind legs. The last was a behavior I wanted, and I wasn't interested in the others at this time. Standing on his hind legs was part of the goal behavior, so I pressed the button only when he stood on his hind legs. I only gave him water when he was near the dipper, facing it, and this happened often enough that within a few minutes, Hobart began to stand deliberately, facing the dipper. It was not long before standing in front of the dipper became a strong behavior. But there were always minute variations in the way he stood. His paws were not always raised exactly the same amount as before. I waited for those times when he stood with his paws just a trifle higher than before, and then gave him the payoff. If his paws were lower than usual, I withheld the water, even though everything else was right. What was once good was no longer good enough. Hobart soon learned to hold his paws higher.

One time, when he stood up, his paws were raised shoulder-high, so he spontaneously reached for the wire and touched it. Of course, I gave him a payoff. When touching the wire became strong, I did not press the button until he touched the wire. Other behaviors, including raising his paws shoulder-high, were no longer good enough. By not rewarding them, I chipped them away and starved them.

For the next few days, I kept changing his target behaviors as he learned each new goal behavior in turn. He first had to grasp the wire, then hold it at least one second, then three, then longer. Proceeding step by step, he was taught a long sequence of individual acts, each leading smoothly into the next, in a chain of behaviors. If you've ever been baffled by the unbelievable tricks you've seen so-called "dumb" animals perform at the circus, be mystified no longer. This is the secret of how it was done. The beauty of it is that it works just as well with humans in all walks of life as it does with the dolphins at Marine World. All we did when we taught Hobart, or when Dr. Skinner taught his pigeons to play ping-pong and to steer guided missiles, was to teach a lot of small steps, one at a time. Each step was easy enough by itself. It had to be, or the chain would have starved right there. Good teaching *always* means making each step easy enough for the learner to grasp soon, and to learn well. We kept Hobart at each step until he had no trouble with that target. When one step was well learned, we moved him to the next step. Does this sound familiar to you? We were repeatedly following the first three steps of programming, according to the procedure we talked about in Chapter 11: 1) We observed were we were at that moment. That is, we saw which behaviors were already present; 2) We decided our goal; and 3) We broke the learning distance down into steps small enough that Hobart could learn each one easily. That is the key to it.

During many years of association with public schools and universities, at all levels, I have met people who called themselves teachers, and this includes some of the world's most famous scientists, scholars, musicians, writers, mathematicians, and artists (people you might expect to know better). Some of these illustrious greats seemed to take a perverted pride in making their courses as tough as they could. By doing so, they said, they raised the standards of their school, because the incompetent students dropped out or failed to pass.

This philosophy is nonsense. Screening is done better in other ways. If the instructor is more interested in impressing people by showing how many obscure things he knows, he is not doing genuinely good teaching, no matter what his other qualifications might be. It takes very little skill to assign more and more reading, or to give more and more problems to work. It doesn't take much talent to make lectures hard to understand. The really gifted teacher is the one who can take the same material and organize it into steps that are so logical and close together that the learner progresses smoothly from one to another without excessive frustration from repeated failures. The student works hard and steadily, but it never seems like "work." A monumental amount of material can be covered and learned by the student without his ever feeling that he had to work excessively for it. *That* is truly fine teaching!

Hobart could not complain about how much homework we assigned him. If the assignment we gave him was too tough, he just dropped out and stopped working. But if we kept the steps small and in the right sequence, he learned what we asked him to learn. The only thing we did was punch a button and give him his payoff. But we had to do it at exactly the right time. We could not wait for the chain to occur spontaneously. Still, we got the same results by going at it piecemeal. That is why it is called the reinforcement of successive approximations. *Successive* means one after the other, in a certain order, or sequence. We strengthened successive steps. Each step was only an approximation to the final behavior, which, you must have noticed, was an entirely new behavior for Hobart. It was a behavior so unusual I will lay odds that not another rat in the world had ever done it before. You don't find rats in nature doing things like chinning and turning somersaults. They must be trained to do them. Hobart must have developed the largest biceps of any rat in California! And yet, any time he got too little payoff, he was free to stop, and at times he did. At such points, our program had failed. We could not blame it on Hobart, as teachers and therapists are so prone to do. We could not say that Hobart was a slow learner, or that he lacked motivation. These excuses only work for professional people who have to explain why their programs failed. It was our job as arrangers to furnish the motivation (which we did with water, given only after certain behaviors, all done while he was thirsty), and to keep the steps small enough. The learner may not be at fault if the program fails. In fact, the learner is always right. If you want the learner to succeed, the program must be changed to make failure a more remote possibility. Only the programs can be wrong.

Thus, it is possible to get entirely new behaviors, or to re-establish old behaviors which have died out. Both are best taught by degrees. We have all learned a lot of behavior chains, little by little. We learned to walk in a number of stages. First, we stood with support, then unsupported; then we took one step with a pause to regain our balance; etc. Most people learn these steps spontaneously, without much help, but the steps are still approximations. The learner here is an infant, and is always right. He stays at each level until he has become fairly comfortable there. The shaping takes place naturally, from easier to more difficult, as it always must.

I have worked with severely brain-damaged children who had never learned to walk. It was necessary to teach walking to them one step at a time (no pun intended). Sometimes I even had to break the first step into smaller steps, because these children, although in their teens, could not do such simple things as standing with support. It would be pointless to try to teach something more advanced, such as lifting one foot off the floor, if the learner could not do the more simple behavior first. I will mention other behaviors from time to time which need prerequisite behaviors.

Speech is another spontaneously learned shaping procedure. You started talking by making easy, crude sounds, and you gradually refined them until you learned speech patterns that are really very complex. You went from simple to difficult. This is also true of any complex motor skill—that is, any skill that involves moving muscles. Some of these skills include flying an airplane, brushing teeth, playing the piano, roping a steer, skiing down KT-22, making a clay pot, toilet training a baby, eating with a knife and fork, making a pencil sketch, welding a smooth bead, tying a shoe lace, figure skating, and riding a bicycle.

Every one of these, and hundreds of thousands of other skills, was learned, either as a crude approximation which was gradually refined, or as a single small bit of behavior, which was joined to other bits to form a chain of behaviors. I doubt if anyone spontaneously learning those skills gives much thought to the step-by-step nature of shaping. But the teacher does, or should, and we all do implicity. If you've ever tried to learn any of the more difficult skills I named, you realized and accepted the fact that you'd be at a certain level for awhile before you could move on to more difficult skills. You'd stay on the bunny slopes doing snowplow turns before you were ready to ski the Cornice.

Good teachers have instinctively recognized all along that you go from simple to complex, or from crude to refined, in a logical, well-organized sequence. You start with counting, then learn to add and subtract, then multiply and divide, then learn algebra and trigonometry, analytic geometry, and finally calculus. You can't understand analytic geometry very well until you understand algebra and plane geometry. Many college students fail history because they did not understand geography, and the relationship of one country to another that was just the result of their locations. They often failed geography because they were poor readers. And they might have become poor readers because they could not sit quietly and concentrate long enough at the time they were learning to read. It seems almost ridiculous to blame their failure in college on their inability to remain seated (something which their teacher might have been able to take care of rather neatly if he had rewarded the child when the target behaviors appeared). But each skill has prerequisite skills, and these must be learned, either early in life or later, if the target behavior is to occur. Before you walk you must be able to stand unsupported, and before you can stand unsupported you must be able to hold your head erect.

Some people do not love music, mostly because they have never learned to listen properly. That is, they do not listen actively, remembering the melodies they hear, the rhythms, patterns, key changes, instrumentation, and other devices used by composers to make their music more interesting and to make it mean something. How can anyone love the Eroica Symphony if they do not understand some of the things Beethoven was doing? People whose musical experience is limited to simple popular tunes played as background do not learn to listen actively. They do not learn to seek out what is there. Muzak and commerical pop tunes often limit the listener to a lifetime deprived of the pleasure of real music. But *listening* to music can be taught, and the learner must develop the ability to remember melodies, rhythms, etc. and to recognize them when they are played in different forms, different keys, or even inverted or backward, for great composers do just that kind of thing. Like any other skill, music appreciation can be taught in steps, and the steps (*e.g.,* listening, becoming familiar enough to be able to recognize the styles of various composers, historical periods, or countries) can be broken down still more.

There are a number of things you should keep in mind when shaping behavior:

1. **Go from simple to complex, or from crude to refined.**
2. **Teach as big a step as you can get by with successfully.**
3. Always **teach as small a step as necessary,** so that success is as frequent as possible.
4. If in doubt as to how large a step to take, **it is better to make a mistake by choosing a step which is too small, rather than too big.** Too small merely slows down the learning by keeping the learner at a lower level of performance for a longer time, but too big may result in the loss of the entire chain by starving. Then, you'd have to start over.
5. **Reward each step often, until the step becomes easy.** Remember, weak behaviors will die out after they happen only two or three times without payoff. I make it a rule of thumb to stay at each step until the learner has gotten ten consecutive payoffs. Sometimes this moves the

learner a bit too slowly for my taste, but it is better and usually faster in the long run to be on the conservative side. This is especially true for arrangers who are beginners at the shaping game.

6. Once a step is well learned, hold out for a bit more. Never be satisfied unless you are making progress, which means that you must be changing targets frequently.

7. You will constantly be changing the form of the behavior you are rewarding, refining as you go. That is, **expect your targets to change frequently and rapidly.**

8. You will always be adding new targets as you go along, and letting behaviors you once rewarded starve, as they become no longer adequate.

9. Psychologists often say that behavior shaping is still an art. You are responding at each moment to very subtle changes in behavior, and trying to capitalize on them. Nobody can predict exactly what the next behavior will be. **Behavior shaping is full of surprises. You must be ready to make the most of them when they come unexpectedly.** Even when you expect a change you still might be surprised, because it might take place at an unexpected time. Much of the time there is some element of surprise. We knew ahead of time that we would eventually get Hobart to touch the wire, but we thought we would have to go through many more steps than we actually did. We didn't realize he would reach up and touch the wire when we were just trying to get him to raise his paw shoulder-high. But we had to be ready for it when it did come along. An infinite number of behaviors might appear, and you won't think of a fraction of them ahead of time. Sometimes targets you want do not come when you expect them. Other times, an expected target appears, even though it was not supposed to appear at that point in the program.

10. It is almost impossible to get good data. I have not yet seen a single article in technical journals where anyone so much as tried to take data in a behavior shaping program. I once submitted an article which did try. The editors rejected it because I had not kept my program consistent! I had changed the targets and the ratios often, which meant many program changes, for change is the essence of shaping. Here is one kind of programming where **you are free, and even encouraged, to improvise as much as you wish.** The targets will change, and the ratios may change, because this is done in all shaping programs.

11. Sometimes, you might chip away too fast. This often happens when the learner himself gets ahead of the program, such as when

Hobart grasped the wire. He only did that once, but even though we rewarded it along with other paw-raising behaviors, we were careful not to starve raising his paw above his shoulders. In other words, we didn't insist he touch the wire again, but continued to strengthen raising his paws higher. As it turned out, he quickly learned to touch the wire, so we could soon wait for that response and starve the others.

Remember that at each step we must eliminate the payoff for behaviors which, one by one, have become "not quite good enough." Since starving the earlier parts of the chain is a big part of shaping, you must be careful it does not gain the upper hand. If you eliminate too much too fast, you may suddenly find the entire chain of behaviors has stopped. Hobart will "drop out," just as millions of high school students dropped out, and for the same reasons: The learners no longer got enough payoff to justify taking all the punishments involved. This is just as true when Ricky stops putting his clothes away as it is when Hobart stops chinning himself.

Just as an entire chain can be set off by a cue, so an entire chain can drop out and starve. **When the learner stops the entire chain, the best thing for the arranger to do is to start completely over, or go back quite a way and pick up again at a place where he *can* start.** This time, the weaker links of the behavior chain—that is, those behaviors where the failure occurred—should get extra payoff a few more times, to be certain you do not lose them again. The most common mistake made, by experts and novices alike, is to push ahead too fast. You must make haste slowly. You must not go on to a new target before the older targets in the chain have been learned well enough. You will find, however, that relearning a chain will proceed much faster than learning did originally. This is also true of any other behaviors which have died out or been forgotten.

12. The name of this game is success, and **the more success the learner has, the more successful the program will be.** Success means payoff. When you say that someone has done something correctly and his consequence is a payoff, it means he has been successful. An error is just a behavior which does not get rewarded. With good behavior-shaping techniques, errors will be practically non-existent. If you make lots of errors, or if there are lots of times when the learner stops responding altogether, you should pay special attention to getting the payoff coming more often, and more times. And this means whittling down those steps into smaller component steps.

13. If you are not getting the changes you want, it could be because you just do not give enough payoff. One of the most common reasons is

that the steps between where we are now and our chosen goal are too long. As the learner tries for a step which is too big, his odds of failure increase. Failure means no reward, and can even mean punishment as well, for nobody likes to lose. Either way, you are weakening the behavior you are trying to make stronger. Trying to get the too-hard target again means repeated failure, which is the same thing as saying the behavior appears without a payoff. That is the exact prescription for starving a behavior, so **be sure you are giving enough payoff when the right time comes along.**

14. Shaping takes place quickly, if it is skillfully done. **When you get stuck and can't seem to go beyond a certain level, it could mean that you're not rewarding often enough or soon enough, or the reward may be too weak, or the step you're working on is too big.** The solutions: **Try to find a more powerful payoff,** but in any event, **give immediate reward more often,** and **check to see if the step you are working on can be broken into still smaller steps.**

A certain amount of shaping occurs when you change your program. We started with Clifford saying, "Pardon me, please," even though he often said it at inappropriate times. But he was closer to our goal than he was before, so we did not hesitate to reward that response at first. When saying, "Pardon me, please" became strong, we were in less danger of losing it when we accidentally missed giving a few payoffs, so we demanded a bit more. He now had to wait. We taught by successive approximations. Each new task was just one step along the way. We chipped away the behavior that didn't look like the finished product.

Behavior shaping resembles the childhood game of "Blindman's buff." In order to lead the blindfolded player to a certain person or object, his companions tell him, "You're getting warm," as he moves closer to the object. We try to do the same thing here. Each step should be just a bit "warmer" than the previous one. You should always try to move forward just a bit, and you do that by waiting for behavior successively closer to your goal, and then rewarding it at once. You also withdraw the payoff for older behaviors which are no longer good enough. Do not hold out trying to wait for too much change, unless the learner has given you some reason to feel that he can and will do it successfully. Your guiding rule should be, *Nothing succeeds like success.* Success is one of the most powerful rewards known, so use it wisely, but use it lavishly. Make every step small enough so that the learner can succeed. Sometimes, the learner loves challenges. At those times, you can hold out for a bit more, but even then, he must eventually succeed or he will stop trying. He gets no payoff until he solves the problem successfully, and no payoff—repeatedly—means the behavior will starve and die out.

It is sometimes best to start shaping at the last step and work backward. This does not mean that the finished behavior will be done from the end to the beginning; it refers only to the sequence of steps used in training. It is not the same thing as backward conditioning, which means that the payoff comes before the behavior you want. As you recall, backward conditioning usually doesn't work. Working backward, or what I will call *reverse chaining*, often does. Let me first demonstrate what I mean, and then I'll try to explain.

Reverse chaining means learning the final behavior of the sequence first and learning the first part of the chain last. Suppose you wish to teach a young child to put on a pair of long pants. A task analysis could look something like this:

Step 1. Child goes to the dresser, opens drawer, finds pants.

Step 2. Child removes pants he is wearing.

Step 3. Child holds the waist open and spreads it apart with both hands.

Step 4. The child puts one foot through the correct leg hole.

Step 5. The child puts the other foot through the other leg hole.

Step 6. The child bends down and grasps the waist of the pants.

Step 7. He pulls the waist over his knees.

Step 8. He pulls the waist over his hips.

Step 9. He zips and/or buttons the pants closed.

Step 10. He threads the belt through the belt loops and buckles it.

In some cases, you might have to make it more detailed, or less detailed. For example, you might want to add a step between steps 6 and 7: Pull the waist over the ankles, if the child has trouble there. And if the child had just dried himself after a shower, step 2 would obviously not be necessary. If the child has no trouble, you should try for as much as possible. I like to start with step 10, because it Step 10 is the easiest step, so I like to teach it first. I dress him completely except for buckling his belt, and say, "Put on your pants, please." All the child needs is to buckle his belt. If even this gives trouble, I might use a physical prompt. That is, I place the child's hands on the belt and help him. I then reward him well, just as if he had done it alone. I repeat the process a few times, eliminating the prompt as soon as possible, and give him a payoff after each time. Sometimes, where there are two separate skills involved, such as putting on his pants and putting on his belt, I might omit step 10, and start with step 9. Step 10 would then be taught separately later.

As a rule of thumb, I usually keep the learner at each step until he has done it without error ten consecutive times. That might be too much, but I would rather make an error by giving him too much training at each step instead of too little.

Once he has learned step 9 well, I go to step 8, and teach him to pull his pants up the last few inches. I dress him completely, pulling his pants up over his hips, but leave them a few inches too low. I then say, "Put on your pants, please." All he needs to do is pull them up. If even this little task gives trouble I could use a physical prompt, placing the child's hands on the waist band and helping him pull the pants up. As usual, I reward him after we have done it together. When step 8 is learned, I go to step 7. I pull his pants down below his hips, and once again give the same command. When he has pulled them over his hips, he nearly always pulls them up all the way, because he is now doing something he knows how to do. Pulling them up over his hips becomes strengthened by his being allowed to do the part he already knows. His success at pulling them up the last few inches rewards the behavior of pulling them up over his hips. Step 8 becomes a payoff for step 7, which is a bonus added to the reward I would have given him anyway. The next obstacle is the knees, so once he has done step 7 ten consecutive times without error, I pull them down below his knees. You can see that each step is slightly harder than the one which was learned before. The use of reverse chaining lets us use success at step 7 to reward step 6, and success at step 8 to reward step 7, etc. The steps which are learned first are the ones which are actually performed later. Each later step in the chain becomes a payoff for doing all of the earlier ones correctly.

When steps 7 and 8 have been learned, step 6 is taught; then step 5, until eventually the entire chain of behaviors becomes quite easy for the learner. The chain would of course include such behaviors as going to the dresser for his clean pants, as in step 1, and could be extended later to include a step 11—placing the dirty clothes into the clothes hamper.

Most of the time, such a detailed program is not necessary. We use them in training severely retarded children and adults to dress themselves, but most normal children will be able to learn well even when a number of steps have been combined, unless the child is very young. But training severely retarded individuals, or even animals, is good learning experience, because you must break behavior chains into their most simple components. When you know how to do that, it is no trouble to do less. The trick is always to see how many errors the learner is making. If he makes none, you should ask for a larger hunk of the chain at one time. Where the steps are, and how large they are depends upon the level of the learner, and you must find this by observing how well he does when you give him the command. But the principle is still the same, regardless of who you are teaching.

A similar shaping program can be used to teach children to make their beds. The arranger should make the bed at first, but when he is finished, he should turn down a corner of the bed spread and have the learner merely smooth it into place when asked to "make the bed, please." This is normally an easy matter to teach a child of three or four years' age. It is even simple enough for preoccupied teen-agers who do not do a good job of making their beds! Earlier steps can be added once the later steps are learned. The last things they should be taught are those early steps in the chain—stripping the bed, putting on the sheets, etc.

Don't forget that each step should be rewarded as it is learned, and of course, repeated a number of times, so that the learner has no trouble performing it. Incidentally, it is not necessary to limit bed-making to a once-a-day process, just because the bed is normally made only once daily. We are talking now of a training program, and there is no good reason why training in making beds must take place at the usual bed-making time. It would be wise to turn down the corner of the bed spread many times each day, and ask the learner for the same behavior again. One twenty-minute session can expose him to many training opportunities each day. I am astonished when I visit institutions and see the staff trying to teach their residents to brush their teeth. Usually, the residents are never trained in this task except in the early morning, when they are crowded together in the bathroom, in a hurry to finish dressing before breakfast. Each resident has only one opportunity to learn to brush his teeth, and this is not under the best of conditions. Why not teach a special session of toothbrushing, or dressing, or bed making, where every individual gets dozens of training trials each session? One such training session can give the learner as much experience as he might otherwise get in two weeks, or even a month. Can't you see how much faster learning would be?

It is also important to remember that rewards should come frequently, whether for toothbrushing, making the bed, dressing, or other tasks. The learner should be told, "That was good." Criticisms by the arranger should largely be positive comments. Instead of stalking the learners, trying to catch them doing something wrong, stalk them and try to catch them doing something right, and then don't forget to reward. They need those payoffs to sustain their good behaviors. If they didn't, the program wouldn't be necessary, for they would already be doing a lot of the targets spontaneously.

Don't think that just because I used the example of parents and children that the process of behavior shaping cannot be used in other settings. Employers: When was the last time you checked on your employees to see if you could catch them doing what you *wanted* them to do? And then looked for slightly better performance next time, and the next? Did you try to catch them doing the things you pay them to do? The things you hired them to do? Or do you make the common error of ignoring the employees when their behavior is worthwhile? Do you take them for granted, or say, "Well, why should I reward that? I'm already paying them for it?" Of course you are, and you are right. You do pay them for good targets, or you hope so, anyway. But often, you pay them whether or not they do their best, and on top of that, you know about how much and how good each of the workers does, and you accept that as what he can do. On top of that, their salary comes at the end of a week or two weeks or a month, almost never at the exact moment they are doing what you want them to do. You already know what happens when payoffs come at the wrong time. You also know what happens when they are delayed too long. The result will be that most employees do just enough to get by and avoid being reprimanded or fired. If you want more effective performance out of them, catch them when they're good and reward them immediately, even if their payoff is only a smile and a kind word of encouragement. But also remember that "being good" will change its meaning, for you will no longer be satisfied if there has been no improvement.

A monetary bonus at such times might even result in a much higher output of work which would eventually pay for itself, if you don't go off the deep end and get carried away unrealistically. It is fine to give one big bonus at Christmas to everyone, regardless of his performance during the other fifty two weeks. It is a generous and kind thing to do for its own sake. But many employers give yearly bonuses when their motive is increased production. If the bonus is an installment payment for productivity in the coming year, it is backward conditioning, and not likely to help much. If it is given as a reward for what they did in the previous year, the rewards should have been given at the time the behavior took place. You already know that the longer the delay, the weaker the effects of the payoff will be. If you give many smaller bonuses, much more frequently, right at the time the behavior is at its best, or preferably, a bit better than before, you can often get much better results. You can hold out for improved performance next time around. You might have to fight it out with your accounting department to figure which fund the money will come from, and of course, you will need to keep good records to protect yourself and your business. But if your profits increase substantially, isn't that a good enough reason to do it? If the payoffs come on an average ratio, you can use the principles of behavior shaping to get more productive behavior from your employees. That should be the main function of the supervisor, for it is what supervision is all about—or should be.

If this seems to you like exploitation, try to understand that happy employees are not as exploited as miserable ones, who tend to do as little as they can get by with doing, thus in turn exploiting their employer. This tends to make them parasitic, and any biologist can point out examples of parasites that eventually die because they killed their hosts and are left to starve. The learner has much to say about the direction the shaping will go, too. After all, if Hobart had not reached up to touch the wire before we expected him to do it, we would have had to continue shaping his paw higher and higher until he did. Even after he learned the behavior we wanted, the choice was still his whether or not he would do it. If our payoff was not good enough, we got no performance from him, and this will be true of all other learners, too.

Working with a teen-age "delinquent" was very difficult, because he so rarely came on time. In fact, it never happened at all. Usually, he arrived more than an hour late, when I was already seeing my next client[16]. But if you think of "delinquency" less as a group of problem behaviors than as a group of target behaviors the boy had not yet learned, you will understand that coming late was not his problem. If he is to succeed at alternative life styles which are less damaging to himself and others in his society, he will first have to learn "responsibility." One part of "responsibility" is coming to work on time, and if he has not already learned to do that, it is most unlikely he will be able to hold a job very long. Since holding a job is very often the most crucial behavior to compete with delinquent behavior, it was important to teach him to come on time time.

One day, when Jeff arrived only thirty minutes late, I slipped him fifty cents, saying, "That's for coming earlier than usual." He came still earlier next time, evidently expecting fifty cents, but I gave him fifty five cents. The next time he was only thirty minutes late I gave him thirty five cents; next, nothing; next, seventy five cents, explaining each time, "I can't promise you how much you'll get, or if you will get anything at all. That will be my choice. But I can say that if you're late, it's your choice, and I can guarantee you'll get nothing if you come too late."

I had to be very liberal in my interpretation of what was "late." But he soon came to nearly all sessions about thirty minutes late, which was a substantial improvement. Once, however, he slipped up and arrived only fifteen minutes late. I gave him ninety five cents. The following time, when he came thirty minutes late, I gave him nothing. Within a short time, he was coming on time to all of his sessions, and on a few occasions was even waiting for me when I arrived. He also began to require less and less money to come on time, because during the sessions we did things he liked to do, and which he knew would be of real benefit to him. The tasks I gave him to do were carefully chosen so that he would make progress, but which were within his means. Thus, he was nearly always successful, and I gave him much praise for his success. It was one of the first times in his life that an adult had praised him. Before long, success became a strong payoff, and he learned the skills I was trying to teach him—skills such as improved reading, arithmetical computation, and some vocationally oriented tasks.

In all, I had spent less than $9.00 to teach him a very important lesson. He learned to manage his time so that he could do more and more things which would help him adjust to society. In so doing, he became less of a burden, and more of a contributing member of his society. Had I not paid him, he might never have learned this lesson. I could have threatened him with all sorts of punishments, but what effect would it have had? He had already been in and out of juvenile hall more times than I can count. I considered the $9.00 I paid out of my pocket to be an investment. It helped teach a young man some skills which might have kept him out of prison which costs in many ways aside from the money the taxpayers spend every year (between $7,000 and $10,000 for each California inmate in 1975). I felt it was not a bad investment.

The crucial thing in all of the examples I used is that we started with target behaviors that were not very adequate, as behaviors go. Coming to a session thirty minutes late is not very good behavior, but it was better than not coming at all. In every case, we wanted more than we got. But remember step 1 of our basic programming rules: *Where is the learner now?* If Jeff could not or did not come less than thirty minutes late, we would have had little luck trying to aim for on-time behavior at that stage. People had tried to get him to do so for many years, and it didn't work for them. I had no reason to hope it would work for me.

Little feet make little steps. You must walk before you can run. These clichés mean the same thing. Turning down the corner of the bedspread is not the best a bright teen-age boy *can* do, but if it is more than you got before, you may have to settle for it at this time. Reward it generously, until it is good and strong. You must be satisfied at first if the behavior you get is only a bit better than you started with. You don't have to remain satisfied, and you shouldn't, if you want any progress from the learner. But you should be happy you got that much improvement. After all, arrangers also need success to strengthen their correct programming behaviors! Reward the improved—but still inadequate—behaviors repeatedly, until they are good and strong. Then, hold out for a bit more. But never wait for so much behavior at a time that the entire chain dies out. Keep the steps small, repeat each step as often as necessary, add new limits, and keep the payoffs coming!

And *that* is how to carve a statue of an elephant!

Chapter 14

Special Applications:
A Bit of This and a Bit of That

This chapter will be devoted to a number of odds and ends which I think are important for you to know, but for some reason they just didn't fit very well into the other chapters. We have talked about programs dealing with some problem behaviors in children, some interpersonal problems loosely called "marital," or "relationships." We have also touched upon some employer-employee relationships. There is still an important case which we haven't talked about very much so far, and that is when the learner and the arranger are the same person. We call this type of program a *self-control* program.

Before I talk about self-control, I'd like to clear the air, because the word *control* is a very emotional one. People often feel that the only way one person controls another is by force, usually extreme, so that one person becomes a helpless robot being driven by the other person. "I have you under my control," says the mad scientist, and the unfortunate victim can do nothing at all about it.

When control exists in this form, it is a frightening state of affairs, but that is not the only kind of control, and it comes in all degrees. Most people practice very mild forms of coercion all the time, which they sometimes call *putting pressure* on someone else, to make them respond in a certain desired manner.

There are still other ways in which control takes place. Control may be good or it may be bad. When a psychologist talks about control, he does not always mean that one person is a dictator, forcing someone else to obey his command. The word is also used to tell how the consequences of a behavior are arranged. In other words, if I reward or punish your behavior, or if I fail to reward it, I will change the strength of your behavior. That means I'm controlling you (more properly, it means I am controlling your behavior). Any time one person dishes out the consequences, good or bad, he is changing the behavior of someone else. He is controlling that person's behavior. It should be obvious from this that control is *always* going on, whether we try or not, and whether we like the idea or not. This is still true when you enjoy the control, and its effects are beneficial to you. A good example was found in Chapter 3. Kathy felt good when I complimented her, but nevertheless, I controlled her behavior. Didn't she enroll in another one of my courses?

I mentioned that she said I was the best teacher she ever had. Wouldn't that make you feel more like complimenting people in the future? We may rightfully say that Kathy controlled my behavior as well.

In every case where one person gives another a payoff, the arranger changes the strength of the learner's behavior. We are justified in calling this control. I am not denying that people can control in evil ways. There has never been any question of that, because force, threat of force, or exploitation are usually involved. I am only saying that control doesn't have to be bad. Why limit deliberate, intelligent control to the bad guys taking advantage of the good guys (namely, us)? Why not insist that the good guys also learn to control, so that they can have their day too? Why can't people learn to control other people so as to benefit the one being controlled? People can be controlled for their own benefit, you know. Isn't control the whole purpose of a good teacher? You *want* the teacher to control behavior. If he doesn't, he's a pretty lousy teacher, because no control means no change in behavior. And no change in behavior means no learning, for that is what learning is. And if no learning takes place, there has been no teaching. The rule to remember is that **whoever changes the consequences of the learner's behavior controls that behavior.**[17] Nobody controls all of anybody's behavior. He only controls certain behaviors, for which he makes or has made consequences take place. If I change the consequences of your behavior, I control your behavior. If you change the consequences of my behavior, you are controlling me at that time.

On the other hand, if I make the same changes in the consequences of my own behavior, *I* become the arranger. We have a situation called *self-control.* If I give myself payoffs as powerful as the ones you give me, I will be controlling my own behavior just as effectively as you did. In practice, of course, you can give me social rewards I cannot give myself, but I am speaking of the two of us using rewards of equivalent strengths. I can arrange with you to ignore me when I'm acting out some problem behavior. If I design a program with the proper consequences, I should expect my behavior to change as a result. Here I am the arranger and the learner at the same time.

A true self-control program would deal with the consequences of an individual's targets and/or problem behaviors. Most of the target behaviors people try to change with a self-control program are behaviors they don't like, but which they want to make stronger. Don't be confused because I said that a target is a desirable behavior, and yet I am talking about targets people don't like. There is really no mystery about it. The target can be a necessary behavior which is still not much fun. For example, I hate to jog, but I wish I liked it, because I know it would be good for me to jog every day. I also hate to prepare my income taxes each spring, but I know that I must. Figuring my taxes is no fun, and it results in a lot of avoidance behavior every year. I would still have to call it a target, because it is behavior I wish would happen—at least, until I get the job done. Let us see how I might design a program to help change my behavior in such a way that I can stick to the job of figuring my taxes.

First, let's analyze the situation. Why does it take me so long? This conversation may give us a clue:

SUSAN: Last night you told me to remind you to work on your taxes tonight.

ME: I will, sweetheart. Just as soon as I relax a bit. I'll start on them right after I play the rest of this sonata.

Does that situation sound familiar to you? First of all, playing the piano, aside from being such a strong reward, gets additional payoff because it helps delay something I don't like. It is avoidance behavior in that sense. But this incident is also a good example of backward conditioning, because the payoff comes before the target behavior. And what did I say before about backward contioning? It seldom works.

What would you think we could do in order to make it work better? Answer: Turn things around so that the consequences come *after* the target. Lock the piano until I have done some work on the taxes. How much is not easy to answer, but it should be enough to help toward the goal of finishing, yet not enough to delay the payoff too long. Too long a delay would weaken the target, making it less likely that I could use the piano to control my other behaviors.

A lot of other avoidance behaviors compete with working on my taxes. The more time I spend fiddling with other things, the less time is left to work on the job at hand. The things I like to do—such as relax with my family, read, ski, play the piano, take pictures, and much more—are all potential payoffs I might use as consequences in a program to make me stick to the job of working on taxes. Avoidance behaviors are not necessarily super-strong payoffs, either. They could be very minor, day-to-day things which are immediate. I have already showed you how things which are unimportant can sometimes compete with—and win out over—things which are really big, important, and significant, provided the big one is delayed and the minor one happens now. That is what crazy behavior is all about.

I might use a program such as this:

Behaviors		Ratio	Learner: Self-control program Consequences
Targets	Working on taxes 60 minutes	1:1	15 minutes of piano
Problems	Avoidance behaviors	1:1	Starve

Change Level: None

Figure 22. *Target behavior:* One hour of work on taxes. *Problem behaviors:* None specifically defined. All avoidance behaviors are considered problem behaviors.

The only problem behaviors are the many other behaviors, which might be targets under other circumstances. But while they compete with my work on taxes, they impede my progress toward my goal, so they are problems for me.

To proceed with my program, I set a timer and I follow it. When the timer goes off, I get up at once. I do not stay and work, even if I have picked up steam and really don't feel like stopping just then. Why not? Because I'm trying to get my target on cue. The timer is the signal which controls my behavior. Although I might be all fired with enthusiasm this time, the next time I might not feel like working the full sixty minutes. If I had not already learned to obey the timer, my program could break down at that point.

For this reason, I reset the timer for fifteen minutes when my hour is up, and I use those fifteen minutes to play the piano and enjoy it all I can. When the timer goes off, I get up and set the timer for another hour. At the end of my fifteen-minute break, I must be just as precise as after the hour. I must not get up before and not after, for the same reason. It is not hard to resist the temptation to continue, after the timer has rung, but if I get up before the timer goes off, or delay getting up when it rings, I will be weakening the control that little machine will get over me, and I don't want that to happen. This is one time when control is my friend, and I don't want to chase him away.

I often hear people complain that I am making myself a slave to the clock, but that is a strange distortion of the truth. Only by developing that control can I really make myself the master. I can then use time the way I want to, in order to accomplish things I can't do now. People who do not "live by the clock" may in reality be the slaves of Time, because they have less control over what happens to them. They are like a cracker box floating in a stormy ocean. Adding a rudder gives them more control. I *want* to be in control, and that means I must learn to become the master of Time. And the best way to do that is to use Time for my purposes.

If it turns out that I cannot stick to the job a full hour, it means that I have started the program at too high a step. I should not try to hold out for such a big hunk of behavior at first. I'll re-write my program for only thirty minutes of target behavior, with a five-minute break, or perhaps even fifteen minutes, with a five- minute break. Using free time as a reward, there is little point in giving less than five minutes, which would be almost meaningless, in terms of having any fun or pleasure.

The rule should be to select a length of working time short enough to be sure of success nearly every time. This is true whoever the learner happens to be, and whatever the program happens to be. Stated in different words, **It is important to program for success, whether you are the learner, the arranger, or both.** A lot of times, it helps to have other people join in the program, to help you keep control when you might be tempted to slip back a little. This is especially true if they are key people—that is, people such as your spouse, employer, grandparent, child, close friend, grandchild, lover, minister, parent, teacher, or anyone else really important to you, including your therapist or counselor! A person's importance is in a direct relationship to how much payoff he means. You can discuss your program with these people and appoint them to help control your payoffs. Here is an example of how that might work:

ME: It looks like a beautiful day for a hike. How would you like to go up Sonoma Mountain to the redwood grove?

SUSAN: I'd love to, but last night you told me not to let you do anything until you had spent at least an hour on your taxes.

If she is firm, she will help starve avoidance behaviors. After I work an hour, she might then say,

SUSAN: Good! You've done some good work on your taxes. We can
go on the hike now, if you still want to go *(putting her arms
around me).*

I have deliberately asked for her help. Her consequences help control my behavior, but I have *asked* her to control my behavior. Susan is
now a part of the team of arrangers. I am a team member. And she can
help me guarantee that the consequences of my target behaviors and
avoidance behaviors will be the correct ones. While this might not look
much like self-control, it is, because I have worked out the arrangement
with her, and we agreed on the program together. After a number of
successful programs of this nature, programs may be written which are
not as dependent upon other people. Independent self-control can
also be shaped by successive approximations, but you must start at the
step where you are now functioning, and not just where you wish you
could function.

Eventually, I always get my taxes done anyway, program or no
program. But it would certainly be desirable to shorten the time as
much as possible, for I am told that I am not the most pleasant person to
be around when I have that hanging over my head, even when I have a
large refund coming. The sooner I finish, the sooner we will have more
time to enjoy together, doing things we both feel are more pleasant and
worthwhile. If we have overpaid, we will get our refund check that
much sooner, so it is to Susan's advantage to help me, for even though
she may call them "your taxes," they are hers as well. While it is true that
I do not always like to hear her tell me "no," the fact still remains that
two people can hold their ground when one might be swayed by
temptations—that is, by competing payoffs.

I have found that it helps to write out a schedule, and it has been so
valuable to me that I have printed special forms, and use them every
day to help me organize my time. Within the first month after I started,
my efficiency in some areas increased as much as 50%. Even though it
takes time to fill out and follow the schedule forms every day, it has
been worth it to me, because I waste less time, and get more done. I set a
timer and follow it, even scheduling my breaks. Setting the timer is
important, because it makes the goal more tangible, and serves as a
mild pressure to stick to the program. It also helps me remain aware
during the day of how rapidly time really passes. If a bell rings every
thirty minutes, it is harder to waste an hour without becoming aware of
it. Each "ding" of that timer reminds me of the job I have at hand.

These schedules work very well for me, if I fill them out realistically.
You might find a slightly different form to be better for you. Look at

the form I have made; it is in Appendix A. You can make similar forms just as good or perhaps even better, but you should have some form worked up that will help keep your day straight.

As you can see, I have organized the schedule into half-hour periods, and each time I follow the schedule for that half hour I check it off in the narrow column. Each of these tasks is given a point value, and at the end of each day, I can count the number of points I have earned that day. I also give myself points simply for following the schedule. The points given for the targets are assigned on the basis of how hard they are for me to push myself to do them, or how important the goals they represent are to me. These points become my way of earning a big payoff. For example, I have set a goal for myself. When I earn 5000 points, I'll renew my physical examination so that I can re-activate my old pilot's license, which I had not used since 1963. Even though I'd like to do it today, or this week, the knowledge that I have not yet earned my 5000 points keeps me working to bring my goal closer to reality. Furthermore, it is with real pleasure that I can look back on a "productive" day, by tallying a large number of points. Many points means to me that I have done many things which were not my favorite things, but which were necessary—such things as working on taxes, writing psychological reports, losing a pound, or some other goal which the point value made a bit easier for me to accomplish. I have less tendency to put off target behaviors which work for future rewards, because the points I get now will give me some immediate payoff if I need push to keep going. The points are now, and flying is in the future. In this way, I can pay off good behavior that much sooner. Equally important, I can be rewarding a number of target behaviors simultaneously.

These points which I give now for a tangible reward in the future are sometimes called *token reinforcers,* or simply *tokens.* I can use tokens not only to keep myself going, but I can also use them as payoff when Ricky makes his bed, puts his toys away, cleans his room, or takes care of Emily. Stars in his book were tokens, and you are surely familiar with other forms of tokens already. The most familiar is money, and tokens which are paid off with this token, such as checks, stock certificates, etc. But money has no value at all until a person learns that money can be exchanged for things which are more important, such as food, clothing, shelter, and all of the other things that money buys. These include toys for people of all ages, cars, jewelry, a new stereo amplifier, a trip to Europe, a new digital watch, a new dress, a new set of tires, the services of a skin specialist, a bouquet of flowers, the services of someone willing to clean your house or repair your automobile, television set or toilet, a ski lesson and lift ticket, a movie, the latest best seller (or your own autographed copy of *Winning the Games People Play!*), and almost anything else you can name, including at times friendship and power. Money is always in demand because it buys the things people really want, whether it is bail money, an air mail stamp with an inverted plane, or a lid of Acapulco Gold. Regardless of whether they are things you might want, somebody else does, and will pay money for them. Paper money, the economists say, is valuable because it can be redeemed for gold, but unless you are a jeweler or a dentist, gold itself is probably worthless, except that it too can be traded for the real goods that people need and want. It becomes worthless as soon as it fails to buy true rewards, and this is exactly what happened with Confederate money, the German märk and will possibly happen to the American dollar as well. It also happens to the tokens we give in programs we devise, unless the tokens result in some tangible reward for the learner.

You can make artificial token economies, and they can be very useful and effective, too. The tokens are only symbols of reward. Therefore, they can be anything you choose them to be. Even the clicks on my counter became tokens for Mark. Ordinary poker chips, stamps, specially manufactured coins, such as those used in gambling casinos, printed cards, gold stars in a book, buttons, punch cards, or bonus points have all been used successfully as tokens.

There are a number of advantages to using tokens. First of all, you can give a small reward immediately, even though the learner doesn't receive the big one for some time. Second, since the token can be traded in on a variety of goodies, the learner is never likely to become satiated on any one of them. This contrasts with the use of rewards such as food, for the learner may soon receive enough food that he will not work for more of it. Hobart would begin to slow down at the end of the training sessions, when he was beginning to have enough water to slake his thirst somewhat, but if we had been using a variety of rewards, he could have been kept motivated longer by switching from one reward to another. This is exactly what we do with money and other tokens. We buy our food, but do not wish to spend our entire paycheck for groceries (although it is getting harder not to). We also pay for our shelter, but we hope to have some left over for other things as well. Even if we love movies, we do not spend our entire income seeing two or three movies every night. We say that we would grow tired of them, which means that they would no longer function well as rewards. But the money we use to buy the movie tickets could also have been spent on a ticket to a baseball game, concert, airline trip, or a new fishing rod, a new sweater, or millions of other things. Money stays valuable, even for multi-millionaires, because, and just as long as, there are always so many more things that we want than we can buy. In other words, the demand for money exceeds the supply.

Another advantage of tokens is that they teach the learner to tolerate delays in payoff. This is especially important for very young children, or others who have not learned to accept any situation where they do not get their wish at once. People are paid in money, but there is still a delay while they wait to go to the stores, or write a check to be sent in the mail, etc., before their real reward arrives. The use of tokens thus interposes a delay, although some reward happens at once. It is drinking the best of both worlds—the present and the future.

There are many different ways to use tokens, and they are limited mostly by the arranger's ingenuity. But all of them require: 1) The token be given as *immediate* payoff; 2) the tokens be held, or saved for a later time; and 3) there must be a variety of rewards the learner can obtain in exchange for the tokens.

My example of working on taxes may have brought to mind my earlier talk about will power and self-discipline. To those people who complain that they have no will power, consider this. "Will power" really means nothing more than the ability to stick to a job you don't like, such as computing your taxes. Therefore, to increase your will power, your task will be to extend the time you can stick to a job you don't like to do. You might have to start with short times, like ten minutes, and work up to an hour. If so, don't feel ashamed and don't feel guilty. Just start with short times. As you reach your change level, gradually make your times longer and longer, until you can work for an hour or more at a time. Your program will look something like this:

Learner: Self-control program

	Behaviors	Ratio	Consequences
Targets	Sticking to the job more than 10 minutes*	1:2	1. 5 minutes free time* 2. 5 points
Problems	None	—	— — — — — —

Change Level: Progress from 10'/target/5' break to 15'/10'; 20'/10'; 30'/15'; 45'-15'; 60'/15'.
Goal (5000 points): Physical examination to reactivate pilot's license.

Figure 23. Program to increase "will power." *Target behaviors:* Sticking to the job 10' (later, 15', 20', 30', 45', 60'). *Problem behaviors:* None.

The important rule to remember is that your free time must wait for your target behavior. Anything else is backward conditioning. Sneaking unscheduled free time will weaken your program, so don't permit it. If you find that you simply *must,* then you should revise your program to make it simpler, and insure your success at each step of the way.

When I talked about behavior shaping, I mentioned behavior chains, and in talking about odds and ends, I want to say something more about them. Sometimes a chain ends in a target behavior, but starts with a problem behavior. Here is an example:

Emily is tired and hungry, and very cranky as a result. She is whining, crying, and demanding, as two-year old children can sometimes be, even though they are happy and sweet most other times. "I want some milk," she cries repeatedly. We surely want to give her whatever food she needs, but we do not want to teach her to ask for it in a way that everyone dislikes.

By the time a child is old enough to ask for things, he is old enough to ask for them in a decent way. If we can teach Emily a good way to ask for something while she is still in her infancy, she will not have to unlearn it and learn a better way later in life, when it will be much harder and less pleasant. Therefore, Susan and I have both tried not to give her any payoffs when she cries and acts in ways we do not like, and know other people dislike as much as we do.

"Ask for it nicely," we tell her, and most of the times this is all it takes. She will say, "Please," so we let her have what she has asked for. But when she is tired and uncomfortable, she is more easily frustrated and annoyed than usual. Aren't we all cross when we feel lousy? Even for an adult, being nice can be too much trouble to bother with at such times, so it is unrealistic to ask for perfection from a toddler.

It sometimes happens that we try to starve Emily's tantrum-like behavior at times like these, but the longer we wait to give her the milk, the hungrier she will get, and the more likely it will be that we will get more problem behavior. If we *insist* that she ask nicely, our refusal to give milk to her will add one more frustration, and sometimes draw the lines in a battle of wills. And don't forget that we should expect a surge when we begin to starve a problem behavior anyway, as I described in Chapter 6. We don't often want to go through all that, so we are tempted to give in, even though we know it means we are paying off problem behavior. "She is becoming more and more hungry," we tell each other, "And it is cruel to make her wait." This is probably true, but we don't want to reward screaming, either, so we try to find some good behavior to reward. We say, "Ask nicely, without screaming, and we will give you some."

That is usually enough, and we don't try to be too strict and hold out for impossibly good behavior. If it seems to us that she is trying, we give her the benefit of the doubt.

So far, there doesn't seem to be anything wrong with that. But if you will look more closely at what we have done, you can see that we have rewarded and probably strengthened a *chain* of behaviors which began with crying, screaming, and demanding. These behaviors can become our cue to tell her, "Ask nicely." Once we have told her, she then asks nicely and gets her reward. An entire chain, starting with problem behaviors at the beginning, and ending in a target behavior, has become strengthened. Since we don't want to strengthen the problem behaviors in the chain, what can we do?

First of all, we should always be aware that it is possible to shape an entire chain. We did it piecemeal with Hobart, and did it deliberately. We can also do it by accident, as we might have done with Emily. But when we give any command, such as, "Ask nicely," we are trying to get a target behavior we can strengthen. We should not give commands when the odds are against their being obeyed. When Emily is screaming from hunger, we are in an emergency situation; as I pointed out before, we may have to be content with putting out fires. We might not always be able to do the best thing in a crisis. I repeat: The best time to deal with an emergency is when it is not happening. Therefore, we should make a much greater effort to strengthen her target behaviors (such as asking nicely) at times when hunger or other physical discomfort is not as extreme. It becomes easier for these targets to crowd out the problem behaviors when the targets are much stronger than the problems. As long as it only happens rarely, rewarding a chain such as I described will not make it strong enough to compete successfully with really strong target behaviors.

Pupils in a classroom often get up and roam around when they should be working. When they are told to work on their assignments, they usually do so. But the pupil gets attention when he roams around, and even though he eventually does his work, these targets are at the end of a chain that starts with problem behaviors. Many times, pupils learn to start off their work by a period of restless roaming. When this happens, it might be because the entire chain has been rewarded and shaped.

Why are we so concerned with chains when Emily screams, and yet we let Ricky scream fifty two minutes? Isn't that showing her favoritism?

I think not. There is a difference. When Ricky dropped his bubble gum, he was not suffering from actual physical discomfort. His only pain came from not getting his way. This can be painful enough, to someone who has not learned to tolerate even small disappointments. But his discomfort was not likely to increase and escalate if he did not get his bubble gum. On the other hand, the longer a hungry person waits for food, the more he suffers. We don't want to subject anyone— learner or arranger—to the inconvenience and distress of behavioral starvation if the problem is aggravated by food starvation. (In reality, Emily was not that starved, for she is a very well-fed young lady. Nevertheless, she has not had to live through much hunger, so a tiny bit to her must seem like more than it would to us.)

In general, if a chain begins with problem behaviors which become cues to perform target behaviors, a delay between them will help prevent the formation of chains. Such a delay should be at least one minute long, and better, five minutes or more. This helps break the association between the problem behavior and the target behavior, and helps reduce such situations as, "I know I will have to ask nicely, but they won't come into the bedroom unless I scream first," or "I can get a lot of attention by getting out of my seat and roaming around. I'll raise hell for awhile, and then the teacher will ask me nicely to be seated and reward me for sitting. But how can I get the reward for sitting unless I get up first?"

There are many other ways to use the principles of Part One to help you become more of a master of your own life. When you understand the forces which control your behaviors, you will be then be better able to use those forces in your favor. For example, you now understand that behavior can be on cue, but let's see how we can use that knowledge for more than just getting a bit of overlap.

Let's suppose you are taking a night school course, or perhaps you are a student in high school or college. You will have to study many hours, and you may find that you cannot study easily. Let's examine some of your study habits—that is, the behaviors you use when you study.

First, what do you do when you study? Is there a lot of avoidance behavior? You know a behavior is avoidance when it keeps you from doing something you should be doing. Typical avoidance behaviors are "piddling around," watching television, talking on the telephone, eating, or even starting other jobs that you really should have done months ago, but never got around to doing. While it is great that these targets have finally gotten some attention from you, that doesn't stop them from being avoidance behaviors. They are payoffs which compete with studying, and even though you might not enjoy them a lot, they do postpone studying, which you might look upon as a still worse punisher.

Many people have associated so many avoidance behaviors with studying that their study desk becomes a cue for avoidance behaviors. In other words, all the learner needs to do is sit at the desk, or sometimes just look at it or even think about it, and behold! The urge to study is gone—wiped out by the competing avoidance behaviors. Let me tell you how I used knowledge of signals to get study behavior on cue.

If my desk is cluttered, and if the room where I study or write is cluttered, I find it hard to concentrate, especially if the subject matter is involved or complex. I am easily distracted. But what does that mean? Translation: *A distraction is nothing more than a competing payoff.* You are distracted when a competing signal is a stronger payoff than the ones which are strengthening your target. The competing signals control your behavior, because you react to them in preference to the material you should have been studying. Your studying is on cue.

It would be logical, then, to study in a room which is as bare and unstimulating as possible, because there would be fewer things to distract you. Why add more, when Nature provides enough already?

An important source of distraction is your own history—what happened to you in this room in the past? You will recall my example from Chapter 11, when I described how the training we gave the self-injurious patients became associated with the rooms where their training took place, and we had to start special programs to get the overlap we wanted. Your own history in the study room might be a cue to a number of distracting signals. If you are serious about studying, it is always wise to build up the kind of history which will help you study in the future. Use your study desk for one purpose only, and that is study. Do not sit at your desk when you read light novels, newspapers, eat, listen to music, "rap" with a friend, nor anything other than study and concentration. All of the "distractions" I named are competing behaviors, and if they are rewarded in the presence of your desk, that desk can become a cue for competing behaviors. Your behavior will then be under control of the wrong signals. In other words, the desk will become a cue which sets off a lot of irrelevant behaviors. These compete with the ones you really want. Therefore, try to keep one place apart from all others, and reserve it for concentration only. Do *nothing* there but concentrate.

If you find you are getting tired, and your attention begins to wander, get up at once and leave the immediate area. That also includes the times the telephone rings, or friends come by to talk to you. It is better to concentrate for only five minutes in the area and put studying on cue than to spend an hour in half-hearted effort. You do not want attention on cue, with fatigue as the controlling signal.

It is also possible to make imaginative use of cues in programs which you design to help you stop smoking, overeating, or other excesses. For example, many people are not aware how important signals can be in habits like smoking. A typical chain smoker starts before he gets out of bed in the morning and lights a cigarette. Before or during breakfast he lights another. At coffee break, he lights cigarettes. It is of more than passing interest that most of these times he also takes a cup of coffee as well. With many, and maybe most smokers, coffee becomes a cue for a cigarette. One just doesn't feel right without the other, like pizza without anchovies, or ham without eggs, etc. There are many other cues. It will make control of smoking easier if smoking is always done *away* from the usual signals. A special place might be made into a smoking area. Nothing else should be done there—no coffee, no morning paper, no social payoffs, no radio, no TV news broadcasts, and even no sitting down. You might mark the place by strips of masking tape in a box, or a cross on the floor. The learner (the smoker) would stand in the center of that box or cross, possibly even on one foot. All members of the family must ignore him completely—as long as the cigarette is lit. In other words, remove the usual signals and rewards and permit as few payoffs as possible. The family will have to cooperate by refusing to interact with him in any way, never talking to him, answering him, or looking at him as long as a cigarette is lit. Their role is to monitor and prevent accidental payoff while he is smoking.

All of these payoffs—attention, coffee, etc., should be given to the learner if he wants them, but at other times, as you learned in my discussion of crowding. And of course, you can write behavioral contracts to give the learner special favors when he does not smoke at all for an agreed-upon time.

You may use cues in programs to control overeating. While eating, the following behaviors are forbidden: Watching TV, reading, driving, studying, or doing any other thing you usually do when you snack or munch. If you confine *all* of the learner's eating to the dinner table, during his regular (scheduled) mealtime, you will find it much easier to control weight through other programs you design for such goals. If the learner feels he "cannot help it," he should at least take the snack to the dinner table, which should be bare of everything other than eating utensils. None of the signals associated with eating will be present in settings other than the dinner table; where eating is not appropriate in the program, these signals will not become (or remain) cues for eating.

Sometimes you can make use of mechanical help in your program. To teach Ricky the notes of the piano, I drew them on some acetate sheets and mounted them as projection slides. I then hooked up my slide projector to a darkroom timer. This way I could set the projector to turn off at whatever time I wanted. I started with ten seconds. Each time I turned on a slide, the timer turned it off ten seconds later. Meanwhile, Ricky had ten seconds to identify the note correctly and/or play it on the piano. It was more than enough time. When he was able to go through a series of screenings and get more than 92% of the slides correct, I changed the timer setting to five seconds. Still later, I changed it to one second. For each length of time, my change level was 92%.

I gave him points for each correct answer, and when he got five hundred points, I gave him a prize. He got a second prize too—he learned the notes, and it was fun for him.

Another type of program uses *behavioral contracts*, which I mentioned a short while ago. They are just what they sound like they should be. The arranger discusses a program with the learner until they work out some settlement agreeable to both of them. The arranger promises the learner some payoff in return for the behavior change he wants the learner to make. The contract, as I said, should be agreeable to both parties, and should never be made under coercion. In other words, never base a contract on avoidance, like, "If you agree to stop smoking around me, I will agree not to punch you in the nose." Instead, you should write the contract so that the learner *wants* to live up to his part, because it is the way he will get something he wants from you. For example, "I want you to do something (or stop doing something) for me. Now, what do you want me to do (or stop doing) in order to make my request worth your while?" Phil agreed to stop swearing in front of his wife, and she agreed that if he did, when a bill collector called on the telephone, she would not simply say, "He's at such-and-such number," but would tell the debtor to stop hounding him—that "Phil intends to pay you and he is making every effort he can to meet payments. You'll get paid, so please trust him."

Sometimes the learner and the arranger cannot come to an agreement at first. In this case, you must ask, "Well, which do I want? Shall I offer more, ask less, or just give up altogether?" The arranger and the learner negotiate back and forth until they reach a compromise that both parties can live with comfortably. The contract should then be written on paper, dated, and signed by both parties. It should also be considered binding, just like any other contract which has been signed and entered into freely, without coercion. And you must be very careful to avoid coercion—that is, *forcing* someone to contract to do something he really doesn't want to do. If you still want him to do it, you must make a richer offer. But remember that it is very easy for adults to overwhelm or frighten children into contracts they do not really accept, because adults are bigger. When you draw up a contract with someone else, to make him do something he doesn't want to do, you must expect to give him enough in return to make it worth his sacrifice. He will then do it because he wants his prize (what you can do for him) badly enough. That is the secret of all successful negotiation. It is the reason you can get men to catch red-hot rivets thrown to them while they walk along a steel beam forty five stories above the hard Manhattan pavement. You would not want to do it unless someone was paying you a lot of money, or giving you some other payoff you felt was so irresistible that you are willing to risk death for it.

If you can, you should get someone else to help you by becoming a second arranger. Dish out the payoffs when the contract has been honored, and not before. That is, be sure to avoid "bootleg" payoff, or backward conditioning, and let your other arrangers be your allies and helpers in doing this.

The use of peer control is a valuable resource often neglected by most arrangers. Let me explain what I mean:

Peers are people who have some social role in common. If you are a child, other children in your schoolroom or neighborhood are your peers. If you are a farmer, other farmers, or other people who live near you, on a standard about like yours, are your peers. Friends are usually peers. Fellow students, men in the service, sorority sisters, or members of the same motorcycle club are peers.

Peers account for a large percentage of the social payoff a person gets in his everyday life. This is especially true of children. It has been estimated that a whopping 85% of their payoffs comes from peers. Only a bit more than 10% comes from parents and family, and less than 5% from professionals, such as teachers, nurses, psychologists, etc. Although it is obvious that these figures are averages, the figures for any child are probably somewhere in that ball park. And yet, probably more than 95% of all books and articles studied by the clinical psychologist, teacher, and psychiatrist are about what happens in their classrooms, or on the analyst's couch or therapist's office. It seems impossible that almost every clinician in the past half-century—certainly since Freud—has written mostly about what the therapist says or does in his office with the client, or the teacher in the classroom. Recently, more attention has been paid to what goes on in the family, but there is still nowhere near the number of articles and books as there is about the office visit. Even more strange is the fact that so little has been studied about the peer group. And clinicians still wonder why their clients behave so well in the office during therapy, but go home and get into trouble with the law, beat someone up, or in other ways goof up their own lives and those of others.

We may sometimes use peers as part of a program. We *should,* not only because so many payoffs come from peers but also because they often spend more time with the learner than the arranger can spend. A mother or teacher may see a child only a few hours a day, but when you add up all the hours the child is with his peers, you'll see how much more power your programs can have when you use them as additional arrangers. Maybe even more important is the fact that to children, and especially teen-agers, peer approval can be more important than parental approval. If you don't believe me, ask yourself, "Would a teen-ager rather please his parents or peers?" Whom does he listen to when it comes to making a choice about clothing styles, music, marijuana, language habits, political ideas, hair style, or any number of other controversial things? Even though he might follow the commands of his parents through fear of getting caught disobeying, the teen-ager would often *prefer* to go along with his peers.

The big problem is how to get the peers to be adequate arrangers of the kinds of behaviors you want. Many times, the peers reward behaviors which are the opposite of the ones the parent tries to teach. How often have you heard the tearful story of the child who was "led astray by his friends," even though the parent claims, "I tried to teach him right from wrong." The problem is that what is a payoff to the parent might not be a payoff to the peers.

Here is a story about Mike, a sixth grade boy who was not doing well in school. He could not relate well to his peers because he lacked certain skills. They did not like him, and you would not have liked him either. Mike *wanted* to be friends with the others, but did not know how to do it. He was clumsy, and most of his attempts to reach out to them turned them off. For example, he might run up to a peer, shove him, and then run away. This was attention-getting behavior, and it got attention, but it did not work when it came to its real purpose of making him friends.

Because of his failing school work, Mike was called in for counseling, and a psychologist was brought in to help[18]. The consultant began to feel that Mike's poor work was at least partly due to his disturbed peer relationships. He noticed on the other hand that most of the children flocked around the best athlete in the class, so he asked the boy, "George, they tell me you're the best football player here. Is that true?"

"Sure is."

"Are you really that good?"

"Sure am!"

"Are you good enough to teach someone else to play football, even if he can't play well at all?"

"Sure can."

"Well, let me tell you who it is. You know Mike, don't you?"

"Yeah, I know Mike." During the conversation, other children began gathering around George to hear what was going on, and they too sneered at the mention of Mike.

"Do you think you're good enough to teach Mike how to play?"

George was on the spot. He looked around at all the expectant faces of his admirers, and said the only thing he could have said.

"Sure."

"Let me give you some hints first. The most important thing to remember is that if he misses the ball, you never say anything, but if he catches it, always tell him, 'That was good, Mike.' Got it?" [Accentuate the positive].

"Yes."

"The other thing is this. Make it easy for him. When you throw a pass, do it from up close, so he can't help but catch it. Later, you can make it harder, but never make it so hard he will fail most of the time. Got that?" [Behavior shaping].

"Yes."

The psychologist was telling George how to program for success.

"O.K., George. I think you can do it. In fact, I'm so sure you can do it that every time Mike catches the ball, each of your friends will get a little piece of candy."

Instantly, all of the peers became interested in Mike's success. For the first time, they began to encourage him. "Come on, Mike! We know you can do it!"

It was a new experience for Mike, and he responded very well. He improved almost from the start. And in the process, George became even more important to his peers, because he was the one who would be responsible for their payoffs.

It worked so well that the psychologist returned to the playground a bit later, and said to the children, "You really helped Mike learn! Now let me ask you something. You know the way Mike shoves you and runs away?"

"Yeah, we know," they said, with clearly audible disgust.

"How do you like it?"

"We hate it!"

"Would you like to change that?"

"Sure, man. We'd like it."

"O.K. Here's how you do it. When Mike shoves you, don't fuss at him, don't say anything to him, and don't even look at him. Just turn your back on him and walk away. Got it? But if you see Mike standing by himself when he's not bothering anybody, and he's got nobody to play with, talk to him and be as nice to him as you can be. But remember: *Everyone's* got to do it, so be sure your friends understand it, too. Got that?"

They understood.

"All right. I'll watch, and every once in awhile, if I catch someone being nice to Mike, you'll *all* get a little treat."

It didn't take any more explaining. The psychologist's total time spent on the playground was less than an hour. He returned to the school a few times later to follow up, but during that first short hour, he had created a self-perpetuating system that kept going the rest of the school year, even when he was not around. As the peers tried to help Mike, they got to like him more, and he learned new and better ways of relating to them, too. When the summer vacation arrived, Mike was one of the more popular children in the class, and one of the best athletes, thanks to George. Incidentally, I wouldn't be surprised if some of the peers' positive behaviors began to overlap into their relationships with each other, and I'm sure that the skills they taught Mike would result in his getting some payoff in places other than the school.

Do you see what I mean by peer control? At first, the peers were rewarded only by the novelty, and by the treats the psychologist gave them. But through his clever and creative programming, they learned to get reward for being coöperative. That is, they got payoffs by helping someone else get payoffs. Does that give you any ideas about how to deal with some of the neighborhood children who have been so sassy? Does it tell you something about how to help your employees do a better job? Wouldn't you work better at your job if you knew your boss was giving all of your co-workers a small bonus if you did a better job? And don't you think everyone would coöperate with each other, instead of trying to sabotage the efforts of the most enterprising one there? Other workers would not worry so much if an eager beaver looked a bit better. They would *want* him to succeed, because they would have a vested interest in his success.

You can count on it. When someone is competing with other people, he'll do what he can to get the best of them, with only the training we sometimes call *conscience* to limit him. And the things he'll do to get ahead might not always be fair and just, either. Competition means that one person gets payoffs at the expense of someone else, because there are not enough to go around for everyone. The trouble with competition is that it so often results in anti-social behaviors—that is, those behaviors that help do others in. People can also get reward through coöperative behaviors (*i.e.*, everyone helping others to get rewards). Coöperation is the opposite of competition. With coöperation, everyone wins, because there are no losers. Even the employer gains, because productivity is increased and improved, and working conditions become much more pleasant. There are fewer personnel problems, less absenteeism, less sick time, and fewer grievances. Last, but not least, it helps to build the kind of world we'd all prefer living in.

It takes a lot of planning and a lot of organization, plus a lot of work, but it is worth it. Why not give it a try?

I do not want to close this chapter without talking about the role of feelings. We seem to be on the verge of a greater understanding of how feelings work. At this point it appears very likely that feelings follow the same laws as other behaviors. Reward strengthens them and starvation weakens them. They can be summoned by certain cues (*e.g.*, music) and they can also be cues for other behaviors (*e.g.*, if we feel "apprehensive," our feeling becomes a cue for avoidance of the signal which set off our feelings of apprehension).

There is a tendency to explain all behavior as being the result of underlying feelings (instead of viewing feelings simply as a signal, or as a consequence of certain behaviors). Somehow, many people will believe whatever their feelings tell them. They believe their guts are infallible, or at least, should be believed when their brains tell them otherwise. I think that what I said in the past still goes. People can starve fears by the use of properly designed programs, and they can build up favorable feelings as well. The story of Mike was only one example, and that of Mark was still another. These stories show what is becoming more and more obvious, and that is this. Once behaviors change, the feelings associated with the behaviors often change as well. While there are undoubtedly many cases where the feelings "cause the person to do things," these are not as mystifying once we realize that the feelings were only an example of cues which control behaviors. But as important as they might be in that regard, they are not the only cues that control behavior, and shouldn't be treated as such.

The moral to the story is to try to get your feet on the ground. Even such subtle and mysterious things as feelings are often—and maybe always—potentially under your control, and the control exerted upon you by other people you contact. Don't overlook the role of these arrangers in your programs, and above all, remember that you can be in control of much of your life situations in spite of your feelings. Don't assign them a power they don't really have. Instead, look more carefully at the consequences of the behaviors that are always occurring around you or a learner you are interested in helping, and the signals which operate in their fields of action. Once having done this, you are in a much more powerful position to influence what is going to happen in the future.

Chapter 15

The Rights and Wrongs of Controlling People

The proper use of the things you've learned in this book will give you a lot of power over other people—more than anything else which has been discovered so far that doesn't need force. Thus, it raises some important questions about ethics—that is, the rights and wrongs you can do as a result of your power. As long as what you're doing doesn't work very well, you won't get a lot of control over others, so people have not been too worked up over ethics in the past, except, of course, where force or threat of force were involved. But these are not the kinds of programs you will be using, now that you realize how much more effective and better reward can be. The power you should get from these programs will be painless—that is, the use of punishment will be minimal. I feel this so strongly that I once considered naming this book, "The Painless Way to Power."

It is a good thing that these ethical questions are finally being brought up, because when you change someone's behavior, it is your responsibility to insure that nobody will get hurt or exploited in the process. Therefore, you must learn to ask certain questions as you design and carry out your programs, or even as you live your day-to-day life, because every time you are with someone else, you will be changing some of his behaviors. You will pay attention to some of the things he does or says, and thus strengthen those behaviors. You will ignore some things he does or says, and thus weaken those behaviors. You will put some on cue. You will be his arranger, but in return, he will be an arranger of your behavior as well, and you will be his learner, on the same basis.

Until recently, this was not understood so clearly, but now that we know what we do, we are no longer able to avoid the moral responsibilities that are implied.

Here are just some of the questions we must learn to ask ourselves:

1. Do I have the right to try to change this learner's behavior?

2. If I do change it, am I using a program that infringes on his basic human rights?

3. If I change his behaviors, will the results hurt him?

4. If I choose *not* to change his behavior, am I also depriving him of rights?

The last question is especially important, because there may be times when we are in a position to help somebody and we do not do it. If I can teach a teen-ager to read better and I do not do it, aren't I robbing him of an opportunity to make a better living? If a neighbor's child visits Ricky or Emily at our home, do I have the right to refuse to give the child a drink of water unless he asks for it in a respectful way? Do I have the right to take it on myself to teach someone else's child good manners, when he is in my home? Do I even have the right *not* to ignore his bad manners nor insist on respect, knowing that the world will punish him severely for bad manners in the future? Or must I strengthen his obnoxious behavior just because someone thinks it would be cruel not to give him a drink of water when he is thirsty, without demanding proper behavior from him first? Must I, and my family, suffer because I am unwilling to take a firm stand and insist on proper respect? Do I owe that child a drink of water, even though he punishes me? Every time I make a decision I control someone else's life. Do I have the right to do that?

On the other hand, every time I *fail* to make the same decision, I am also controlling someone else's life. Do I have the right to refuse to make a decision, when my refusal might alter someone else's future in some way? A cop-out is still a decision, but simply a decision made without the courage required by a positive stand. Do I have the right to reward obnoxious behavior by giving the child a drink of water when he asks for it in an insulting way?

Looking back on some of the examples in this book, do the arrangers really have the right to make Clifford wait until *they* feel it is convenient? What about Clifford's rights? Why does their convenience matter more than his? Or does it? If so, why? If not, why not? Who decides? Must it always be just the one who is bigger and more powerful? Or smarter? Or more knowledgeable, having just read, *Winning the Games People Play?*

Obviously, the arrangers decide, since they control the consequences of the learners' behaviors. Where the arranger is equipped with sophisticated knowledge of human behavior it puts him even more into a position where he can potentially abuse someone else. It gives him so much of an edge that questions of ethics become especially urgent. These are not easy questions to answer. In fact, there might not even be right and wrong answers. Maybe the best we can do is just ask them, knowing that answering will be impossible. For every *no* there are *yeses*, and for every *yes* there are *noes*. I'm afraid the best we can do at this time is to try to use our best judgement. Whether we like it or not, people control other people, and it happens every day of our lives. We do it whether we like it or not. We may hate the idea, but that does not make it any less real. We may pretend, or even believe, that we are different; that we are moral; that we do not control others. But the bare truth is that we are not different and we do control and that's that. We may hate gravity, but we still fall, and no amount of verbal nonsense can alter that fact. We must face the question squarely, and be aware of our responsibilities.

For example, I have had to struggle with this question: Since I will be selling this book to thousands of people, I cannot personally vouch for the ethics and motives of every person who reads it. What if a potential Adolph Hitler or Joseph Stalin buys this book because he wants to build power for himself that could damage others? Just because I am talking about ethics, and urging my readers to act responsibly, that does not mean that I believe every person out there in the audience will listen to my pleas, and obey them to the letter. Do I have the right to sell this book so indiscriminately, knowing that someone might try to abuse other people with the information the book contains?

My answer is: Of course this power can be abused. If I didn't know that I wouldn't have bothered to write a chapter on ethics. But just because a felon can abuse the use of a knife, is that a good reason to forbid a surgeon to save your life with it? There is nothing in this book which has not been available elsewhere, although it is usually in technical psychological language most people cannot easily understand, in journals not everyone has available. Of course, anyone who cares to spend enough time in enough libraries can still get most of this information, even if they miss out on some of my golden interpretations by taking that route.

Frankly I do not feel there is any danger of a dictator using this book to overthrow anyone and rob him of freedom, and here is why. Dictators use force or threat of force to control others. I think I've made the case against the use of force (punishment) pretty conclusive in Chapter 8, and if he tried to use punishment he would ultimately fail anyway. Aggression always begets counter-aggression. The only way a dictator could rise to power by following the laws in this book would be to use so much reward for so many people that they would all insist he stay in power. Would that be so bad? Even so, once the payoffs stopped, he would have lost his power. The only way he could remain powerful without using force would be to keep pleasing his constituents, which is the basic idea on which democracy is based anyway. Isn't that why politicians make pre-election promises, and try to make the public think they are doing a good job?

Any program of social control must please the learners, or else it loses their support (this is also true of the programs by a single arranger for a single learner). Governments in the past have wriggled around this issue by lying about their success, and I must admit, that much is still true today. But a lying government loses the trust of those being governed, and this is what Watergate should have taught us. Even in America, where people have it much better off than in most other countries, we have become so accustomed to lies that not very many people are still naïve enough to believe official statements of any kind.

I can also feel that I have done the right thing because I know that any person who wants to do evil can learn how to control for evil purposes without my help. He will use force. But what right have I to deprive those who would like to use this book to give them more happiness, or who would like to give more happiness to others? Do I have the right to keep people of good will from using these laws to make a better life and a better world, just because somewhere there may be someone else who might abuse them? Finally, just because of a remote possibility the material might be abused, do I have the right to rob all the other people of benefits that I know I can give them? Do I have the right to know this information and not share it?

Today we are learning to understand things about human behavior we didn't know before, and it is now clear that we have the beginnings of a true science of behavior. We have enough knowledge and experience already to be able to design better societies than we have—maybe not yet perfect, if there can be such a thing—yet still a society which can furnish each member with more freedom, more ability to create good things, more happiness, better health, and more justice, without using punishment, or certainly, using far less. Some people may draw the line here, saying, "Do we have the right to design the society so that nobody has any choice?"

I say, "How much choice do we have now? " While nobody can know just yet what the best kind of society might be, it will not be long before we know a lot more about it than we do now. Any designed society must have built-in safeguards, so that it may change when change is necessary. The arrangers must never be in a position to get excessive rewards through abuse of their power. Attitudes toward power struggles must be changed, so that instead of glorifying too much political power, it may even be seen as something we should look upon with pity, or even scorn. The arrangers should be hired to do their job and make their decisions based upon accurate data which show their ongoing competence in creating payoffs for large groups of people, and when they begin to fall down on the job, their behavior must be changed, or they should be rotated to a different job, where they *can* be successful. And success here would mean giving large numbers of people enough rewards—in other words, meeting a lot of human needs for a lot of people. Somehow, through all this, we must also learn how to keep dissenting individuals from being swamped by conflicting desires of the majority, for the minority must never lose their rights in the process of catering to the majority. Perhaps the near future can bring us advances in computer technology which can help us solve that kind of problem.

There is much more to be learned, but we have made a very strong beginning, and if you follow the information in this book, most of the time you will be able to design adequate programs to change behaviors, just as I promised you. There will be a small percentage of cases where you should look for professional help, from highly trained experts in behavior modification or behavior therapy, and this will be especially true where you might have serious consequences of the learner's behavior, such as violence, or some medical problem. But what you have learned here will help both you and the professional consultant get better results together, and should rarely conflict with good clinical advice.

If you have studied this book carefully, you will have learned much of value. Not all of it will be easy to use, but I never promised you it would be. Counting behaviors is not always much fun. But I never promised you it would be fun.

What I did promise you is what I have delivered to you: Information. If you study it carefully and learn it thoroughly, then you will have learned how to aim at your worst problems and hit the bullseye. I have not promised you anything magic, even though the results might seem like it at times. You have here an intelligent approach, which might not appeal to some people, for today we are living in an age where there are strong anti-intellectual forces operating. Millions of people are abandoning sane, reasoning pursuits and turning instead to fairy tales, astrology, psychic explanations, and other rejections of common sense and sound, scientific data and methods. Millions of others are apologizing for using their brains, as though this made them deviants, or freaks. In a world dying from lack of knowledge about human behavior, the survival of the human species and perhaps most others will surely be dependent upon how we use the intelligence we have.

I would like to take this opportunity to wish you the best results. Study hard, and use your knowledge for your benefit and for the benefit of others as well. Keep asking questions about human rights, and then try to answer them the best you can, knowing that in most cases there really is no final answer. Still, keep trying to answer them, but above all, keep asking yourself the questions. And may all your targets increase and strengthen.

Footnotes

Chapter 1

1. Berne, Eric. *Games People Play: The Psychology of Human Relationship.* New York. Grove Press, 1964.

Chapter 2

2. After you read Chapter 3 you will understand why it is better to translate the statement into, "I don't get enough reward or satisfaction." The solution then becomes more clear: Learn the specific skills of getting more payoff. Furthermore, we can measure payoff, but we cannot measure happiness.

3. Orwell, George. *Animal Farm.* New York. Harcourt, Brace, Jovanovich, Inc., 1954.

4. Technically, a target behavior is *any* behavior you wish to change, including problem behaviors. But I will not include problem behaviors in my own use of the term *target behavior.*

5. Mercer, Johnny (lyrics); Harold Arlen (Music). *Accentuate the Positive.* Copyright 1944, Harwin Music Corp., 31 W. 54th Street, New York, N.Y.

Chapter 3

6. Author unknown. I would appreciate hearing from any readers who can identify the author and publisher, so that future editions may include permission. Please send information to me c/o Mission Press, Box 740; Sonoma, California 95476. Thank you.

Chapter 4

7. As a demonstration of the power of reward, consider this: A few weeks after this book was completed, Ricky joined a local ball club. He needed adult help with his practice. Reluctantly, I did my duty. He turned out to be so much fun to work with that to my surprise, I found I was beginning to enjoy playing baseball with him!

8. Conditioning is a word which means about the same thing as *learning*.

Chapter 8

9. However, the arranger might be more prone to give payoffs he likes, and he might not bother to give payoffs he cares nothing about himself. Thus, he exposes the learner to a different set of consequences. Just the opposite could be true as well, for we often reward those behaviors we like least. At this point I am not concerned which of the two situations actually occur. The issue here is that our likes and dislikes may influence the way we treat the learner, but the rules are not changed.

10. When the same behavior is both rewarded and punished, a situation known as *conflict* takes place. If the punishment and the reward are both strong, and just about equally matched in strength, the conflict can be very disturbing. (See page 147). Most people can tolerate a higher level of punishment than of conflict. Prolonged periods of strong conflict can result in extreme discomfort, and serious behavioral (or even physical) disorders, sometimes severe enough to result in long-term hospitalization.

Chapter 11

11. It is customary to take baseline data for two weeks, whenever possible. In this case, however, the parents were so impatient to get started that they jumped the gun and began the programming on Day 8.

12. Needless to say, events such as concerts, church services, weddings, funerals, and other occasions where adults want children to remain quiet are not the best times to be training them to remain seated. Instead, they may be considered tests of how good a job you did on the training you already gave the child at home. You should start by teaching him to remain seated at the dinner table until everyone is finished, or to be seated during a "family time," or "quiet time," just before bed. Remaining seated might be a weak behavior which starves easily, especially since so many competing behaviors will reward him for getting up and becoming more active. Once you are in a public place with the child, you might not be able to reward him as often as necessary. So if you would like your child to be able to sit through solemn occasions, do your homework in the leisure of your home, not in a setting where you will have to put out fires.

Chapter 12

13. These widely quoted figures have been used as a demonstration of the ineffectiveness of psychotherapy, and they just might be right. They might also be wrong, for there are many possible sources of error in studies like these, not the least being that errors are always more likely when the experimenters who did the statistical tests want them to come out a certain way.

14. It would be wiser to consider the problem not as an adult being too dependent but rather, the adult child cannot make certain independent decisions. In this way, the problem is seen more as a behavioral deficit than as a problem behavior, and furthermore, can be more easily translated into terms such as those described in Chapter 2.

15. The line of best fit between A and B may be considered baseline data for a new program which begins at B.

Chapter 13

16. A similar case was discussed by Robert Schwitzgebel, Ph.D., of UCLA.

Chapter 14

17. Technically, I should also include cues, ratios, and other relationships between behaviors and their environments.

18. This case was treated by Gerald R. Patterson, Ph.D., of the Oregon Research Institute, Eugene, Oregon, and has been paraphrased here with Dr. Patterson's kind permission.

Date_____

0700				
0730				
0800				
0830				
0900				
0930				
1000				
1030				
1100				
1130				
1200				
1230				
1:00				
1:30				
2:00				
2:30				
3:00				
3:30				
4:00				
4:30				
5:00				
5:30				
6:00				
6:30				
7:00				
7:30				
8:00				
8:30				
9:00				
9:30				
10:00				
10:30				
11:00				
11:30				
12:00				
Total:				

Sample form for organizing daily schedule

Appendix B
Conversion to Rate/minute

Hours Between Behaviors	Seconds Between Behaviors	Minutes Between Behaviors	Behaviors/ minute	Behaviors/ hour
24		1440	.00069	.0416
18		1080	.00093	.0555
15		900	.00111	.0667
10		600	.00167	.1000
8		480	.00208	.1250
6		360	.00278	.1667
5		300	.00333	.2000
4		240	.00417	.2500
3		180	.00556	.3333
2		120	.00833	.5000
1		60	.01667	1.0000
.7500		45	.0222	1.3333
.5000		30	.0333	2.0000
.3333		20	.0500	3.0000
.2500		15	.0667	4.0000
.1667		10	.1000	6.0000
.1333		8	.1250	7.5000
.1000		6	.1667	10.0000
.0833		5	.2000	12.0000
.0667		4	.2500	15.0000
.0500		3	.3333	20.0000
.0333		2	.5000	30.0000
.0167	60	1	1.0000	60.0000
	45	.7500	1.3333	80.0000
	30	.5000	2.0000	120.0000
	20	.3333	3.0000	180.0000
	15	.2500	4.0000	240.0000
	10	.1667	6.0000	360.0000
	5	.0833	12.0000	720.0000
	3	.0500	20.0000	1200.0000
	2	.0333	30.0000	1800.0000
	1	.0167	60.0000	3600.0000